Acknowlegements

So many people helped me with the creation of this book. I would like to thank my mother Lotte for urging me throughout my life to share my imagination with the world. My father Julian for instilling a respect and love for animals which we both shared.

Thank you Island, my beautiful daughter for her patience and understanding during the times we were apart so that I could follow my passions.

Thank you Eugene for being the tree I leaned on all during those wonderful years.

I thank Juan Jose Rojas for honoring me and my work and giving me a chance to grow.

To the Solano family for being my surrogate family and keepers of the wilds.

To Alex, who made my dreams come true and teaching me the importance of oneness in this world. To Juan Carlos Crespos for allowing me to fly. Mark MacKay for believing in me. Bonnie Casper for awakening my spirituality and her relentless efforts to push me through. and a special thank you to Stefano whose love carried me every step of the way. For all of those not mentioned you know who you are and you have a place in my heart always.

My tech team, well I could not have done it with out them.

Sonja Herbert	my editor
Derek Boccara	Artwork@racsa.co.cr
David Zeledon	(Book Design) www.escazuweb.com
Nick Kraemer	Computer genius
Mark MacKay	MacEye Productions
Nano Fernandez	Audio
Mario Araya	Costa Rica INMOTION

Introduction

This is a true story, a once upon a time between a woman, a puma, and a small country. The woman of courageous beauty, the puma from death's door at a hunter's mercy, the country of jungle paradox that brought the two together. Costa Rica and its splendid, unique in the world jungle with its elusive fauna, where though reduced by uncontrolled poaching, is still possible to encounter various felines in the wild, is the scenery of this tale. The book is at the same time the diary of a rare experience between a woman and a puma, a denounce of the lacking of a political system in maintaining one of the most complex and richest eco-systems in the world, and an invitation to deepen and appreciate the relationship between man and animals.

The narrator, through her personal journeys with different animals, elaborates an ability to communicate with the animal kingdom which is outstanding. The results obtained in curing the injured animals by the author, are the blend of understanding the beasts through communication, and the use of natural medicines learned from the millenary tradition of the indigenous people.

Pumas, Jaguars, tigers, vultures, monkeys, tapirs and many other animals enter into the life of the protagonist teaching something and adding another piece to the mysterious and immense puzzle that compose the wilds.

These animals received in exchange, unconditional love from the author and the door to be open to their cages, their kingdom to behold. The extraordinary and contagious energy of this woman created a task force of dedicated persons that fight several battles gaining unbelievable results in changing the individuals mentality, veterinarians practice and the governments politics toward animal conservation.

The climatic walk back to freedom of the puma is a rare if not unique experiment that confirm the worth of Julie's theories and work which she finally decides to share with a larger audience through this book.

Thy Kingdom Come

"The last babies have already been born." This comment, spoken to me, prompted a series of events that lead to writing this book. For you see, it has been waiting to be written. Yet life doesn't always allow us the luxury in which to free ourselves to do so. I finally got free...

The wild animals of Costa Rica became my life. It is their story to be told, they simple chose my hand to do so!

Since as long as I can remember, I knew more about animals than I knew about myself. It was something inside me, just in me. I understood animals. I saw their emotions.

I never questioned this thing I had with them. I guess at first I simply felt everyone did.

It was as much a part of me this instinct as my foot is. I was to be, "people's imagination"...

Through the maze of animal experiences which became my life, I learned how to feel the instinct in each and every living thing.

This is a cat's tail!

Bushmaster 1

Moving to Costa Rica was like searching for unknown treasure. Costa Rica is beautiful. The jungles seductive, the scent of rain in the forests, the heat of scented air, the smell of life. Warm grasses swarming with insects playing their music to the winds. Everything was new to my senses here, the language, the people, the sights and sounds of a whole different world. I loved it.

Costa Rica was a different place from what it is now. She was freer, wilder and more challenging. Horses were more prevalent than cars. Highways, shopping malls or the litter of plastic did not exist.

There were few foreigners at this time, the country was still unknown and we were some of the first. Many people came here to get lost or hide from something, yet in reality they were really trying to find something, inside of them, they just didn't know it yet.

I lived in San Jose, the capitol, for the first year. I met some of the most memorable characters which were to become my dear friends and helped me through my discoveries of a new world. We all came from different walks of life and to say the least we made an interesting bunch. This was the year to meet the people who ran the country, from government to underworld.

We learned the *Tico ways*. Tico is the commonly used word to describe a Costa Rican. At any given party or dinner affair we all were one. Protocol, rank, cliques, nationality or creed was not important. The ambassador sat with the cattlemen, high society women bonded with their maids and drug dealers toasted with doctors. We had come to live amongst the beautiful lands comprised of the mighty jungles. Some wanted to save it, others to rape it and take home its profits. Fortune hunters of an unspoiled wilderness waiting to stake their claims.

Most simply came to live a better quality of life . It is a great place to raise children. The original teacher, Mother Nature, allows them to integrate and become one with the world. What they see, feel, touch, smell and experience stays with them for life. Children are numero uno here, they even have a national holiday for them. September 9 each year is the dia del nino, day of the children.

I came with my husband Mitch who had been living in Costa Rica since he was sixteen years old, and my daughter Island. Mitch had first lived on the Carribean side of Costa Rica in a town called Cahuita. He had chosen this spot for it had one of his most favorite surf breaks in the world. We were to enjoy this for many years until the earthquake came and changed many of the surf spots dramatically. Cahuita park has a coral reef and a transparent calm sea. The extraordinary phenomenon that took place here was the tectonic elevation of almost one meter high as a result of the earthquake of April 22, 1991, which measured 7.5 on the Richter Scale.

This coastline is very beautiful. White sand beaches, waves of every color, and an endless menagerie of wildlife. Thousands of coconut trees line the shore, and the majestic bloodwood tree is the predominant master. Their roots grow long and high off the ground. This is a most unusual tree which is vital to floodland areas. They seemed to me to be walking on long legs of heightened roots.

Birds and their songs lull one into euphoria. My favorite are the orependulas. Their body is brown with a striking red bill, long yellow gold tail feathers with a black head accented by a white patch on both sides of their eyes. Their song is very distinct, you recognize it immediately. As this bird begins its song, the body bends over, head down, tail feathers raised up. From end to end a ripple of a shake then shivers roll down its form. Throwing the head then up and back over its body, comes into a climatic release of sound. A trill, an exercise of form.

Everywhere you look, their nests catch your eye, unique in their architecture. They are like long hanging baskets. Unusual.

The ocean life is amazing. Fish of every size and color, queen angelfish, holacanthus tricolor, different species of coral, anemones and venus sea fans. The varieties will astound you, and there are constantly new species being discovered here. The tidepools were my daughter's and my favorite pastimes, and the monster surf seduced my husband. We spent a good bit of the next year living in Cahuita. The black Carribean man is more dominant here than the Costa Rican. They are a strong race of people but riddled with poverty.

Limon, the port city, has a typical port town reputation of pirates, drug smugglers and poachers. Cocaine was free. Corruption was on the rise. Everything could be bought and sold. *"The vulture is the national bird of the Caribbean."* That was the saying of all the locals, as Limon was covered by these winged dark demons all the time.

The vultures are the most important species to the survival of any living species. They clean and detox the carrion which carry disease and would otherwise rot in the baking sun and create perfect hosts for plagues to take over.

I like vultures and later on you will read of my experience with them.

Crime was as usual here in Limon and one thing the criminals feared were dogs, especially pit bulls. Mitch had one of the most feared pit bulls in the country. He was a champion pit fighting dog. Mitch had rescued him from this sporting life. His name was Baron, and he was all white with half a ear ripped off. He weighed about one hundred pounds, and it was solid muscle. So whenever we needed to travel around with money or important documents we would put it in a pouch which fit nicely around Baron's neck and go about our business worry free. He would also sit like a statue in the front seat of the truck and guard with pleasure. No one ever came within 20 feet of that truck.

There was however, one thief who stole from everyone repeatedly and was dealt with by the so called," laws of the jungle."

A random tourist, an elderly American, was asked to carry a briefcase and use the local downtown public telephone to make a call. The briefcase was to be placed in an inviting position to tempt the thief. Only a few minutes needed to pass, and sure enough the thief came, grabbed the briefcase and ran off. Some of the locals which had put this scheme together chased him. He ran harder, the briefcase jumping up and down in his hand. The locals stopped the chase and just sat down with great big grins on their faces and waited.

Ten minutes went by, then we all heard a piercing high pitched scream rattle the jungles. I had been watching the scene over breakfast at the local soda, which is a typical small food stop, peppered throughout the country. Upon hearing the scream I knew what had happened. I froze. When the thief stopped to open the briefcase he said hello to a very angry, very hot, very beaten terciopelo (fer-de-lance), the most deadliest snake in the jungles. The Costarican's call him the bush-master. A just and fitting name. He ended this thief's career. And so this is how it was. Jungle justice.

The jungles and the mountain range which run through the Caribbean are full of mystique. They are lush, thick and strong. Impenetratable, these forests, one would have to swing vine to vine to enter into its core. They are home to some unique native indigenous people. The medicine women hold secrets the white man is dying to know. They speak to no one. Not but three years later, Costa Rica was to be flooded with pharmaceuticals companies cutting deals to extract the jungles herbs. At any cost...

I took all this information and stored it in my brain.

Poaching was rampant and uncontrolled in these jungles, this shocked me to see. One hears about all that is being destroyed in our world, yet nothing prepares you , when you are there, for the onslaught of mankind. Whether you are against it or for it, you are a part of it in some way. It calls for choosing hot or cold. But never be just lukewarm.You might as well be dead.

I saw beautiful margay and rare tigrello skins set out for sale, formed in the shapes of ladies purses. One of the locals offered me a meat to eat so sweet, as like nothing I ever tasted in my life and then a raw egg I sucked shell dry, its rich golden form giving life to my own. I later found out this was turtle eggs and turtle meat. The natives make a soup called rondown, which is turtle meat cooked in coconut milk. I had never put anything more delicious into my mouth. It is one of the foods of the gods. Still it was poaching. I never ate this again.

I spent every day in the jungle amidst waterfalls, or tide-pools and the ocean. I was beginning to feel that perhaps I could make a difference. Maybe like I had heard, one person could initiate change to happen. That was what I was all about. I wanted to save man from himself. Each and every day I learned more about my purpose on this earth, in this lifetime.

I never gave up when I set my mind to something.

You see it was hard for a blonde white newcomer in this land to gain any respect from a society of macho men. They looked at me merely as something to slack their lust upon. And I had been fighting it all the way, every day. There were times I wanted to pack up and go home. But maybe this was home.

My husband was passive to everything, he did not want to make waves, only to ride them. At the end of the year's school term we left the Caribbean and the central valley where my daughter attended the american Country Day school and moved to our beautiful jungle beach property, located on the pacific coast in a town called Dominical. Mitch had purchased this piece some years back, before he had met me. He had always wanted to return to it and settle down but had given us a chance to acclimate to the new frontiers of a third world country by starting us out in the city. Whether we were ready or not, I knew in my heart it was time to give him what he needed as he had given my daughter and me the same. In this I was both grateful and lucky to have him.

The pacific property had a small surfer house with bamboo hammocks, no electricity nor hot water. Our indoor plumbing was but a hose set inside a river nearby that more times than not got clogged with debris every time it rained, and it rained almost all of the time. But we were in pure paradise on one

hundred acres of jungles, rivers, waterfalls and animals. The
toucans lived here, the coati mundi, tigrellos, margays, jaguars
and monkeys of three types. We had several families living
amongst us. One of them was the congo mono or howler monkey, which has the largest larynx of any animal. These monkeys howled louder than anything I have ever heard. It sounded like giant gorillas attacking. "Who! Who! Who!" at a deep
din which was deafening. They are the quarter of the size of a
gorilla. During the morning feeding hours and early evening
you would hear them roar. At times the males would become
rivals and their howl made one stop dead in their tracks. These
episodes would have made classic King Kong movies.

We became their friends. They hate dogs, most wild animals
do, and we had by this time collected a few. Street dogs lit-
tered the roads of Costa Rica. They were so skinny and sickly
that my heart went out to them. Spaying and neutering was
unheard of thus the population grew out of control. I brought
some home, sneaking them by Mitch till he got used to the
idea. He always did. He had a heart for animals too. One street
dog was Monster, named because of the grotesque condition
I found him in. His supreme trust in me astounded me and
embedded a great respect for man's best friend in my mind.
His story…

One day, I was driving home from San Jose over the high
mountain road. This was a long drive on a treacherous four-
hour jungle highway. Most of this road consisted of dangerous, winding turns. No markings on the roads, no cat's eyes
and no street lights. On one of the long stretches I saw what
appeared to be a tall leggy deer-like animal standing directly
in front of an oncoming semi truck. I beeped my horn in hopes
of making the animal move, and then, as I speed to its side, I

saw it up close. I was shocked at the hideous sight, a tall bag of bones with an enormous head and sunk-in eyes ringed in black and blue. This dog wanted to die and knew this highway was his ticket to a quick death. I screeched my truck to a halt right on the road, not even taking the time to pull it over, opened the door and jumped out. He stood there just watching me and then collapsed. I grabbed his front paws and dragged him as fast as I could to the side of the road, the semi roaring by, barely missing me and clipping the dog's left hind leg. I laid the dog gently on the grass and went to move my truck over to where he lay so still. I thought he was dead. I stroked his head and he opened his eyes and asked me why had I stopped him. I cradled his head and cried silent tears for the injustices of mankind. I lifted him onto the back of the truck. I told him I would make him better and to hold on till the next truck stop where I would feed him. This animal had not eaten in weeks. He understood and in one mighty attempt stood up on wobbly legs, favoring the one which was crushed on the foot and showed me how proud he was to be chosen as my guardian. When we give a purpose to our animals, it gives them the will to go on. His tremendous determination was something to see.

I drove to the truck stop a few miles down the road and bought him all the food I thought his stomach could handle. He devoured it without chewing any bite. I dressed his leg wound and took him home. Monster recovered quickly and I found him a wonderful home just ten days later. As I drove off the howl he let out to bid me farewell and thank me was not of this world. He was an experience of courage which made my own grow.

One of the first things I taught our dogs was not to chase the wild things. We were surrounded by a massive mountain range, all protected rainforests. The property had a magnificent 180 degree window of the pacific. Out in the sea you could see *Isla Cano*, a beautiful little island which Mitch remarked had some nice waves for surfing. Cano island is a promontory of basalts that belong to the Nicoya complex. It is progressively energizing due to the tectonic elevation caused by the subduction of the Coco's plate beneath the Carribean plate which date from the eocene 50 -56 million years ago. Isla Cano is an uninhabited biological reserve. The forest on the island is evergreen with very tall trees.

We had a southern exposure view of the ocean,. We looked out at the bahia de ballena, which means bay of whales. The whales migrate in winter and calve here. Greys, humpback, sperm and others all travel this passage. The jungle runs down and kisses the sea. On one of my morning walks at dawn while Mitch had his morning surf, I saw jaguar tracks throughout the sand. The sand here is grey black. There are many streams and rivers that break through from the jungle and empty into the oceans. Fresh water is abundant.

Three rivers ran through our property. I saw life in them like I never knew possible. One of my fondest memories of my first outings on the property came from a stream close by to our house. I wanted to get wet. I scooped up some water in my cupped hands to splash on my face and let out a scream to Mitch .

"Mitch, come quick, I just found some jewels, rubies and emeralds. Quick! Run!" At this moment the jewels moved, they jumped out of my hands. Cheerfully colored frogs that impait a venomous mucous which can kill. Blue with black feet, reds and deep forest green. So soft, so tiny. They became one of my favorite jungle animals . Even the tree frogs that stick to your hands, with faces so docile were abundant here. People told me the colored frogs were poisonous, but this never stopped me from carrying them around in my hands every chance I got. I loved the way they felt. Later an Indian friend of Mitch's told us the poison arrow frogs, as they were called had a gland . When pierced on the tip of an arrow, it carried a deadly shot. This was its danger and its protection.

The constant rains in this area served as the perfect climate for these frogs. This coast stays green all year round. We were up on a mountain top. I could see for miles.

The townspeople all knew Mitch and greeted his family with open arms. They were a quiet, hardworking lot, from farmers to fisherman to squatters and women surrounded by lots of children. For the most part they were poor but none were starving. There was always food in these jungle lands. It soon became apparent to them all that I loved animals. They brought me all sorts as gifts. I thanked them but discouraged their

future efforts and began my teachings of animal conservation to this group of Costaricans. One by one the animals came to me. I soon had quite a group. The antics of my animals were a constant source of entertainment. They all had quite a personality, and were so warm and loving. Except for the birds, which were very one-on-one with only one person. Handling them was tricky. I received my first set of scars which tattoo my body, from them. I look at the scroll-like marks on my body from animal scars and read it as my prayer.

My first gift was a baby green small parrot. My daughter and I named it Baby Birdie and I must tell you how heroic he was. One day while I was cleaning up the house, a new man Mitch had hired to work on the land came into the house to ask for a glass of water.

I knew only a few words in Spanish and just stood and watched him. Baby Birdie was hitching a ride on my shoulder. He still was too young to fly. The man came closer. I sensed then that he had ulterior motives. I didn't mistake his hidden glances and lustful looks. It is customary for workers never to enter houses uninvited. They drink water from the hose outside. The man came closer. Slowly. As I called out to Mitch, Baby Birdie sensed my unease and dove into the man's face. Unfortunately he fell short of his mark and dropped to the ground with a thud. I became so angry; I grabbed a machete from off the table and went to attack the man. He ran out the door and down the driveway right past Mitch. Mitch grabbed him and threw him to the ground. He fired the man on the spot. Baby Birdie was okay, and shortly afterwards became the greatest flyer.

Our home was a jungle dwelling. It was a retreat for us in many ways. But we needed a real house. We were not ready to make any commitments to building one yet. We looked into rentals which were few and far between. Luck was with us. We moved into a great big mansion, the first and only of its kind, built by a family from Arabia, just twenty minutes up the mountain road from our ocean place. It was very big, very beautiful, and it was new. Everyone thought we were royalty. It was three hundred dollars a month. We still went to the ocean jungle house almost every day. Mitch lived to surf and these beaches had exceptional, unridden waves. Mitch was one of the first guys to ever surf here. Each day the locals gathered around with wonder in their eyes and watch as

Mitch danced on the water. He was a hero in many youth's eyes. The local lads would run to pick up the pieces of many a broken surfboard smashed by monster waves. It was funny to watch as they tried to ride the shore break with these chewed up remnants. He taught many to surf. He called it his morning meditation.

The name of our new town was called Platinillo. There were only twenty houses in this little town. This was to be our home for many years to come. Again we were in the midst of a dense wet tropical forest, but being higher up in the mountains from the beach brought fewer mosquitoes. The altitude made the evenings fresh and cool. The air was clean and fragrant with a multitude of exotic blooms which made you sigh as you exhaled.

Behind the house were rolling hills which sloped down into a river which cut into the jungle. Much of the surrounding large pieces of land were cow pasture. There was also a great deal of deforestation. Mitch was becoming quite knowledge-able on trees. He was to become the leading man responsible for reforestation projects on this coast line.

He planted thousands of trees and encouraged others to do so.

We had about ten acres. We were on the main road and had one little pulperia, which is a type of staples store, with a pool table and a bar that sometimes served food. We had a running tab here as we always needed something. The bills were more for the candies and sweets my daughter became addicted to and always bought for all the other kids with her. I laugh as I think of how her little groups of friends would think they were hiding from us all under the big mango tree by the side of the pulperia, munching to their hearts content.

Island attended the American school, Escuela de Valle in the big city a half hour up the mountain called San Isidro Del General. Within a short time, her Spanish was so good, including all the local slang, that people thought she was a tica. I learned from what I heard and most of what I learned came from my dear friend and housemaid Majudy.

I started to feel at home in this country.

Thus started a daily routine of driving over the mountain ranges to take Island to school, then Mitch would go down the mountain and surf and I would either join him in the mornings at the beach or practice my archery. I loved this sport and became quite adept at it. I also loved to ride my wild horses through the jungles down into the waterfalls. Those morning rides and baths in the falls were my alone times. I was quickly gaining a reputation for helping the wild ones, hence I started one of the first rescue shelters. It all came to life with the story of Rasha.

Rasha Rescue/Release Center 2

One afternoon, Mitch came home from the beach with a present for me. Of all the animal species, I had a passion for felines. Later I was given the nickname cat woman. I ran to see what type of animal he had brought me. One of my dogs, a beautiful Austrian/German shepherd mix named She-dog, always alerted me to any animals before I ever saw them. She was my nurse with the little ones. She ran up to Mitch to see what he had brought home, softly whining so as not to scare the little one, came bounding back to me, looking me straight in the eye to tell me what it was. She was super excited. Sure enough, inside Mitch's hands was a tiny baby margay, a small tree dwelling feline. She was undernourished and sick with a viral infection. Mitch told me that one of the cattle farmers had found her in a hollow tree they were cutting down. No one knew where her mother was, or if they did, would not tell. When this man found her, it looked like this baby had gone too long without feedings from its mother. Someone had given her raw, rotten meat which she was not able to digest properly.

I gently took her in my arms. She was incredible soft, her coat with its markings so artistically made, a fawn-like brown with black spots. So beautiful and rarely seen. I fell in love with her immediately.

I named her Rasha and carried her up the stairs to my bedroom. I laid her on the bed, purred and nuzzled her. I whispered to her that I would take good care of her and keep her safe, she need not be afraid. Her soft, shiny eyes became mesmerized by my hypnotic voice, as if holding her in a trance.

She curled up into a little ball and slept on my bed. I went to find one of the local farmers which had goats. I purchased some fresh, warm goat milk and hurried back to the house. I poured some into an earthen plate and offered it to Rasha. At first I rubbed some on her mouth and whiskers and she tasted it. She promptly began to drink every drop and dropped back off to sleep. I was so excited that she took the milk. It was a good sign. For the next week I fed her every four hours, sometimes dropping a raw egg in with the milk and adding the herb goldenseal for the viral infection.

She started to gain some weight. Every time I came home I would run up the stairs and see her. I rarely left the house during these weeks. She remained in my bedroom. She would make small sounds, bird-like almost, whenever she saw me. Rasha was also using her legs. I mimicked her mother in every way. I would take a warm damp cloth and rub it over her coat and stomach, much like a mother does to wash her. I would curl my body around her and stroke her softly, slowly. She loved this. She would stretch out full length and purr. Her scent was a baby's heaven. Margays are amazing cats. They are tree dwellers and are the only cats capable of climbing down a tree head first. They have the ability to turn their front forefeet completely around which is why they can climb down the tree twisting each paw to move front first. They also can jump from tree to tree with amazing agility. They have long tails which act as rudders in their leaps.

It had been two weeks, and she was getting stronger. You can't believe how fast one gets attached to something this helpless. I spent hours just watching her. My family watched me do little else but be with her. They were happy for me though. Rasha fascinated them as much as she did me.

I learned a lot from Rasha, the ways of the wilds were being shown to me by one of their own. She was so sweet to me, never bit nor scratched me. She trusted me. One day a veterinarian from San Isidro stopped by on his way back from the beach where he had gone to inoculate some cattle and horses. He had become a friend of ours and had heard we had a margay. He walked in with a big welcome grin on his face and hugged me. We talked for a bit, I fixed some coffee and sweet biscuits. And then he asked to see the margay.

I was hesitant, I don't know why. I was very protective about this little one and really did not want anyone seeing her. I bit my lip, stalling. Mitch nodded to me.. Reluctantly, I went upstairs with him and Mitch to show her . The vet marveled at how well she was doing. He watched me take her in my arms. He didn't ask to touch her and I did not offer. Wild animals are quite cautious about new people and I did not want to make her nervous. She stayed in my arms a few minutes, then jumped to the floor and defecated in front of us. The vet noticed some worms in her stool. I told him I knew she needed to be deparisited but did not feel that now was the time as it was more important to get her fully strong and healthy first.

I had studied herbal medicine while I was stateside with a shaman from Sri Lanka called Dostora. Needless to say, I was against most modern medicine and had never been to see a doctor, nor my daughter for that matter. But veterinarians were a new frontier for me. It is my belief that when an animal is sick, the first thing to be addressed is the illness, then to deparisite, as this process depletes the system which is already overtaxed by the illness. The same rings true for detoxing the liver. The stress on the system is too great in the presence of a disease. However, the vet disagreed. He felt she needed to be deparisited and he had the injection with him to do so.

Mitch said, "Lets do it," and I was outvoted, and the vet administered the shot.

Rasha died within twenty-four hours of taking the shot. I
could not believe it. I sobbed uncontrollably and my family
stood by helplessly watching my screams shake our walls. I
cried into the night. The house was filled with an eerie silence.
I waited till dawn to bury her. I told my family I had no reason to run up the stairs anymore and I stopped eating for five
days. I mourned her in such a deep way that even now the
tears flow as I write of this.

I vowed to learn everything there was in these jungles full of
medicinal plant life . The lethal injection, Ivomec, that took her
life is a poison, any way you want to look at it. It affects the
liver and kidneys and should never be administered to young
babies or sick animals. There are many natural remedies that
work gently and with no side effects. I wanted to teach the
veterinarians a better way. So I went in the jungles to learn. I
spent quite some years with the indigenous people of our forests. Their knowledge of medicinal plants is tremendous. Their
respect for all living things goes hand in hand with the way
they live. I witnessed cures to many diseases which the white
man's medicine cannot do. One indigenous in particular put it
quite simply to me.

"You have a choice, god's medicine or man's" he said.
"Which would you trust?" The Rasha rescue center was growing. I cured all the animals with natural remedies. I never lost
one and I never had a veterinarian come out again. There were
birds of every sort. Those animals that could be released back
into the wilds were released, only in a area more remote from
the town, to discourage their contact with humans. We had a
pair of palhuelas, which is a small, lean, wild type of turkey.
When it was time for them to be on their way, I opened up
their habitat and set them free. Funny thing though, they did

not want to go, even though there were several other wild ones around. They stayed living on top of their old home for days. I finally took the house apart, and they stayed on the rubble left behind. It was so funny to observe their behavior. I knew they were scared and just gave them the time they needed. The following week they did go and would return every now and then to pick some fruit off the multitude of trees.

Then there was Maria, a congo monkey given to us by a friend in the next small town who had her as a pet. We guessed her to be about eight months old when we got her. She thought she was one of us. My daughter became her best friend and they would do the silliest things imaginable. One such episode occurred when the rains had started, and it was quite a heavy downpour, so we all were inside for the day. We had no television. Island took Maria out of her habitat to play with her in the house. We had her on a harness when she was let out. It helped us keep her out of mischief. Our house cat was walking around with Baby Birdie on her back, yes this bird and cat actually were real pals and Baby Birdie still liked to hitch rides.

Well, Maria decided she wanted to join in and with a great big flying leap broke free from my daughters grasp. She grabbed the cat's tail and swung her around and around. Baby Birdie had flown off by now and was noisily scolding the monkey. I heard the commotion, my daughter laughing so hard she peed her pants, and I grabbed Maria and returned her to her habitat. The cat was shaken but safe and she avoided the monkey in the future.

Maria's release was difficult. Monkeys need a family, their social behavior is so much like ours. I had been watching a family of congo monkeys nearby for some time. There were two mothers, one with a baby and one without. So I decided to introduce Maria to them. We waited until late in the evening when the group was making the beds for the night. This particular type of monkey makes a new bed every night, out of soft leaves and mosses. Mitch and I put her on a harness and as we approached the group Maria became very excited and nervous. I spoke quietly to her. I knew I was going to miss her a lot. It was hard enough explaining to Island that this was the life she was born to live. As I unhooked the harness I set her in a neighboring tree. I was careful not to leave the human scent on her. I had been touching her as little as possible these last few days, and when I did I always smeared my hands with earth and mud. The earth has such a rich scent to it especially after the rains. We walked away about five hundred feet. The group of congos watched Maria curiously. They communicated amongst themselves. Maria was scared, she truly did not think she was a monkey. But instinct told me she understood the language of her kind. She was afraid of what she was hearing. This was new news to her, even though I knew she heard and smelled them and knew of them from their co existence by our home. She bounded down from the tree and ran full speed past us straight up the hill and into the house. Exasperated, we hurried after her. We found her in Island's room sitting quite nicely on the bed. My daughter just had a big smile on her face. Mitch and I looked at each other and burst out laughing.

There was no monkey sanctuary in Costa Rica at this time and the only other place we could take her to be with her own kind was the zoo. I never put an animal in the zoo. It was against my religion. Captivity was not an option. The best I could do was to find another person who had congos as pets and put them together. We eventually found a wonderful loving women who had been living in the jungle on a farm for sixty-seven years. She had three other orphaned congos and was delighted to add Maria to her family. She told me they all had the option every day to go and play in the jungles behind her. If they took to the wilds then that was their choice. She would not interfere. She was just there for them. She was wise and warm to all who passed her way.

Maria of course was both shy and curious about the woman. She did not want to go. I placed her into the arms of her new surrogate mother. Maria touched her face. Slowly they walked outside to a patio table laden with tropical fruits. Maria picked up a piece of papaya. Contently she ate. Mitch and I chose this moment to quietly slip away and left.

Island visited with her over the next few months which made it nice and easier saying good bye. Upon each visit the woman always told us the same thing, Maria is a human not a monkey, so it was...

There were two other animals at my center which had a story worth mentioning. A kingachu and cachuyo, a green parrot. The kingachu, Ringo, came to us much in the same way Maria did. He was a pet in a family whose little girls brought us fresh milk every day. They lived deep inside the river pass. It always amazed me how much walking these girls did to come to me and go to the little local school near the church in town. Every town in Costa Rica, no matter how small has a church and a school. People did not think twice about having a baby wild animal as a pet, however the fate of most wild animals which become human's pets is they outgrow their cuteness and become their wild selves. This kingachu was such. He was now a nuisance to the family, so we took him in.

Kingachus are fascinating animals. They are nocturnal. Their bodies are like five different types of animals all rolled up into one. A prehensile tail like monkeys, tongue like an ant-eater, claws like sloths, rounded ears and soft, brown fur like a feline. with big dark bulging eyes like bats. Martilla, was the spanish name for this animal which translated means hammer also. It puzzled me as to why this name was so. Ringo was really friendly and affectionate.

He slept all through the day. Like *Dracula*, he drew his blanket over his head with first morning light. We built him a cave-like box to spend the day in. His habitat, like all our animals, had a tree for play, exercise and shade. I changed his bedding every night. One early morning as I put him to sleep, he urinated on me. Since I spent every morning cleaning out habitats and feeding the animals, I did not change my shirt.

By midday, when I was done I was drawn to a very erotic scent. It was his scent. The ammonia had evaporated through the morning and all that was left was a musky seductive smell that I wished I could bottle.

Ringo caught a cold that rainy season. He was always sniffling. At night I brought him in out of the chill air. It was a hard, long rainy season this year, nine months to be exact, from March to November. We get a lot of rain in this part of the country, attributing to why it is so beautiful and green here. Rain is the main ingredient of a rainforest. I decided to help Ringo with a natural remedy Dostora, the Sri Lankan herb master had given me for people.

Basically the same herbs work on both humans and animals. Animal DNA is ninety-seven percent the same as humans. The remedy was a type of yucca leaves from a tree in India called yucccinara.You boil the leaves covered, then get under a sheet naked and steam your whole body, taking deep long breaths. I got under the sheet with the martilla and spent twenty minutes each evening with him steaming, like a Turkish bath. He got over his cold in four days. On the last day he spent in the bathroom during his flu, for it was the only safe place to keep him from tearing up the house, I was awakened in the middle of the night to someone taking a shower.

Guess who? Ringo had been jumping around and playing and had accidently put the shower on. He was acting differently, very wild, he wanted something.

After the rains had ceased I spotted a wild martilla on one of my jungle walks. I had been riding my horse hard on a trip to the Diamante,which means diamond, the largest waterfall in Costa Rica. I was excited over the sacred caves I had come upon set on the top of the falls. The writings and drawings on the wall were from another time. I was anxious to talk to Mitch about them.

I did not know if this kingachu that I spotted was a female or male, but I sensed that Ringo was looking to mate. The call of the wild was coming to him and he wanted to roam. It was becoming more difficult with each day to keep him in his pen. He would look about the pen for openings to escape, so I took him out at evening time to see what would happen. He sniffed the air for a long time, then he caught her scent and scrabbled out of my arms. It was difficult to see what was going on as he bounded into the brush. I stayed in the same spot for three hours. Just as I was about to leave, I spotted both of them under the moonlight. They were definitely a pair, and with her help in learning the wilds I knew he would be fine free. All animals have the innate instinct in them. Born wild, but raised among humans it remains on the surface awaiting their return. Born in captivity, instinct is tampered with yet never extinguished.

I never saw him again; hopefully he became a father that spring. Nocturnal animals were hard to watch. I had nothing such as night vision binoculars. Wish I did. The final animal release at the center was a beautiful green parrot, a lora, named Checuyo, which is the name of this species in Spanish. I confiscated him from some Ticos who stole the eggs from nests and sold exotic baby birds to tourists.

He sure was an ugly thing when I first got him. He ate like a pig and grew up fast. I fed him a mixture of corn meal with smashed up bananas and papaya and even a few drops of milk. Later on he ate many different things. He liked to try people food. He was very curious and had a mean streak in him. I observed him mimic the dogs to a T. My dogs were guard dogs except for She-Dog who licked and cared for every baby animal that came my way. She was wonderful about the way she handled them. She made them feel comfortable in their human space.

Checuyo was like a pit bull. He screamed a shrieking sound whenever anyone came over. Our house was always full of people. Mitch was selling some real estate and was the idol of every foreigner who wanted to have the life he did. We had guests every night. Most spent the night, as accommodations such as hotels were non existent in these parts. Checuyo was rarely put in his habitat. Only when we were away, otherwise he was free to fly about. He never left our area. He knew the boundaries without being told. Birds are the only animals that actually rebuild brain cells. They are very intelligent.

On several occasions, he flew into the windows of our guest's room and stole things, a set of diamond earrings, rent-a-car keys and anything else that caught his fancy. We never knew where he hid them. He also woke up very early in the morning and bothered the guests to get out of bed. He became a legend and a story to take home. I remember how vicious he tried to look when he was trying to intimidate someone. He puffed up the feathers around his face and walked around all big and proud, slowly circling like a lion.

He stayed with us for two years, then made his own decision to go free. One morning I could not find him. I was worried, this was not like him. I asked my maid Majudy who came every morning, except Sundays. She too thought it odd that he was nowhere to be found. I had just lost a toucan to a snake that bit him in his habitat one night, and I feared the same fate had happened to Checuyo. I searched for his body everywhere. Mitch was away this morning so I couldn't ask him. At lunch Mitch returned. He too helped me call and search for him. About an hour later, Checuyo appeared with a female. This we could tell for the colorings are different on the female and male. He was so sweet to her.

What a change had come over him. He wanted us to know he was in love and it was touching to see him bring us his mate so we knew he was leaving us in a good way. I wonder if he gave her the diamond earrings he had stolen? My heart sang as they flew away...

In my years of living in the wilds I observed many phenomenons. Creatures living amongst mankind. Accepting man's children, nourishing them, protecting them and teaching them. Many instances have been observed of this. And many people have observed a dog feeding a kitten or a mother cat feeding puppies. Even wild ones. I witnessed a video tape of a tiger in a zoo that had lost her babies and went into a depression which the handlers could not cure. A last ditch effort was made with whatever baby animal they had in the zoo. It happened that there were only a group of baby pigs available. Incredibly the mother tiger is shown lying down with 6 little piglets nursing off her teats. People who live in the territories of wild animals share a special relationship with each other. Creatures are drawn to man and ready to serve him with a heartfelt desire. Why is man's love so important to them? City folk and their pets also see this, even seeing different pets get jealous in which one receives the most attention. We take this for granted, yet even in the jungles all animals aspire to feel the invisible ray of light emanating from man. What it is called may vary but this is a real natural phenomenon, and we need to understand its specific purpose.

Our domestic animals are people's creation. Each species originates in the wilds. Pampering animals turns them into what we ourselves lack in our lives. Give each animal their right to that wild space which is inside each and every one of them. Our history beginnings depict man hunting and killing animals. This is but a great misconception. In truth man and animals shared a love and respect for each other.

There are those domestic animals which have been so over breed that they no longer retain the wilds in them. Neither in dna nor spirit. This worldwide massive disorder between domestics and the wilds plays a major role in wildlife dehabitation, disease and deforestation. Man needs simply to stop breeding domestic mutations to restore and co create the wilds once again. He will find that everything he thinks he needs from our domestic's in the wilds.

There is a series of books called "The Ringing Cedars of Russia". It is *Anastasia's* story and I strongly urge all of you to read up on our true history. They have become my favorite books.

I had greatly influenced these scattered small towns and their people in the rights of wild animals. No longer were the people taking wildlife as pets and pretty soon I wanted to expand my work with animals. I was also speaking to local vets about natural alternatives and some were listening. By the end of that year all the animals in my center had been returned to the wilds or placed in the best hands possible. I too started a new chapter in my life.

The Beach 3

The beaches of the Osa peninsula encompass the district our ocean property was on. This is the most beautiful coastline in the entire country. Raw, untouched and unspoiled. The only national marine park, called Uvita, is located only twenty minutes south from our land. There are a series of distinct rock formations out in the oceans with beautiful names to match. From our mountain top we are able to see Uvita and the island of Cana, a small island abounding with sea life. It was just a short trip by boat and surfing was good on the leeward side. Mitch finally took me out there. I saw the giants of the sea. The whales migratory pass cut through these waters. Swimming in rhythms, breeching and rolling with the seas. They are abundant here. The coastlines of Costa Rica are protected by a law which states one can not own or build any structure within three hundred meters of the high tide line. This is what impressed me about this little country. One does not see rows of condos or homes and hotels. Virgin jungle lines the ocean shores.

On a typical morning I was riding bareback on *Neblina*, one of my horses into the ocean surf. Neblina, which means mist, was my sea horse, a petite beautiful palomino. We would swim through crashing waves and beyond. Then wonderfully exhausted and hungry, I picked my breakfast off the trees and shared it with the gorgeous scarlet macaws watching me from the tree tops. Their favorite treats were almonds. Almond trees and coconut palms held hands with each other. Always in pairs for they mate for life. But beware, these birds caw so loudly, you cannot hear yourself think. When they take flight, it is as if you are watching a flying rainbow.

Whales and dolphins are here year round. Some species are migratory, others live here permanently. The surfers get a rare treat here, they surf with the playful dolphins. I spent many long lazy afternoons watching how these cetaceans play with the humans in their waters. It is as if they know the minds of the surfers. They calculate their moves and joyfully bound in and out of the waves. These creatures are masters of the surf. Showing off comes second nature to them. They spent most of their time playing and only a relatively short time feeding. During that time I read of two women who spent three years studying dolphins in the Bahamas. They determined that humans are closer to dolphins than they are to primates. Our brain size, our skin texture, even equal to our emotions. A little known fact about the species itself was interesting to me. All animals mate solely to procreate and do so only during a certain time known as their heat, while dolphins make love all the time to all they come in contact with and they have orgasms. No wonder they always have a smile on their face.

I am a fish sign and have been told I am whale pisces. I have a great love for whales. They are the record keepers of our world. This the indigenous people taught me. They taught me that every animal has a spirit which carries a power we can all call upon. From the smallest creature to the grandest, they all serve a higher purpose. The bay of whales, *bahia de ballena*, located at the bottom of our land, is teaming with them. From our lookout point we would count how many there were every morning. We would spot anywhere from five to fifteen in this magical spot.

I spent endless hours sitting on the beach talking to them, and sending messages with my mind. Trying to talk with them, wondering if they indeed hear me. I play the piano and

I wanted to play music to them. Their soundings and songs seem so sorrowfully deep to me. A visiting friend of ours from the States gave me the opportunity to play to them. He had a magnificent sailing ship and aboard it he had put a piano. We set out early one dawn to greet the whales. The morning mist greeted us. It was so peaceful on the sea, no other boats in sight.

The wonderful smell of brine filled my lungs. I stood at the bow watching the movement of waves lulling the ocean to awaken. We did not need to go out far, we spotted a pod almost within minutes. A rush came over me as the gentle giants rolled with the waves. We sheeted in the sails and I began to touch the ivory's. I closed my eyes and let the swaying of the ship take me into that dimension seldom felt. The music I played was one of my own making. It was a bittersweet melody. The notes crescendos, then pierced the morning air.

A remarkable thing happened then. The whales started singing along. Note for note they matched my tune. An uncanny schronicity. It sent chills up my spine. I opened my eyes for a brief second then fell back into the trance I was taken under. Some of the men on board closed their eyes as waves of emotions flowed through them.

This continued for a half hour. They stayed close to the boat for another half hour and then went on their way. I watched the expressions of the men aboard. I knew the whales had the power to make us see things deep inside of us. The vibrational range of sonar in which they communicate amongst themselves from ocean to ocean carries tunes and tones in which they express themselves. They give us a balance, and they receive our thoughts as well. It is an experience I will never forget. These whales were humpbacks, but greys were also out that day. The silence that came over us was as if the whole world for one holy second was at peace. We had all received a healing from these great ones. We were struck with awe.

The next day I walked a new beach in my exploration of this coast and found a huge ivory bone piece. It was whale bone. It weighed a ton and looked as if it had been there a long time. Very brittle and sun bleached white. It was the piece that holds the brain in the back base skull of the whale. I carried it, more like dragged it, to my truck and with the help of a passer by, lifted it up and drove it to the jungle house. It remains with me still to this day. My good luck charm, my gift from the whales....

Pro-Felis 4

Along the beach of Uvita I had come to learn about Pro-Felis, a new rescue feline center. It was headed and run by two German biologists, Siegfried Weisel and Sabine Weber. Minae, the enviornmental government branch, placed small wild feline species into the care of Pro-Felis. They worked with ocelots, margays, and tigrellos. This was exciting news, as for the first time I saw a change in the country's attitude to protecting its precious wildlife.

I went to visit. I had just come from surfing, I was wet and pulled my truck up to their gates and began to change my clothes. In the middle of my doings I heard a soft , warm chuckle and turned around to meet Ziggy. He stared at me, not knowing what to think. He had piercing eyes, a serious face, thin statue, and strong hands. I liked him immediately. I sensed his no nonsense approach to his work. I smiled and introduced myself as an animal behaviorist and herbologist. He invited me in, but told me they were not open to visitors. I told him I was not a visitor, I was there to help. I told him I wanted to see his cats. He was hesitant, but I matched him glare for persistent glare. He relented. What else could he do, I was not leaving...

I followed him to the thatched bamboo structures which made up the encampment. Nestled amongst the jungle in a clearing close to a stream, the center looked much like an African safari camp.

As he offered me some coffee, I set my bag, a fake spotted cat purse, down on the table. Sabine walked in and burst out laughing at my bag. I thought, well at least I am proving entertaining to this group. Sabine was very warm and loving. She had a soothing, soft-spoken voice. I knew the animals liked her voice. The most savage of beasts responds better to low decibels. We all sat down and talked of many things. They were very by the book in their work. They were working on introducing the felines to a new protected area in the jungle along the coast. The cats would wear tracking collars, and Ziggy and Sabine collected information and data with the aid of these collars. Ziggy informed me that Costa Rica had never done any collective studies on any of their wildlife. No one knew how many species, how many counts, where their range came to or what was really out there. I liked his tenacity. He agreed with me that the government was slack about their parks and even though there were many national parks throughout the country, none were properly protected and accounted for.

The government lacked funds they said, when in actuality they dictated monies out for all the wrong reasons. Selfish to a fault, yet there were some worthy people working at Minae that really did try.

Any feline a farmer saw passing on his property would be shot on site, even though these wild cats were highly endangered and protected by international laws.

No one enforced the laws.

Ziggy also guarded the areas where the cats would be released. I met the felines and was happy to see they were well cared for. Their pens were large and on natural ground. Food was fresh and alive. Contact with humans was minimal. They were situated on a river running into the sea, very private and away from human habitation. I went home that day and talked my family's ears off about the center. I prepared some herbal formulas, simple basic remedies such as a parasite cleanse, a hairball remover, a skin condition treatment and a kitten formula. Pro-felis was open to accepting my herbs.

One area we disagreed on however, were vaccinations. Ziggy vaccinated all the cats. This was proven as being detrimental to the existing wildlife in the areas the cats were being introduced to. Since the live vaccine carries the disease itself, it is picked up by the wild ones through the defecation of the new releases both on the ground and in the rivers where the animals drink and hunt, thus infecting healthy wild cats with the deadly disease. Whole areas of wildlife have been wiped out because of this.

On New Years Eve night Ziggy took me to the site where his first release would be. He had four margays ready to go. He brought a pair of military Russian night vision binoculars. I had never looked through these binoculars before in my life. When I put them on I let out the longest *woww* I ever heard myself say. It was so cool to be able to see at night. I could pick out a tiny bug on a huge green leaf. Things were shaded red, but it was so remarkable to be able to see. I saw the jungle like I had never seen it before. It becomes so alive at night. I wanted to stay there forever. New's Years Eve was a night in which I always did something which would honor the coming year. This night the three hours I spent having the power to see at night was a vision unto myself. My family knew this night was important to me, and as I quietly snuck back into the house, I found them still up and waiting to hear all about it. They had spent the evening playing scrabble which Island always won.

The release took place the next day and I was allowed to join the group. Ziggy tranquilized the cats and put tracking collars on their necks. When they came to, Ziggy gave them some time to become accustomed to the collars. They didn't like the unnatural collars. I wouldn't want one on my neck either. But again I could not say anything. This was not my project and it was the only way to keep tabs on their progress.

Sabine opened the traveling cages, and the four margays immediately bounded into the jungle. Ziggy spent the next month tracking them on foot and via an ultralight flying machine. They all did well except for one male which Ziggy found dead one day from a bullet to his head. He contacted Minae. They did nothing.

Ziggy was learning, like all of us who worked to save the jungles and their inhabitants, that you had to do all the work yourself.

The No Name Hurricane 5

The season was changing. The rains would be upon us soon. Mitch had covered a top story porch we had in our house in Platanillo with a heavy plastic, transparent roof. We spent a lot of time up there as the view was quite nice. Gentle rolling hills, connected to an emerald rainforest mountain range, and there was always a nice breeze blowing. We would relax and smoke a joint. It was about 4:30 in the afternoon. Mitch, a couple of his surfer friends and I were up there hanging out. Suddenly the winds picked up, but something was different. I couldn't put my finger on it, I just sensed something forbidding. I turned to the guys and said, "There is something wrong, this is not a good wind."

Mitch looked at me and said, "Don't worry. We are probably just in for a good rain."

No sooner had he said this than a strong gust took the plastic roof right off.

I said, "Mitch I have a feeling we need to leave right away." My instinct was so strong, I could not explain it.

Smiling down on me Mitch asked, "Where would you propose we go?" I said, "Away from here. This is not a good storm."

He put his big strong arms around me and held me tight. "Come on," he said, "Let's go inside and close the windows. It's just a storm."

We went inside and our friends went on their way. It started to rain buckets, such mountains of water I never saw in my life. I looked at my animals and saw their fear growing. The land was beginning to run. Earth shifting into mud. Animals in the wild always sense impending danger. It is the instinct that tells them so. My instinct, too, came alive.

44

It rained all through the night. I fell into a deep sleep. I had a dream that haunted me for years. In my dream I saw wild cats, trapped in cages, drowning, their screams ringing through my brain. I woke in the middle of the night and shook Mitch awake to tell him about it. He was worried about me, he had never seen me like this. He helped me back to sleep.

The next morning, dark, angry skies replaced the curtains of rain. We woke to an unbelievable devastation . The road by our house was gone. It had sunk down like a crater and had been washed away by the monsoon rains. As far as one could see, mountains of earth had been toppled and pushed. Houses were down.

This morning even the birds were silent. We found out a hurricane had hit the coast. It was unforeseen and the wreckage it left in its wake was monumental. The winds were still blowing; the president of the country flew out via helicopter to see the damage. There were two helicopters; one was pushed by gale-force winds into a mountain. It was smashed to pieces. The president's helicopter made it, and after the investigation the president declared the catastrophe a national disaster. It made worldwide news. This hurricane was named Cesaer, and it came without warning.

To some of us at least...

We were fortunate, our house intact. But many others were not so lucky. Many people had died. We helped as many as we could. No one had water, even though it had rained a hundred inches. The parts of the road that were still there, were impassable, for giant landslide mounds of earth covered them. No one could drive, so we walked. Mitch was worried about the beach farm. We needed to access the damage to our land. We walked all the way down to the beach. It took us three hours.

Huge parts of jungles, trees and boulders were ripped out of the ground. It was sad. Whole sections of acres at a time were gone. The farmers who clear hundreds of acres of rainforest to turn it into pasture for their cattle, had created an erosion of the lands upholding the jungles. Thus when such great forces of water arrived, nothing kept the trees from falling. A lot of the rainforest that was wiped out was virgin or primary, and like the wildlife, was greatly endangered.

Climbing the final ridge before the beach, we saw a different ocean. Grossly engorged, major rivers had carried the debris from the hurricane into the sea. Thousands of trees and homes floated in the ocean. The water was an ugly color, brown for at least a mile or more out to sea. A family we knew, who lived up the ridge on a hill, was in trouble. We had just begun our descent when I heard the mother screaming. I ran up to see her. The going was tough and slippery. Our plastic boots were collecting mud up over the tops and my socks were soaked and I sloushed and squeshed at every step. Mitch was behind me guarding my back in case I fell. I could hear the dread in the mothers choking throat as she moaned and sobbed with her tears.

When I reached her she waved her arms frantically. She told me a horrible story. In the middle of the night her husband awoke to the crashing of trees. As he looked out his window at the mountain top, he saw the entire mound surface coming down, headed straight for their home. It looked, he said, like an enormous ocean of mud. He woke his family and instructed them to run. The mother carried the infant and the other two daughters, ages six and thirteen, had to run on their own. The six-year-old did not make it. When I arrived, they had just found her body, which had tumbled a kilometer downhill with the mud. She had been buried alive.

I helped wash the mud off her lifeless mangled body as the parents sobbed. We took the family down to the church at the sea where an emergency outreach was set up. I held the mother for a long time, Mitch gave the father some money and we continued on. We stopped and talked with the townfolk. Everyone was frantic.

The hurricane's major center damage was a corridor starting at San Isidro, running along the mountain range all the way to the beach of Uvita. My heart sank when I heard this. I remembered my dream of the night before. I thought of Pro-Felis and the cats. We could not make it down there, but one of Ziggy's workers, who had come into town early this morning by boat, told us that Pro-Felis was gone. He told me the whole story, and it was just like my dream. At the same time I woke Mitch up last night to tell him of my dream, Ziggy also woke up. He and Sabine could tell the felines were in trouble. They ran out into the dark night and pouring rains. The cats were screaming. As they made it to the habitats and cages, the river running alongside the center had tripled and was sweeping everything out of its way. Some cages were already washing down the raging river.

Ziggy ordered Sabine to open all the existing cages as he went into the river to try to rescue the trapped cats. He was only able to reach a few and watched, sickened and helpless as his cats drowned in their cages. I was numb after the news. A coldness crept over me. It was what I had foreseen in my dream and now I was shaken in fear at the ability I had to have foreseen it. Mother Nature had taken her toll. It took months, almost two years, to repair the damage. It was forever, before we forgot it.

Move n' Change 6

About this time, we decided to send Island back to California to continue her education, since Costa Rica's higher level schooling fell short. She was going to live with her father, whom she had seen only three times in her life. It was ultimately Island's decision, but we all had mixed feelings about it.

I took a place in the central valley, up in the high cold mountains above San Jose. This area was called Monte De La Cruz. It was on the border of the central valley and the magnificent national park, Braulio Carillo, which was the passage of forests covering the mountains down to the Caribbean side. The trees were all pines, the grasses, long and soft and I used the fireplace in our new home every night. Mitch remained on the coast to continue his work and look after our land.

Shortly afterwards I flew to the States with my daughter. She was both excited and a bit fearful, yet Island had a strong beaming spirit which shone through her apprehensions. I held her close the whole flight and buried my tears deep inside. I spent a month getting her ready for her new life. I would miss her so much so I kept myself insanely busy. I also took advantage of being stateside and spent my free time researching wildlife work and herbal formulas. I became a student of master herbologist Joel Hyman and created a natural animal remedy line which I carried back to Costa Rica. Animal herbal remedies in the Western world were a relatively new frontier. It was important to my work that I gained as much knowledge as possible on the subject. I respected Joel's methods and their effectiveness. Joel had a kindred spirit. It was easy to learn from this man. The last week I was there Mitch flew in to join us. He was helping me stay strong through the parting and I could see he too was finding it hard to say goodbye to his little girl. He was more of a father to her then any man ever could be and my heart went out to him.

We planned a trip to Nevada to check on a wild animal center. They had asked for my help in curing some sick animals. I strongly disapproved of these wildlife breeding facilities, yet I sensed there was a calling coming from this trip. As we drove through the Nevada desert, endless miles of cactus and dry thorny shrubs, there on the side of the road we saw a string of cages, covered from the scorching heat by a mere piece of newspaper. The woman slouched on a broken plastic chair by the cages was huge, she looked like a circus freak, with several missing teeth, rolls of fat squeezed into spandex pants and her hands had not been washed in weeks. She sold rare white Alaskan wolf cubs for five hundred dollars. I was furious. We stopped the car and I let her know what an outrage it was for her to be selling wolves, let along in the middle of the desert. She only seemed to get turned on by it. She smiled wickedly and then spit. I wanted to vomit.

One of the four male cubs, the smallest one, smelled the worst. His whimper raked against his dry parched mouth creating a raspy low whine. I wanted to save him. I wanted to save them all. But this woman was big and no doubt had a rifle in the rusty brown trailer toilet she used as her room. Mitch created a ruse to distract her while I stole the small wolf. I quickly threw the little guy into the backseat of the car, got behind the wheel, opened the passenger side of the door for Mitch to jump in and we drove away. Looking through the rear view window I saw the woman running into the toilet and as I accelerated the cloud of dust hid us out of sight. I floored the car and we were gone in a flash. After but a few miles I pulled over to change places with Mitch so I could examine the little guy. He was shaking with fright but I knew this moment of fear was worth it for him. I wrapped him in a towel and put the air conditioner on high to cool him down. He did not stop shaking till we reached our motel which thankfully was quiet and small and set in a small group of trees. I snuck him into the room, put him in the bathroom with water and food. I rushed off to see my client and Mitch stayed to keep watch over the wolf. Within an hour I was back. I set about checking out the condition of my new charge. This cub was sick with worms, poor diet, malnutrioned and desperately needed a bath. The first night he howled his heart out. It was a motel so I put him in the bed. I slept as close to him as I dared for I could not give him a bath until we returned back to California the following day. He had a bacteria infection in his stomach, which was part of the acridness I smelled on him.

I can diagnose many conditions simply by the smell the sick animal gives off. I have an acute sense of smell. It guides me well. This sense tells me more than my eyes, since I know how to read it and to interpret it.

The drive back was torturous. Hot, slow, for wolves get motion sickness faster than any wild animal I have known. Poor thing, I couldn't wait to get home. I had three days to ready him for the trip to Costa Rica. With the help of Joel's herbs I cured his condition as quickly as possible. He helped ready the paperwork to exit the country. It is illegal to transport a wolf out of the country. To do so takes months of paperwork and a lot of money. We had neither. We listed the cub as a German shepherd and gave him a natural herbal sedative for the five hour plane ride. We flew Lacsa, the airline of Costa Rica as they had a red eye flight which was perfect for our needs. It is always better to fly animals at night. They sense less of their imbalance. Also the night is cooler. The rumble of the plane's engine are probably the worst vibration animals feel. It creates fear. I prayed.

Everything went fine. We arrived in Costa Rica and the airport baggage handlers immediately gave me my precious cargo. Mitch had tipped a guy and he ran to do our bidding. The cub was fine. The sedative worked very nicely. It was effective, yet harmless. When we got our baggage and went through the customs check , the cub began to howl. Everyone in the airport turned around to look. Could they really have heard a wolf's howl?

Customs at this time was pretty lax about paperwork and usually very accommodating to tourists. Normally, they greet you with smiles and are always ready to help with your questions whether they understand you or not. But their curiosity was up now. They asked if this was a wolf and I smiled sweetly and showing the papers said, of course not silly, it is just a little German shepherd. They let us through. As soon as I took our new baby out of the cage, he promptly threw up all over me. We started the forty-five minute drive to our lodge house in Monte de la Cruz. This cold temperature was so much better for an Alaskan wolf than the desert. I named him Spirit.

Espirito 7

This little wolf cub became one of my greatest animal powers. My time with him changed me forever. The reason he was in my life was to open eyes I never knew we could possess.

When we arrived home, I began to work diligently on his health and well being. I added herbal supplements to his food, wild meat. We enclosed a small part of the forest in our back yard for his space. I exercised him three times a day. I also researched how I could return him to the wilds. I knew he would spend at least his first year with me and even though Costa Rica was not his country, it was a place where I could work in peace with him without the bureaucracy of the States. However, this was a double-edged sword. Those responsible and experienced to work on freeing animals needed paperwork a mile long with red flags thrown at every turn.

The laws in the United States allowed individuals with no experience to own wild animals of all kinds. Beware, they are not a prize. Man never did nor ever will own them. Wolves have long ago become extinct in many countries due to man's ignorance. The myths surrounding wolves were ill founded and grossly exaggerated. Man destroys or cages that which he fears most. In reality, his acceptance of his fears would give him greater power then he realizes. We created the wild ones and in our darkness have sent them further and further away from us.

In my workings with animals men fear, I have found that only in respecting them does one truly gain power. I was to become very powerful. The animals gave me this and more.

Spirit or Cub, as was his nickname, became quite strong. A vet, Villalobos, was opened-minded enough to work with me and my alternative medicines.

In Spanish his name means, " house of the wolves". He
loved wolves and both he and his girlfriend Kattia were frequent visitors at our home.

The little wolf was developing quickly. He ate always and
everything I gave him. The way he ate was strong. He wolfed
down his food, hence the saying, as if it was air. Once he
started eating, no one could get in his way or stop him. Wolves
in the wilds may eat but twice a week, though they hunt daily.
So instinctively they eat as much as they can to store for the
lean days. However they are not gluttons. They are far more
physical than that.

I fed Cub a very healthy, live diet. It cost a fortune but he
was worth it. He grew incredibly fast. At four months he was
bigger than my full grown German shepherd, with a beautiful
coat that was long and white, with grey black streaks running
on the tips. The texture of his fur was coarse, thick and shiny.
Only his underbelly was snow-white and baby hair soft. His
paws were massive. They were as big as my face when he was
still so little. The way he ran was different from dogs. He gal-
loped like a horse, long, loping, even strides. He had stamina
which wore us all out.

I was alone with him most of the time. We took walks
through the forest, and the cold climate was so invigorating
for him. I too, liked the cold. Wolves can not bark. But they
howl a piercing sound, which goes through your bones, for
long spells. It is the song of the whales and wolves which
moves me most. I had always loved wolves, and I was delighted to finally have this opportunity to work one on one with
him. I loved him in a different way. He was my male. Wolves
mate for life like whales and I became his mate. My husband

only came two times a month. I do not know how to explain
that this wolf and our bond made me not need any other male.

My dogs liked the cub when he was little. As he multiplied
in size they wanted very little to do with him, yet I knew it
was important to the cub to have other friends as they are
pack animals. So I had a long talk with my dogs about helping
me out. My dogs were great. They never let me down. Spirit
would run up and roll on his belly submissively to the alpha
female and lick them all over.We became one happy wolf pack.
I soon heard of other people who had wolves as pets in Costa
Rica. Of course I wanted to investigate as I could not imagine
wolves living in this tropical climate. There is a species of red
wolves which used to roam Mexico, but they too became extinct. The only place I ever saw the red wolf is in a cage at the
zoo in Mexico City.

I had my wolf in one of the coldest parts of Costa Rica. The
others here who had them were reported to be living on the
beach in an area called Montezuma. I contacted one couple,
Iala and Akal. They had a white female wolf named Loba.
They had heard of my work and were open to learning all they
could. They truly loved their wolf. Loba was not a full wolf, I
could tell she had a bit of dog in her like so many wolves I was
to meet. It was quite popular at this time in the States to have
a wolf as a pet. Breeders breed huskies, German shepherds
and the likes to wolves to try to come out with a more domesticated pet. But Mother Nature rules, and the wildness of the
wolf always comes through. Like most wild animals turned
into pets, once they mature they become dangerous and their
instincts come alive, telling them this is not their world. After
the initial novelty of owning a wolf died down in the States,
hundreds of them were put to sleep as the owners could not

handle them anymore. Loba had come from a set of puppies brought down by another couple in Montezuma who originally were from Canada. Heart and Honey were their names. They too were nice people, but nice people can be ignorant too. Almost no wolf cub made it past six months. The tropical climate brought new strains of virus and bacteria to animals whose immune system was not accustomed to it. The heat also took its toll on them. Several times I would wake in the night to someone crying on the other end of the phone about their sick wolf cub. It took six hours to get to Montezuma. You drove, you waited for a ferry, then you drove again. The ferry only ran certain hours, limiting you. All on shitty roads with endless potholes and dirt more than pavement. As usual, the local veterinarians did more harm than good and I got called in when the animal was already on death's door. I was beginning to feel as if the animal spirits were solely calling me to help them pass from this world into the next.

I taught every person I came in contact with the downfall of taking a wolf as a pet. I suggested they work on good wolf projects at protecting them instead. If they wanted to remain in Costa Rica and had such love for animals, I also prompted them to work on the local wildlife and leave the wolves up in the northern countries where they belonged.

Loba did well and Iala and I became good friends. Loba loved to sing and at any given moment when instructed to sing, she would howl her heart out. Later on in my story you will read of an endearing experience she had with a group of school children.

At six months Spirit was the size of a full grown wolf and he was not nearly done growing. I received a letter from a contact I had in Canada. They were a grass roots organization that was re-introducing wolves into the wilds. I was thinking of sending cub to them. They were ready to work with him.

With a heavy heart I digested all this information. I could not leave Costa Rica at this time and yet I wanted to work with the cub myself. I knew he would not take to new people. Except for Kattia and Villalobos, Iala and my husband, no one ever saw him. He did not like any other people. He trusted and was attached only to me. This bond was a mental acceptance of truth in all things and an unwavering trust. In him I saw a spirit animal with an intelligence which far surpassed the animals before him. I decided to take my relationship with him to another level. I wanted to work with animal communication. I had read a few short articles on the subject. It was still considered an impossibility by most of the world. And those that believed in it rarely if ever went public with their experiences. People simply did not believe in such a possibility. Yet I knew this was the "missing link" between animals and mankind. I couldn't be the only one with this type of instinct inside of me. The possibilities of different realities inside our minds had long ago been removed from our minds.

I remembered my time with the indigenous people. They told me one could talk to everything, plants, trees, animals and every living thing. I knew animals had strong communication amongst themselves and other species. I researched and read everything written to that point about animal behavior and interspecies communication. One book I liked was When Elephants Weep, by Jeffrey Moussaint Maison . It was the first written of its kind on the minds of animals.

This wolf made me see things I never saw before. Throughout my childhood years I had seen, felt and heard things with animals. It was not clear to me what I was experiencing, however. Science spoke little of these things. Biologists are left brain thinkers. Our minds are structured on polarities. The sixth sense language breaks down all the polarities. It leaves an open book of information we can draw from. Through the minds of animals I witnessed this ability locked inside the human race.

I worked with Cub every day. Through a series of mental pictures I sent simple messages to him. He received them immediately. Even my dogs picked up on what I communicated. You are reading minds when this occurs. The indigenous people taught me that we all are born with the innate ability to communicate without talking. We simply are not instructed to use this method of communication. We instead prompt our children to talk first. Every parent delights in their child's first words. The indigenous people do the exact opposite. Before men learned to speak they spoke with their minds. In opening the ability to speak with our mouths we also created the ability to lie. For the mind can not lie as it speaks to other minds. It is a open window to the soul. Something to think about…

A child, it has been proven, can communicate with animals. This communication is effortless until the child reaches puberty. We need only to instruct them. I guess I am going backwards, we first have to learn ourselves before we can teach our children…

Clinical scientific studies have shown the brain wave patterns between an animal communicator and an animal. Once communication is channeled, the brain wave patterns become in sinc. I will share a story I read from an excerpt in a book by Penelope Smith, animal communicator and author of Animal Talk. She was asked to prove her ability to talk with the animals. So she shared a story with the group, A woman in New

York City, was having a problem with her dog. She dearly loved this long time family friend, so she contacted Penelope in a last ditch effort for help.

Penelope agreed and flew from Los Angeles to New York. She asked to be left alone with the dog. Within a short time she had communicated with the dog. She asked the woman to return to the room where she was.

She asked her, "Where are your roller skates?" Dumbfounded the woman asked why.

"Well," Penelope said, "Your dog is very sad. That is its only problem. You used to go roller skating with your dog and suddenly everything changed," the dog had told her. The dog even told her that they were in a different place and did not like the change. The woman was shocked. It was all true. She had just moved with her family to another part of the city, whereas before they were in a more rural area. Before the move, she skated with her dog almost every day.

The woman ran up the stairs to the attic where she had put away the skates. Upon bringing them down, the dog immediately jumped up and down and changed from his depression of two months. The joy seen in this animal came from the communication. It was finally able to break through to its human companions.

Picture how hard it is when you want to tell someone something urgent. If you were in a foreign country and did not speak the language, image the constant frustration that would arise in you. It is the same with our pets. They need to know you understand them. More times than not, such a misunderstanding leads to a negative outcome.

Through my experiences I have learned that what wild animals communicate and what domestic animals communicate is entirely different. Usually domestic animals speak of their domestic life, while animals of the wilds tell a far greater story. This process comes from our thoughts. Our thoughts have the greatest power over anything on this earth and what we think is what they hear.

My cub, Spirit, enlightened me to this. One day while I was again walking with him in the forest, instead of running about when I unleashed him as usual, he laid down by my side. He then spoke to me as opposed to me speaking to him. He asked me about mankind. He asked me if I knew who I was. His message was crystal clear. He let me know he was not mine. He told me he had come into my life for a purpose and that he would not long be with me. He was of another place, another time. He spoke to me as a shaman of old would. His message was very powerful. I grew in my respect for him tenfold.

My inner voice said, "You realize you have this power and a great responsibility comes with it, a privileged knowledge. You unlock it through your suffering."

Some of his message is not meant to be shared at this time. It was a personal lesson I still carry with me today. I realized that the work I choose would not be easy, and yet it was one of great importance and would enlightened the masses. We walked home very quietly this day.

Mitch and I were going through some problems at this time. He needed me to make a short trip, about five days, to the States. I did not want to go, but I knew I had no choice. He would stay with the cub for the first three days, then Villalobos would come and stay with him at the house. Spirit was not a dog you could move to a kennel, no matter how nice the place was. Villalobos agreed that it would be best to stay with him in his own den. That is basically what my house had become at this time. Spirit's den.

Kattia had taken a keen interest in what I did. Our comradeship gave her the opportunity to read all my work on animal communication, as she too wanted to be closer to the animals in her life. She was a horse woman, a good one, and wanted to communicate with them. I saw that, this would come easy to her. Villalobos did not really believe in such stuff. That was okay. Everyone in their own time, I figured.

I exercised Cub a lot in the days before I was to leave as I knew he would stay in his pen for the duration of my trip. No one else could handle him on a leash, but I rarely had to put the leash on him. I preferred to let him be as free as I could make him. With a burst of tears I kissed him good bye and flew to the States.

I called home every day. Mitch said Spirit was depressed. He let him into the house. Cub found some clothes I had been wearing and took them into his den. I tried long distance communication. I do not know if he got it. His appetite had lessened. Mitch had our dogs spend a lot more time with him. Spirit was the first animal since Rasha's death that I allowed myself to get close to. I had fallen in love with him. I didn't know how much till this separation. Absence makes the heart grow fonder and weepier. How true this saying rang. It was my pure unconditional love that wanted so desperately to set him free.

He deserved his own life, his own kind. I wanted to set an example for others. I wanted to make a difference. I remembered what he had taught me. I knew and felt myself growing wiser. Two more days to go. I called just as Mitch was leaving back to the beach and Villalobos and Kattia were on their way over. Our dogs stayed at the house to keep Cub company. Kattia immediately set upon making Spirit feel better. She spent hours with him while Villalobos had to do his rounds with his veterinarian practice.

He too, would return in the early evenings, cutting short his days because he was so amazed by the cub. He would take in every nuance of this beautiful wolf. He even started to wear only wolf t-shirts and asked me to bring him one upon my return.

The next morning he did a thorough examination of Cub. Spirit allowed him as Kattia who he had a kinship with, never left his side, and he was beginning to trust in her. I think it also had to do with the fact that she was a female. Villalobos decided to give him a yearly worming shot of Ivomec. He wanted Cub to live forever, he was falling for him too. What he didn't know was that Ivomec was never used on wolves. Their system not only repels this chemical but it has been proven fatal. It was an injection. It raced through his bloodstream very quickly and the cub became very ill.

When I called that evening, it was Kattia who gave me the news, as Villalobos had surgery to do at this time. Deep inside of me a moan like the howl of a wolf escaped my lips. No, no , nooo please God, not again.

I tried to change my flight to one earlier but there was no availability. I called Dostora, my shaman in California, and asked him what the antidote to this chemical was. He told me it would be a race against time. I had to go to a volcano in Costa Rica and extract a mud clay, dry it in the sun, and force spoonfuls of it internally. This acts as a sponge, absorbing toxicity caused by chemicals. The blood needed to be cleaned out also, and he suggested making a fresh aloe vera liquid drink and giving him this too.

I tried to reach Mitch to go get the mud/clay . Here in Costa Rica we have an active volcano called Arenal, which houses this precious mud. Rincon De La Vieja is another. But they were both located in the middle of the country, in opposite directions far from where he was.

Just before I boarded the plane, I called Kattia and asked her to find me an aloe vera plant and if possible send someone out to Arenal. I would pay whatever it cost.

It was a two and a half hour flight from Miami. It seemed like eternity. I arrived very late in the evening. As I raced to the house, my heart in my throat, cub's eyes came to me. I saw his journey in front of me. He then send me a picture of him and me howling at a moon. When I reached the house the lights were dim, not even a bark from my dogs and Spirit was laying on my bed. I needed to be alone with him.

I thanked Kattia for her vigilance over the cub. She held me tight and left. She told me if I needed anything through the night to call her. She told me Mitch had finally called but that he would not be able to make it in until the following day. I greeted my dogs, put them away and went to Spirit. I gently laid down on the bed with him. He barely moved. I wrapped my arms around him and petted him softly. He whimpered as he finally recognized me. He tried to rise. I simply held him tighter. I sang comforting songs.

I knew I had but little time with him. He was such a strong animal. He should have been dead by now, yet he was holding on to tell me something. He loved me, he was a Spirit of one of the great ones. His passing was only a transferring of power. He would watch over me forever and never leave my side. He was with me in spirit. He told me whenever I needed him I was just to close my eyes and howl. He would be there. Many times as I called on his spirit in the future I would first feel a rush of air, his running at me and always on the left side of my body I would feel the sweeping touch of his thick, warm fur and every hair on my body would stand on edge.

It was always a bit frightening when it happened to me, but also I would have a sense of being amongst the great ones. This was my higher self. It had been an honor to have known this wild one. The next morning, quietly, Spirit left this earth. I was steadfast.. I did not shed one tear. I couldn't. He would not allow it. I had one breaking point. I lay with him on the floor of the kitchen as he drew his last breath. When he closed his eyes in death, I weakened and selfishly wanted him to remain with me. I shook him and shouted his name, *"Spirit, Spirit, Spirit"* I chanted.

His great huge frame was limp in my arms. And then he lifted his head completely up and opened his eyes, big and bright. For that one moment his eyes held mine. He sent me a force of power and understanding which I will never be able to explain as there are no words to describe this in our human tongue. He ascended into the Heavens. I watched over his body for a long time. I went somewhere deep inside of myself. I wanted to go with him. I wanted to be anywhere else but where I was. In a state of shock I called Kattia. I said but a few words. Kattia was the only one I wanted with me at this moment. She came. We both said nothing. Then she told me to take him to Los Alpes up in the high mountains of Moravia across the valley, where she kept her horses. Neither one of us spoke of Villalobos. We put Spirit into the back of my car and Kattia got back into hers and led the way to the mountain. I don't know how I drove. I was mindless of everything in front of me. I wasn't there.

Kattia and I buried him on top of a mountain which seemed to overlook the world. The hole was already dug for Villalobos had ordered this to be done for me by his workers when Kattia had called him and told him of cub's death. No one was there but me and her. I stood over the deep hole, then I got inside of it and ever so tenderly laid him down. We did a ceremony for and of the gods in his passing, but shed no tears. I clipped a lock of his fur from the nape of his neck. I wore it as a amulet. Kattia and I were to become guardians of the wilds ones, and this had been our initiation ceremony. We just didn't know it yet...

I changed again with this experience, each animal changed me...

I had a great challenge in front of me. One month prior to cub's death I had arranged a teaching seminar in Costa Rica. It was scheduled for the annual veterinarians conference which took place in San Jose. Veterinarians from all of central and south America were to attend. I was hosting master herbalist Joel Hyman to give the lecture on alternative medicines. Now, as my experiences with veterinarians had been so hard, a part of me did not want to go through with this. But then I saw Spirit's eyes piercing me, pushing me to go on. I had worked long and hard hours on this project. It was becoming increasingly obvious that all fields of healing needed to open to each other. I went over and prepared the last details. Finally it was time to pick Joel up at the airport. His optimistic enthusiasm about Costa Rica turned a switch back on inside of me. I was ready to go on.

The seminar was a huge success. So many veterinarians wanted to learn about alternative medicines. I made good friends with some of them and also learned a great deal from them. I needed to change the bitter taste I had in my mouth towards them. It was not their fault that alternative natural medicines were never explored or encouraged in their university teachings. They were considered taboo. The fault lay primarily with the pharmaceutical companies whose only purpose was to make money. I saw this repeatedly not only in animal medicine, but human medicine also. We are all mere guinea pigs to them. And of course it was all about money.

The Class 8

After the seminar was finished, I gave a course to the general public on animal communication and general natural maintenance of pets. I ran an ad in the local English newspaper, the Tico Times. I met Dan Fawcett, a writer at the paper who became my confidant, partner and dear friend. He was a Canadian who had been living in Costa Rica and working for the paper for a number of years. He was a good writer. He was tall, with black hair, and thin as a bean pole. For the most part, he kept to himself and had few friends in the country. I wasn't sure how well received this ad would be as animal communication was a new frontier, I was amazed by the response. The telephone never stopped ringing, I had to schedule two more classes to cover the applicants. Most were Costaricans, some foreigners, lay people and veterinarian professionals.

It was one of the most interesting classes I had taught. Every one of my students had a wonderful or emotional story about certain animals in their life. I met a very interesting, good veterinarian, which had an insight into animals which was pure instinct itself. His name was Dr. Bitters. In class, he shared an experience he had with a group of hammerhead sharks while he was on a recent diving vacation.

In Costa Rica there is an island three hundred miles off the coast, internationally protected, called Coco's Island. It is of unmatched beauty. The island has diverse and unique ocean life. The location of this island brings together two spheres of ocean allowing for a diversity not seen anywhere else. It is also close to the Galapagos. Divers from all over the world remark on Isla De Coco's as one of the best diving spots.

Hammerhead sharks swim there in countless schools. The numbers can be in the hundreds. They are so curious about humans. Dr. Bitters was swimming amongst them.

He said, "I was surrounded by them."

This went on for three days, and he understood everything they said, and they understood everything he said.

There was Alycia the horse whisperer herself, only in female form. She was a school teacher . Alycia had two teenage children with a gift, each with a magic sense. I could see the wizard in Mauricio, her son, the day I watched him orchestrating schools of fish in his bedroom aquarium, to dance through the water. I remember laughing so hard with him that I fell off the chair. Alycia taught her children how to know their gifts. She too was to become part of my team.

Kattia was there, foreign students, zoo techs and an ambassador. This was my class. The money raised went to a zoological park, La Marina.

A New Frontier 9

Costa Rica was changing. It became one of the most popular destinations for holidays in the world. More and more people came to visit and never left. Its rich jungles and abundant wildlife were fast gaining international attention. Costa Rica was the eco-center of the world.

My life also changed dramatically. I was gaining national attention for my work with animals. I became the only twenty-four hour wildlife rescuer in the country. I took a seminar with Minae, the government branch which ruled and regulated the country, and did a Navy Seals ten month survival course. It was brutal. I became a long lean machine.

My partner in this course was a french guy named Derek. He was beautiful. His hair, worn long and loose, fell in a cascade of waves upon his back. He had an easy smile too. I had an instant crush on him. He felt the same, but we went no farther. He nicknamed me Tiger. Today he is still one of my best buddies.

I learned what I learned, then formed my own little army. For, even though Costa Rica was receiving recognition and funding for its biodiversity, none of it was making it out the door of the government. I decided to change this. During the next year, I traveled the whole country, seeing every animal project there was.

I had just been in the area of the volcano Arenal, when I came upon my first encounter with La Marina zoological park and Juan Jose Rojas. I was getting ready to go through the zoo and I ran into Jose at the entrance on his morning rounds. He is the tallest Tico I ever met or saw, at least 6 ft 4. He was strong and powerful and had an eagle tattooed on his massive chest. He said hi, and so did I, and we both got that feeling between two people like they had known one another before. We liked each other, but approached with caution.

I asked him simple questions , told him my stance on freeing wildlife. His mother, Dona Alba, ran the zoo, made all the decisions and turning it into a wildlife release center, was not in the picture. Jose took time from his morning rounds and walked the park with me. I did not push anything on this man, just talked to him about a different points of view in the fate of wildlife. I spoke of methods different from any he heard. He listened to everything. He had a real sense for animals and liked my ideas. His ease with me during the walk, and his understanding of my goals prompted him to open up by the time we rounded the last bend.

He invited me to spend the night in the big family house. I enjoyed an evening of story telling and met many orphaned animals he sheltered in his home. I left the next day and told him I would be in touch. He needed some new ideas on bringing necessary funding to this animal center or his mother would have to sell. It was a beautiful jungle zoo set amongst a national park, bordered by pristine rivers, a volcano, and a mountain corridor, where all animals were treated with care and respect. Through my travels viewing the country's wildlife centers, I had never seen one which impressed me as this place. La marina had so much going for it. I vowed to do what I could to help this man. My little voice was talking to me again.

On my return to the city, the telephone rang and it was Barbara Beck, a wonderful, high energy woman from Cobano, part of the Nicoya peninsula in the country. We had met through my work with wolves in Montezuma. She also had attended my class. She owned a huge piece of property, raised a new breed of stronger cattle to sell to the ranchers, and had a gorgeous home by the ocean. She told me that she desperately needed my help. The local farmers said a jaguar had been attacking their herds, and many had lost cattle to it during the last four months. They had seen the tracks. The men were organizing a hunt to kill the jaguar.

The next morning I started "*Project Jaguar*". This project was to change the fate of wildlife in Costa Rica.

Project Jaguar 10

I prepared to go out to the Cabuyo area in the Nicoya penisula to investigate the situation. I stayed with Barbara. We talked with the local cattle farmers. Some said the jaguar was a big male and roamed the opposite side of the peninsula. Other local farmers said it was a young one.

I decided to track this jaguar. I enlisted the help of two of my Seal comrades. We first constructed a natural platform near the local watering hole on a river, then camouflaged and hid it from sight. All the jungle animals came here to quench their thirst. We left the platform in the jungle for two weeks before we planned on using it. This accustoms the wildlife to it. Our lookout point becomes part of the jungle.

We set up three different shifts and sat quietly in the jungle night. It was hot, humid, and full of mosquitoes. We wore no scent as not to alert the animals to our presence. This meant no bug spray. Instead we covered every inch of skin with clothes. Ironically the bug spray of choice here is a product by Avon called "skin so soft' which is an oil used for after a bath or shower. It does not contain many chemicals and works better then the lethal toxin type of sprays. Something about this scent drives the mosquitoes and night bugs away. So our clothes were always full of sweat and then clung to our skins as the cool night breeze froze it to our bodies. No chance to feel comfortable. My shift was first. Nothing happened. Man two, the same luck, then number three was the charm.

The jaguar slowly, cautiously, stealthy and silent walked into the river bed.

There are few sources of water in this peninsula and this dry season which was upon us was exceptionally dry. The jaguar drank deeply. He was a good size. He did not seem

hurt or sick . When they are, carnivores choose to hunt domestic livestock, for it is easier. This was not the case with
this jaguar. The next evening I set out to examine a cow who
had been reportedly killed by a jaguar the night before. The
farmer showed me the teeth marks on the head. I took out a
measuring device to mark the bite. It was false. The width of
the bite was far greater than any normal jaguar. This cow was
also covered with sores indicating it had been very sick, which
probably was the real cause of death. It looked to me as if the
farmer had hammered a nail into two different spots in the
cow's skull to make it look like a jaguar did it. You see, Minae
pays a sum of money to any farmer who loses livestock due to
an endangered species taking it. These reports are not looked
into and most of the time are invented. I also spoke to one of
Barbara's cow rustlers who was a hunter himself, and he told
me that people were hunting everything out of the jungles,
thus forcing jaguars to find other food, as theirs were taken by
man.

The tepesquanti is one of the most hunted of the jungle animals. It is a large rodent-like animal, black with white stripes
lining its torso, which builds burrow colonies in the ground.
Its meat is full and flavorful and highly in demand at the Easter and Christmas holiday table. These animals mate but one
time a year and only have one baby. It is the main food of the
jaguar and yet was as endangered as they were.

I documented all these happenings and returned to San Jose.
I scheduled a meeting to go into Minae and meet with the vice
prime minister, Carlos Manuel Rodriguez. It was difficult to
get an appointment with him, because he is so busy. I stressed
the urgency of this meeting and was granted one the following week. I appeared in the offices of Minae earlier than my

appointment. I wanted to check things out over there. I kept my nose to the ground and took in valuable information of the workings of Minae. Carlos was late. Finally the secretary admitted me into his chambers. His office was comfortable and simple, except for one thing. He had the entire skin of a jaguar draped on his wall.

The first words out of my mouth were not hello. I asked, "Where and how did you acquire this skin?"

He introduced himself, then explained. This jaguar skin was confiscated from a poacher. The penalty was a fine and one month in a local prison. This poacher was the only poacher in the history of Costa Rica to ever face charges. Unbelievable!

I kept my feelings to myself and made no further comment on the skin.

Carlos heard me out. I had a detailed data sheet in front of me and I reported news to him of his country's problems that he was not even aware of. He asked me if I wanted to work for him, I told him I had a job. I then finally introduced myself and told him I wanted to put together a meeting of all the jaguar people in the country. We needed new laws. Prior to my meeting with him I studied the existing laws of conservation Minae had written. They were so vague, there were a million loopholes to slip through.

He agreed and was willing to be present at my meeting. He offered it to be held in Minae's conference room. I accepted and thanked him for his time. As I was getting up to leave, Mitch showed up. He had just come in from the beach. As he saw me with Carlos he called out, "Hey Charlie," looking right at Carlos.

I said, "You two know each other?" come to find out they had known each other since the "old days," as they put it, and had surfed and smoked the herb in the early years of Costa Rica. Small world.

As I left with Mitch, he told me that money was going to be tight for a while. There had been a problem with the land in Dominical and his partner was stealing from him and he would have to take this to court. Court in this country means ten years of hell...at least.

He was letting me know I would have to find some means of supporting the work I was doing with animals. Even though I worked round the clock, most centers could barely pay me for gas in my truck. Mitch also informed me he needed to sell his truck and would have to use mine. So I had my work cut out for me to find funds soon.

Our relationship had been strained; the separation in our lives, stemming from our different responsibilities didn't help. This news added more rift to it. We were growing apart. Our visits to each other became more and more infrequent. We just didn't have the time. Every time we thought of getting close again, something else came and pulled us apart. Again our marriage was put on the back burner, and I buried myself in my work.

I contacted the following people to attend the forthcoming meeting. Barbara Beck of Cobano, was to be my partner in this, and her help was immeasurable. Then Siegfried Weisel, for he was still working Pro-Felis. They had moved their location after a German land owner in the Nicoya penisula, Peter Kolind, offered his place as the new center. He helped them start up again with funding. Peter Kolind was also on the guest list.

I asked Juan Jose Rojas from La Marina, he was a jaguar expert. Two other biologists that were working with jaguars were invited. I invited Dan Fawcett from the Tico Times, as I wanted newspaper coverage of this event. Then finally I asked eight of the most experienced parks rangers to attend. The presidents of the three nature conservation organizations in the country rounded it all off. They all accepted.

The meeting was set. In ten days, we were about to make history.

Preparation 11

I began looking for ways to resolve the jaguar problem. This problem does not only exist in Costa Rica . I researched some ideas and spoke with the guests on my list of their theories concerning the problem at hand. I met a young Costarican named Roberto Godinez. He owned a technical company, and he had an invention he wanted to present to me. I met with him the next day. His place was quite impressive, very high tech for these times in Costa Rica. This guy was a genius in disguise. He let me first read an article from New York City on how it rid its subway systems from a rat infestation. It dealt with vibrational frequency. All living things contain a network series of vibration inside of them. They emit vibrations too. Some frequencies attract and others deter. Every living creature has a pitch which drives it mad. It annoys them to such a degree that it disrupts them from coming around. This is what the engineers in New York City devised, a frequency much like a silent dog's whistle which interrupted the instinctive signals given to the animal. It worked.

Roberto had rigged a pyramid shaped conductor to be mounted on cattle fences. It would need little power, which would be generated by solar energy. This was extremely cost efficient. It would emit a high piercing vibrational frequency which would discourage the jaguar from entering and interrupt his hunting. It would be as if a person had to listen to a high decibel sound of fingernails scratching down a chalkboard, over and over again. Got the picture...

I also had come up with an additional plan, and I had uncovered a lot of dirt on the subject of jaguars . There was great anticipation and apprehension for the meeting to come.

The Meeting 12

The day dawned clear and bright for our group. Everyone
got there little early. We were all very excited and anxious. We
had spoken of little else these days. I passed out a paper to be
signed by all the guests and asked them to introduce themselves and their reason for coming. The informal introduction
let us get acquainted with each other and showed the different
strengths we all had concerning the jaguar. It was nice to see
Ziggy again. It had been such a long time. Things were going
good for his center, he just needed more help from Minae.

Jose had brought his mother Dona Alba. She was a very well
known advocate of wildlife in this country. Her work with
animals was also quite impressive. She was well respected by
her peers. Her family had worked with animals for forty years.
Barbara was taping the meeting to take the minutes back to the
cattle ranchers,who were waiting for an answer.

Finally, twenty-five minutes late, Carlos Rodriguez walked
in. He looked around the room at the table of experts and
needless to say was quite impressed by the attendance. Then
he looked right at me and said, "You surprise and impress me,
more and more."

I asked him how much time he had for us today and he said
twenty minutes. He ended up staying two hours. For the next
two hours the intensity of this meeting was inspiring. All present wanted to help make a change. First, we set upon dealing
with the situation at hand in the Nicoya peninsula. None of
us wanted the jaguar hunted. I stressed that if hunted, word
would get out to conservation groups in the United States
and abroad and the position Costa Rica held as an ecological
paradise would be greatly damaged. Since Costa Rica depended heavily on the tourist dollar, I might be able to sway

our position in favor of our wildlife. Not to mention if we were to instill a working answer to cattle ranchers and the wilds, we would shine for our ingenuity and create a solution which could be passed on to other countries. Carlos listened thoughtfully. He was a wise man with many years experience. He also looked to the future. He knew the jaguar was an endangered species. He respected our candid remarks.

We needed to set an example, rather than add to the statistics, I said. " Costa Rica depended on the tourist revenue. Nature lovers which made up the bulk of the tourism would not take lightly to bad news." Carlos agreed he did not want Costa Rica to lose its good standing reputation.

We all proposed our ideas. I was proud to see so many people stand up for the king of our jungles. Roberto's idea was accepted for testing. The cattle ranches most problematic with jaguars would be the testing grounds.

Then I made my suggestion. I had been hiding this one from everyone for it was a stretch, but in my eyes well worth the shot.

I proposed that the jaguar be moved to another area. In my research of the area in question, the Nicoya peninsula, I found it was only a matter of time before the ever-growing presence of man, his hotels and farmlands would surrender the jaguars to future maraudings. There just were not enough wilds for the carnivores to safely and adequately live in harmony with man. Data would have to be collected on which area would work best for a new release spot. As I said before, there was no accurate account to date of the existing jaguars in any of our parks and a male needs a great deal of territory to roam. We had to know how many males to an area there were. This idea would take some time. So I breached my secret plan. It was another suggestion along these same lines.

Coco's Island had a problem with wild pigs. Brought over by pirates many years ago, the pig population was growing out of proportion. There were no predators on this island. The pigs uprooted the vegetation and turned the area into something that resembled a mine field. Minae had even organized a hunting season on the pigs and had taken twenty hunters out to the island to bag as many pigs as possible. This did not help at all. But to transport the male jaguar there and let nature take its course would solve both problems at once.

Everybody was curious about this idea. The people talked amongst themselves about this daring choice. It took them so by surprise that some said they needed to think about it

We all addressed another urgent point. The laws had to change for the enviornment. More specific new laws on jaguars rights and stricter poaching penalties were needed. Stricter rules and regulations were a must. Fines needed to be imposed to discourage the endless slaughter. Carlos agreed on all our points. He would turn over all the ideas to Elizabeth Odio, the vice president of the country and president in charge of Minae. She was his superior. The meeting finally adjourned and we had, at least for the moment, bought a jaguar more time. Two of my buddies from the task force volunteered to stay in the jungle area of this jaguar and try to guide him out of harm's way, as well as keeping trigger happy farmers from shooting him . If he was seen by a hunter first, he would be shot. This we all knew. The Tico Times with Dan Fawcett at the helm was to return back at week's end for a statement from Rodriguez and Odio on the final decision made.

The Children 13

The children of Costa Rica are not like their forefathers. They carry a real respect for their animals and natural resources. The see the ravages of their past generations. They are like the hundredth monkey, after ninety-nine get it, the hundredth is automatic. They were the leaders of tomorrow. Alycia, the horse whisperer friend of mine who attended my communication course, invited me to come out to the school where she taught one day and give the class a speech on Project Jaguar. I consented. Children had a contagious energy about them that always brought out the child in me. I loved to play. Child's play. Iala would be in town at this same time with Loba, her wolf. She and I both agreed we could make this more fun for the kids by bringing Loba along. Alycia prepared the class for my visit but kept the wolf guest a secret.

As I walked into the class alone I was surprised to see how eager and anxious the children were to talk to me. They were so polite and spoke only English to me. I was touched. Their English was quite good.

I asked them to share experiences they had with animals. They expressed their individual stories with great enthusiasm. They all stated how lucky they were to live in a country like Costa Rica, teaming with animals. It was the high point of every child's family vacation to go to the parks and experience the wilds. All of them loved jaguars. None were afraid of it, nor thought it to be a bad animal. I told them I needed their help to save the jaguars. They all shouted and cheered.

"What can we do?" they asked.

I explained that they needed to write a letter to Elizabeth Odio, saying why they feel the jaguar should be saved. They raised many questions and gave many answers . We spent

an hour listening to the hearts and minds of the little ones. I
told them their voices needed to be heard, not just the adults.
Alycia said the letters would be ready by Friday. With a bright
big smile on my face I took in a deep breath. Then I told them
I had a surprise for them. I began by telling them that in North
America, the wolf was in danger too. They had the same problem up there that jaguars had down here.

The children asked, "Why does man shoot these beautiful
animals which we are supposed to share this world with?"

I answered, "Because man is afraid of them. He accuses
them unjustly. It is a fact that in all of Costa Rica's history no
one has ever been killed by a jaguar."

The class become solemn with those words. I could feel their
thoughts. Why?

I answered what I could to their worried hearts . At last I
told the children to close their eyes, and in walked Iala and
Loba. When they opened their eyes they all let out a long low
sigh. Their eyes popped out of their heads.

Loba loved the attention and showed off. She let everyone
touch her. Some did so with loving joyful abandon, others
with slow gentle caution. The children marveled at the touch
of her fur and how beautiful and friendly she was. The kids
were making such a commotion, all good of course, that the
neighboring classes stopped their work and look in through
our windows. Iala sat the group down on the floor and ask
them to sing a song with Loba.

They all giggled at first, not believing they could sing with a
wolf. So Loba started first. The minute Iala told her to sing she
started to howl a slow soft ballad as if to the moon. The surprise on the children's faces was priceless. They all joined in
and the ballad crescendos grow louder and deeper. I sat back

and watched one of the most precious moments of communication between animal and children I had ever witnessed. At that point all had become wolves, all were one. It was so emotional .When I looked up, the windows were crowded with other classes of students, and the teachers were spilling silent tears. What came through all of us, together in us, was how we would all imagine it to be in a different world. One that was the Garden of Eden.

As quoted by one of my favorite authors, Peter Matthiessen, in The Snow Leopard,

"And surely this is the paradise of children, that they are at rest in the present, like frogs or rabbits."

This wolf so touched these children's hearts that not only did they write letters for the jaguars, but they also wrote letters to the United States on behalf of the wolves and how important and precious they were. The letters received international attention. I was so proud of them. They were my little warriors.

Alycia continued to work with children for years to come and teach them the ways of animal communication. She was one of the most noted authorities on talking to animals. My experiences with her alone are enough to write an entire book about. She is a good witch. They do exist.

Iala and I also put together a play for the students in the Nicoya penisula which depicted the story of the jaguar in their area. It too, opened the eyes of a new generation...

The following letters from the children to Elizabeth Odio in behalf of the jaguars made the headlines of all the newspaper in Costa Rica.

THE TICO TIMES/ March 20, 1998

CHILDREN WRITE TO NATIONAL PARKS' LEGAL CONSULTANT The Tico Times is happy to share portions of letters from the Methodist School directed to Carlos Manuel Rodriguez, legal consultant to the director of national parks, about the fate of jaguars in Costa Rica:

> *I want the people to stop killing the jaguars. I don't want them sold because I love the jaguars.*
> *-Jose Pablo Hernandez Montero*

> *We want to protect jaguars from the people who want to kill them. I like jaguars. We have to protect them because if we don't they all will die.*
> *-Paola Villalobos*

> *I think you make good work by protecting the animals. The people have to protect all the animals because they are like brothers.*
> *-Elizabeth Aguero*

> *I think that jaguars are very beautiful animals. It is an animal that we need to protect. If we don't help the jaguars they will be extinct and the rest of the people will not know them.*
> *-Karla Lucia Retana Cordero*

> *I think that your job is the best of all. I want to protect animals like you do. The Lord made the animals to be protected.*
> *-Santiago Suarez Mendez*

> *I want you sir to save the jaguars because they are my favorite animal. We have been doing projects to save them, please sir try to save these animals because they are so pretty.*
> *-Daniel*

I don't like the idea of hunting jaguars. They are one of the beautiful presents that nature gave us. That is why we have to take care of them. I think it is the same to kill a jaguar as it is to kill a person.
-David

I would like to thank you if you would help the jaguars because they are very special cats for me. Did you know that the jaguar is my favorite cat? Do you know why I like him very much? Because he is big and strong, I wouldn't like them to be gone forever.
-Michelle Alvarez

It is nice to see that people are trying to save them.
-Ivannia Chan

I learned that jaguars are animals that are in trouble. Mr. Carlos Manuel I really want the jaguars to be protected. The jaguar is my favorite animal and I think we can protect them.
-Juan Pablo

I want to help them to live. They have the right to live and we have the right to live too. We don't want to kill them or hurt them. I want the forest to live too, and I want you to tell the people who cut trees, that we don't want them to do that. We want nature in this world.
-Jessica Chan

I want to tell you that you have to protect the jaguars. I like to protect the jaguars.
-Rafael

This letter is very important to me. I have learned a lot about the importance of the jaguars. They are part of nature.
-Jenny Huang Wu

I want people to protect jaguars because I think they are sweet animals. I don't want them to disappear. God made all the animals of the world and he doesn't want animals to be extinct
-Catalina Morales

I would like to do something but I can't. I think you can do something to help them. I want jaguars in Costa Rica because the Lord put them here and he knows why they have to live in Costa Rica because we have beautiful forests. When I have children I want them to see all the animals the Lord put in the world
-Adriano D'Ambrosio

We need to protect the jaguars because they are very beautiful and they are in danger of extinction. We don't want them to be hurt. I'm very sad because some people are killing jaguars out there.
-Pablo Mora Cascante

I want the jaguars here. I love the jaguars, they are so pretty. I love the jaguars running fast. I want to protect and care about them.
-Luis Diego

God created the jaguars and I think he is very sad because we are not protecting them. If we don't they will all die. We need the jaguars. They are the heart of the jungle.
-Karina Preciss

I have learned more about the jaguars. I wish they will protect them before they become extinct.
-Carolina Padilla Castro

I am sad because all the people in Costa Rica kill the jaguars. I know that you Julie, my friends and my family love jaguars so we will never kill them. The jaguars are so beautiful.
-LizI Alvarez

Mr. Rodriguez we think that you can do something to protect the jaguars. Please do something!
-Stephanie Gouryong

I do not want that the people to kill the jaguars. They need to live like all animals need to live. And I am a person who likes animals and my favorite animal is the killer whales. Well, I just don't want people killing the jaguars. Please help protect them.
-Natalie Mora Cascante

Can you help us protect our jaguars here in Costa Rica? We need them, to balance our ecological system. They are living things like us. We should not kill them, that is why I want you to help us protect them. We have many beautiful animals in Costa Rica including the jaguars. We want to protect them. We don't want people shooting them.
-Esteban Vega Cruz

It is not funny to see the jaguars in jail. I would like to help them. Why do people kill them? They don't do anything to us. This is serious. Please help jaguars.

-Roselia Sagot

I love jaguars. I'd just like them as pets, but it would be like keeping them in cages and I do not like this so I am asking you for help. I'd like you to save these beautiful animals. People shoot them, that makes me sad but I know that you will help.
-Crystal Osejo Rodriguez

I want to protect all the animals. I see the jaguars on T.V. And in pictures. I don't like very much the animals but I want to protect them.
-Daniela Trejos

We have to save the jaguars because they are so beautiful, and because they are creatures like you and like me. They have hearts too. We do not have to kill the animals.
-Monica Perez

We don't want people killing jaguars. They were made by the Lord like we were. They are beautiful animals that can live. We want you to help protect them so they won't be extinct. I will say one more time, please, help them.
-Melissa Herra

Judgment Day 14

Project Jaguar was growing. Global attention focused on
jaguars. Mexico, Brazil and Columbia held government meetings. Hundred of letters came to me from all over the world.
Things were slowly changing for this magnificent species. The
indigenous people told me I was carrying the jaguar spirit and
with it, its power.

Dan Fawcett called me in the morning, wanting a private
meeting with me. I rushed to meet him. His face was grim.
During my investigation of the jaguar's history in this country and prior to the meeting I held at Minae, I had uncovered
some information which I was at present withholding from
the public. I wanted to see what the decision would be before
I unleashed hell and all its fury upon the government. Dan
had unearthed some stuff of his own. We compared notes and
decided to wait till Friday for the final judgment on the jaguar
in the Nicoya.

That night my team of men in the Nicoya who were guarding the jaguar, radioed in with a report. The news was alarm-
ing. It matched one of my findings at Minae that disturbed me
the most.

In the past hunters offered enormous sums of money to
hunt and kill a jaguar. These were not locals, rather they were
dignitaries, rich professional hunters from abroad and even a
nobleman's son from Europe. Their only concerns were to add
another trophy to their walls. Of course this was all secretly
organized, and all involved were greatly protected. No one
wanted to step on anyone's feet. These were people of the up-
per class and their records needed to be kept pure.

I was even contacted by a Texan sportsman, as he called
himself, and offered one hundred thousand dollars to help my

cause, of course, if I granted permits to hunt for sport in our jungles. I wanted to choke this man. I started to plan my own hunt. The hunters would become the hunted. I was pacing like a lioness.

My men told me that there was a lot of talk of another such hunt getting ready to happen in the Nicoya. I could hardly wait until tomorrow.

Tomorrow came, Odio and Rodriguez and three other men from the parks were present. The meeting lasted an hour while I waited outside the door. Carlos walked out first and was a little stunned to see me standing there. He quickly put on his public-eye face and greeted me warmly. He introduced me to the group. I minced no words but got right to the point.

"What is your decision?" I asked.

Elizabeth spoke first. She told me she had received the letters from the children and she thought they were so sweet. She also said she would personally go out to the school and thank the children herself. She never did go.

Carlos, on the other hand, was mastering a speech to me that made me sick. He went around and around without telling me anything.

I asked him if he was ready to meet the press.

He replied, "Yes indeed. I have a meeting with Dan Fawcett later today." He asked me to have lunch with him so that he could talk to me in private. I nodded yes.

At lunch Carlos looked me straight in the eye and told me his hands were tied. His background was lawyer, and he was a politician now. He had to keep the peace with the government.

He really believed in my ideas and was moved by my dedication to my work. Being a foreigner and female to boot didn't make it easier. He understood all this and I let my instinct guide me, I knew inside of this man was some sort of willingness to change, yet he had been part of a system that was more corrupt than the underworld for far too long.

For governments all over the world always put on a mask when dealing with their lies and secrecy. What we the people are told and what really happens is as different as night and day. Promises are made to get people elected into office then forgotten just as quickly.

I asked Carlos if he had even been out to the Nicoya.

He replied no. But he said he would and I was to accompany him. He also wanted to become more involved in the workings of the wildlife groups in this country. Siegfried Weisel invited him to go out and witness the next release of felines. I could then just bide my time with him. I left, knowing the only thing I had gotten out of this man was more time.

Dan Fawcett wrote the following article for the Tico Times after his press conference with Rodriguez.

Synopsis of Project Jaguar

By Dan Fawcett, TICO TIMES EDITOR

Julie Bindas woke me up to a lot of things. I think she has an extraordinary understanding of our environmental crisis - scientifically and spiritually. With Project Jaguar, I think Julie's time has come, because the sands of time are fast trickling away for biodiversity in Costa Rica. While a few grains still remain, I think Julie's views are as timely as the teachings of an Old Testament prophet. For those precious and few individuals who care about nature, her thoughts on the wilderness survival or extinction of the jaguar in Costa Rica are of great gravity.

I met Julie last October, when she appeared in the office of The Tico Times, Costa Rica's English-language weekly newspaper, with a handwritten press release, on banana paper, about her soon-to- be held seminar on communicating with animals. I thought this source presented an inspired opportunity for a humorous take on the news.

I wrote a comic piece about how you could graduate from Julie's seminar walking and talking with the animals, like Dr. Doolittle of sixties-movie fame, and dubbed Julie's colleague, animal herbalist Dr. Joel Hyman, the "Sigmund Freud of his breed."

Julie didn't mind this light- hearted treatment of her life's work. Judging by comments I received from readers, a followup story last November about Julie's herbal and mud treatments for felines' nervous system and skin disorders was one of the most popular stories of the year.

A different dimension of Julie emerged when she convened an ad-hoc meeting of more than a dozen of Costa Rica's leading wildlife experts from government, academia and private organizations in January. The issue: "Problem Jaguars" in the southern Nicoya peninsula. At the meeting, Carlos Manuel Rodriguez, the current Vice-Minister of the Environment, delivered an inspiring address about a " new approach" to livestock vermin.

"New Hope for C.R.'s Jaguars" ran the headline of the story which appeared on Jan. 23, 1998 in The Tico Times. Not until a month later did those at the meeting learn the "New Hope" was the trapping, relocating, caging and hunting of "Problem Jaguars."

Consulting over forty sources for an article on the controversy, the validity of Julie's opposition to the plan became obvious to me, and according to almost all my sources -- ranchers, wildlife biologists, government officials and environmental activists -- increasingly respected and supported.

Largely due to Julie's efforts, I believe, Rodriquez' plan has not been adopted as policy. However, no source claims to clearly understand his intentions. All agree he is a masterful politician.

Jaguar Special Report By Dan Fawcett Tico Times Staff

A declaration of peace in the southern Nicoya peninsula between cattle ranchers and their old foe, the jaguar, has proponents and critics locking horns over a controversial proposal for livestock predator-management under consideration by the Ministry of the Enviroment and Energy (Minae.)

The written appeal Last November by twenty-nine ranchers who suffered livestock losses from a marauding jaguar around the community of Cobano, (TT Jan 23) petitioned Minae "not to agree to the elimination of the jaguar until all other possibilities have been exhausted."

Many area ranchers, environmentalists and wildlife experts now fear the ministry's proposed vermin-control plan will do exactlly that.

Etc, etc, etc,

Project Jaguar Part II   15

The newspaper article was several pages long. One positive thing that came out of this meeting with Minae was that old laws and ways were finally being dusted off the shelves and revised. You can't teach an old dog new tricks... That's how it was with this generation of leaders. Awareness would have to come slowly. They feared any drastic change, for they knew not how to go about it. The vibrational frequency device was to be tried as soon as money from the government became available. That was just a put-off. They were afraid of it. Relocating the jaguar, they feared, would only make it return.

Jaguar experts merely laughed at this statement. Moving it to Coco's Island, the government feared, would endanger the rare bird found nowhere else in the world but on this island. It is a very tiny bird. The Coco's Island Finch which is a subspecies of the famous Galapagos finches that inspired Darwin's revolutionary theory of evolution. The only predator it is in danger of is the ever-growing domestic cat population, which started with the comings and goings of seamen and continued with some of the locals who traveled to this island. A jaguar does not catch little tiny birds while hundreds of juicy, fat pigs are running around for him. Map maker and Skipper Capt. Fradin caleed Coco's a " miserable Pig Island" by the end of the last century, but Jacques Cousteau recalled it 13 years ago "…the most beautiful island in the world." The truth of the matter was that Minae had a small substation out on the island. This is the only structure permitted on the island.

The two officials that stay out there were afraid to live on the island with a jaguar. A boat came once every ten days with provisions, and radio contact was twenty-four hours. But they were still scared. Perhaps the treasure has something to do with it too.

It is told that the richest treasure in the world is buried on Cocos. Not one but two major loads. The first belonged to a pirate named Benito Bonito who sailed the "Relampago". The second and biggest treasure was brought to Coco's by Captain Thompson in 1821. None the less the final decision was indecisive at best. But the final blow was left till last. The Minae government finally came up with a decision, which was just as I had read about in the hidden files at Minae.

In order to raise much-needed funds for Costa Rica's jaguars, they decided that hunting the jaguar would raise a great deal of money for the project since numerous wealthy sportsmen had already contacted them. In short kill a jaguar to save the species.

I shook my head in disgust.

The next week Carlos Rodriguez had a nice, new shiny truck to drive. Wonder where that money came from.

A new law did go into effect in favor of the jaguar with more stringent regulations. The international endangered species act added to it and it had stiffer fines for poachers. However, without enforcement, they served little purpose. Only eight new park guards were added to the entire country's park system. These men were underpaid.

I received many letters from the different groups of people living in Costa Rica. Some of them helped me immensely. Their dedication and support of my work helped change the minds of men. We did everything we could in the next four months to guard this jaguar. After eight months, the jaguar was never seen again.

Kaiser 16

Project Jaguar grew to be an organization. I was called to work on several other projects, so I had a very busy year. One day Danilo, the veterinarian at the city zoo Simon Bolivar, called me. Two baby jaguar cubs had just been born. He wanted me to come and see them. I was busy elsewhere, and it took another month before I was able to go out.

The cubs were beautiful. Agatha and Brutus were their names, a boy and a girl. They were growing nicely and were in good health. The vet took me around the zoo and asked me to help with some problems with their animals. This zoo is not one of my favorite places. In my opinion, it should have been closed down long ago. Small, old rusted concrete cages, poor diets, no possibility of exercise and sickness both mental and physical affected the animals. I came out because the animals need more help there than anywhere else in Costa Rica.

I spent a great deal of time with Danilo, going over step by step what needed to be done to help these animals. As I left, I wanted to see the jaguar cubs one more time. The telephone rang, Danilo had to go answer it and left me alone with them. The cubs jumped on me and almost licked me to death. They communicated with me. I was surprised and happy. It had been a while since I had communicated with the wild ones. They said they wanted to come with me. They liked the way I smelled. For a minute I thought of just stealing them.

Then the vet walked back in.

I asked him if the zoo was open to releasing these cubs back into the wilds.

He shook his head no. "We need them here as fresh gene pools of the species," he said.

I said nothing.

"If you change your mind, call me " Then he laughed and said, "if I could, I would open the cages of all these animals. I am simply a worker here, sorry."

I shook his hand, thanked him for the play time with the cubs, and left.

A week went by and Kattia called me from the zoo. She told me the vet at the zoo was her cousin and he was working with Villalobos on a tiger named Kaiser, who was very ill. The tiger had not drunk nor eaten in three days. The vets would have to intravenously give fluids. Kattia was calling on behalf of the vets to please come and see what I could do. I put together some herbal formulas and was on my way. I arrived at 4:30 in the afternoon. The sun goes down at 5:40 every day, all year round. Not much daylight left.

I went to the cage of the tiger. He was completely down, laying on his side, his breathing labored. He was really huge. He was magnificent. I got closer to the cage and looked at him for a long time. He had an air of greatness around him. He was regal to the end. His aura was powerful. I tried to communicate. Nothing. I knew he must be really thirsty. I looked around the cage and saw three coconut trees behind me.

When a coconut is green and imature it has a water in it the people here call pipa water. It tastes very good and light. Quite a lot of this water comes out of one of them. As the coconut matures, its outer shell turns dark and is covered with a brown dry husk.

Inside, it has a white, sweet coating of coconut meat and a liquid. When blended together, this becomes coconut milk. Coconut milk absorbs poisons from the bloodstream and neutralizes the stomach.

The pipa water is very healing. It cleans the blood, liver and kidneys and has the highest natural form of electroylites.

I asked the zoo attendant to cut some pipas down for me. The vets looked at me as if I was nuts. Tigers do not drink coconuts.

Kattia just laughed, she had seen me do some pretty strange things in the past and she believed in me all the way. I asked the vets if they wanted my help or not. I was not into wasting my time. They apologized and let me go about my work. The pipa was split in two with a machete and poured into the tiger's dish. Kaiser looked at me and thanked me. He drank every last drop of three pipas.

Animals have a sense of what they need. I have given coconut water to all my animals. They all take it. My shaman told me it is one of the foods of the gods for it is the only water that does not touch the ground.

I was exhausted. I hadn't had a day off in fifteen days. I told Kattia, who was going to spend the night with Kaiser, that I had to go home and sleep. I left some herbs to be put in his meat if he should decide he was hungry. I told Kattia to call me if there was any change.

That night Kattia experienced a communication which changed her life.

It was her turn to watch over Kaiser. Kaiser had been a prisoner of the zoo for thirteen years now. One of the zoo attendants had been with Kaiser the longest. This man's name was Manuel and without ever hearing about nor knowing animal communication he came forth with a lesson of his own this night. The minds of animals involve an intellect still undiscovered by most of mankind. Our realities and thoughts are simply molecules trained and retrained to think but one way. But there are those that encounter the possibilities. I have seen a bond occur between man and beast which can not be overlooked time and time again. It is part of the mystery of this world we share. The subconscious lays dormant until a wild one opens it for us. Then it is up to us to choose to walk through that open door. This was Kaiser's last message to our kind, given to Kattia as she held his great head.

Villalobos told her not to enter the cage, for she had asked earlier. She heard Kaiser calling to her as she sat by him through the night. He wanted to be touched. She was told it was too dangerous and the zoo would not allow it. Carlos told her they had to go in now to treat him. She could accompany him since the animal would be tranqualized. It was 6 pm.

Eleven people stood by. Carlos, Kattia, and Manuel entered the small working enclosure of the dying tiger. Carlos tranquilized the tiger. They needed to wait a few minutes. Carlos readied the medicines he would administer to him as he backed up against the open door to the enclosure. The tiger's breathing was laboured. Kattia moved alongside Carlos and squeezed slowly over to the other side of Kaiser. In one great movement Kaiser rose out from under his sedation, clear-headed and focused,. Manuel stepped back first. Carlos moved backwards out the door. Kattia was trapped between the tiger and the door. Kaiser turned and faced them, then turned his enormous head to her. Eye to eye, Kattia felt his breath heavy on her face. She stayed still. A strange calm surrounded her.

Outside the cage, the people were shouting at her. "Get out of there!"

"Hurry now!"

Kattia smiled, where was she to go?

Carlos was shouting the loudest, "Don't touch him," again and again. The din was maddening.

Then deep inside her soul, a silence to their cries touched her. Closing her off from the madness.

Now Kattia heard only the tiger.

"Touch me," he said, and, "I won't hurt you."

She knew this, she reached out to touch him. Her hand, dwarfed by his head, came to rest on it. She stroked him. His breathing steadied, his sigh of relief egged Kattia on. She rubbed his ears, the Tellington touch. He slowly laid down by her feet.

The crowd of onlookers were awed into silence. They watched breathlessly. Kattia spoke even, soothing, rhythmic words to him.

She moved her other hand onto his back and stroked him, long even stokes. She then told him, "I am going to cross over you now."

He let her pass. Slowly and regrettably, she moved out of the cage. Carlos ran to her side. "Are you all right?" he asked.

She said yes, and her legs began to shake.

Carlos turned and administered more sedative to the tiger. Then they all sat down to wait.

Kattia moved closer to Carlos and kept her thoughts to herself. She still felt Kaiser's fur on her fingers. There was so much feeling going through her whole body. A great sadness, a warm kinship, an inspirational courage.

The night grew on. Finally the vets made the decision to put Kaiser down. Danilo would have to go up to the office and phone Yolanda, the curator of the zoo who was presently in Cuba, for the final green light. Everyone decided to go in with the group of vets to grab a coffee.

Kattia stayed behind. It would be the first and last chance she had with Kaiser alone. It was just a little before 11:00 PM. Drums, Kattia was hearing drums. Loud and clear. At times one hears the distant drumming of school bands rehearsing, but that is during the day, at this time these drums were not of here. Kattia later told me her body began to rock to and fro on its own, exactly as mine did when Spirit my wolf was dying. At moments throughout my life when I am in depths of sorrow or suffering my body involuntarily still rocks. This I cannot explain. She knew the end was near and the great ones were preparing for the transcending of one of their own. Kattia walked over to Kaiser's cage. She walked over to his side. He had been motionless for hours.

She began to pray. "Thank you Kaiser for being here, for bringing so many people joy and awe. You are a glimpse of the beauty and power."

He awakened, stood up and proudly walked the distance to her side. He lay against the irons as close as he could get to her. She reached in and touched him. He took his last breath...

A Tiger's Silent Words

I was with Kaiser to the very end. I do not look at it ever as his end but rather as his beginning. He was in agony. He was having trouble breathing. Nine people wanted to put him down. I wanted him to live. When I finally found myself alone with this great tiger, he came alive. At 1: 45 PM. I heard drums. There is a school near the zoo, but at this hour of the night it could not have come from there. The drums were strong, they echoed deep into the recesses of my mind. Then the communication started. Kaiser stood up and walked towards me. He lay next to me. I touched him. His breathing

*changed, it became more normal. Then he started talking. He
had the voice of a young man very clear and sweet.*

*"I know what you are trying to do, but this is my time. You
have no idea what it is to be locked up here for years and not
be able to run. I don't belong here.*

*"We are here to live in harmony, but you human beings
don't know the meaning of the word. There is a balance in this
world and it has been like that for thousands of years.*

*"The balance is perfect, yet fragile, but you don't listen.
rules are being broken, , there is no turning back.*

*"You are here to witness the transition of my soul to free-
dom. I will finally be free, and maybe in another moment in
time we will reach the balance to live together again.*

*"You train us to prove we can be taught, what you don't
understand, is that we could teach you more than you'll ever
know."*

*Kaiser also talked about the difference between animals and
humans. About us having souls and them having souls and
spirit, but that was complicated, remember he talked to me
in English, my second language, not in my native Spanish
tongue.*

I hope all who read this will understand.

Kattia Leandro Esquiver

When I received this from Kattia, I first remembered
thoughts which had come into my head during this night.

Thoughts of far-off distant lands. Of men from different centuries, and they were all fighting and killing. Kaiser's message was deep and profound. Tigers talk not of nonsense. They were created without fear. What an ascension this was for this species. Man is wrong when he thinks of himself as the most intelligent species on this planet. In fact he should be placed on the bottom of the list and begin to climb to the top on the wings of those wild ones' souls.

When Kaiser spoke of spirit and souls, I understood, for I have had more than a number of wild ones tell me the same. Animals know their souls and spirit. We do not. They have evolved to a quantum level which we have yet to reach. None of us know what or who we really are. Nor will we ever, unless we find our spirit and soul. Out here, in the nowhere, it is easy to forget what we came from.

For those who believe no explanation is necessary

For those who don't, none will suffice.....

Of Tigers and Women

Animals know Katia's spirit. For in her lives a story that her life's journeys will unfold. This story was put inside of her from all of her lives.

We all carry stories. We all carry lives. There is a book called, "Of Tigers, and Men." It was the supreme wish of one man to walk amongst the tigers in their domain, come face to face with one, and see what fear really was. Animals awaken us. In each of us lives a soul which, no matter how great mankind's accomplishments, inventions and studies, still eludes us. What is the soul everyone speaks of? It lives on forever, how long is forever? Our instincts are sleeping, then in the space of a moment they are brought back to life by the creatures of this planet that give it life everyday. Theirs do not sleep. They have a knowing we strive to grasp. If man could rule his kingdom as those wild ones , taking only what he needs, day by day, the trust of infinity in our spirits would come to life. We fear, for our spirits sleep. Awaken them.....

Wolves howl,

Lion's roar,

Eagles screech,

Snakes hiss,

Whales moan,

Birds sing

Are they not telling each and every soul the story of life?

Katia walked into a tiger's cage, without fear, with spirit guiding her soul to do. It is why she was able to hear the message.

Listen, listen, listen

For it is all about life, yours and mine....

Wolfensohn and Inbio 17

Costa Rica was changing. Good things were happening with conservation. More and more people formed groups and organizations. Many people like myself were moving mountains. People were doing whatever it took to bring attention to Costa Rica's need for reform. One example was of a crazy, in a good way, Frenchman who had spent a good part of his life protecting one of the most important sea turtle nesting grounds in the country.

The rare species loggerheads, leatherbacks and green turtles would lay their eggs only on certain beaches. The frenchman guarded Ostional beach with its mass nestings of the rare olive ridley turtle. More then 75,000 turtles will gather out at sea and come ashore over the space of a few days, with the possibility of 10,000 reptiles on the beach at any one time in September and October. The trigger of this timing is always associated with a waxing three quarter moon. This man guarded one of the best spots. When a developer decided to turn it into a resort area, he went on a twenty-one day hunger strike. The developer had to go elsewhere.

Then there were the group of international students who lay down on roads to form a human chain in front of the rolling trucks to stop the logging companies from cutting trees in the Osa Peninsula. People were no longer just sitting by and letting governments rule unjustly. They were stealing back what had been stolen from all of us.

I was preparing myself for a visit to our country from world bank president Wolfensohn. The world bank is part of the trilateral commission. They rule the world.

They dictate the monies and the powers of the world. This visit was very important for our country. I had heard through my inside sources that Wolfensohn was giving Costa Rica a sum of monies for its "Biodiversity". I wanted to make sure this time the money went to the right hands.

The president's visit would be guarded. No one was allowed to get near him. I had to come up with a plan. Wolfensohn was arriving at the airport at noon and then was to visit Inbio and hold a meeting at Minae. Inbio stands for instituto nacional de biodiversidad, (national biodiversity institute). Entomology, the study of insects was one of its foremost endeavors. Wolfensohn was to met with the minister, Carlos Rodriguez. Carlos and I had done a few things together during this period of time. In the aftermath of project jaguar our relationship had changed. I had been watching him like a hawk. Better to become friends with your enemy. Then you can keep a queer eye on them.

I planned an unannounced visit to his office at precisely the same time that Wolfensohn was scheduled to arrive. I also sent a sweet little girl, the daughter of a German friend of mine, to the airport to greet Wolfensohn in his native tongue with an enormous bouquet of exotic blooms as a welcoming gift. Hidden inside the bouquet was the list of worthy projects in Costa Rica which needed funding. It worked like a charm.

Through the multitude of armed guards a little girl was given quarter to the president. At his visit to Inbio, the country graced him with a newly discovered species of beetle. They named it after him.

However, it always appeared as if more than meets the eye was going on at this place. It was like a fortress, heavily guarded day and night. One wondered upon first glance why bugs needed such heavy protection. Dan Fawcett informed me that my intuition was right. He told me if I was lucky enough to find a book which had been written on the underground, called, The Inbio Conspiracy, I would begin to understand. It was written by a woman and uncovered scientific and bio-engineering testing.

Everything about this book had become a mystery. It mysteriously disappeared from all those who had carried it. Dan was covering the story for the Tico Times of Wolfensohn's visit. He told me he would keep his eyes and ears open .

Later at the Minae meeting I walked in on accidentally, yes, I witnessed the writing of a check to Minae from the world bank for five million dollars. Carlos Manuel Rodriguez's signature went on it along with Wolfensohns's. That money had the ability to save Costa Rica. Promises were made to fund some of the projects in the environment. Hand shaking and smiles.

But then there were hushed rumors of creating a bio-genetics laboratory, a Jurassic Park, so to speak at Inbio. But no one was supposed to know this. I called Dan Fawcett. My team was put together again and we went to work finding as much guarded information as we could. Getting into Inbio was tough. I contacted a dear old friend of mine who had a pass, which enabled the bearer entry to certain areas of the complex. It was a researcher's pass.

Going through the first doors was easy. The others were posted, no trespassing. But I did. Inside one of the rooms was a gentleman I remembered seeing at the meeting with Minae. He was one of the scientists. He looked, oddly at first, and then waved to me. Good, he remembered me. I told him I was assigned to work on some components of the brief on the meeting for Wolfensohn. He looked at my badge, I held my breath and he told me he would be back after lunch to help me.

Then I was alone. What I found was frightening indeed, documents and laboratory data surrounding a genetic gene pool on the international world market trade, literally worth billions of dollars. I left the room and found a side exit door, through which I hurried. I jumped into my truck and called Dan.

I told Dan, "Let's go public with this information."

We had to watch our backs every step of the way. We hunted employees willing to divulge information through various channels. It took six days and seven nights. The night before the copy was to go to print at the Tico Times , Dan received a phone call warning him if the article went to print, Dan would be bodily escorted out of the country.

The caller was anonymous. The owner of the Tico Times also received a threatening call involving closing the newspaper down if Dan's article went public. The owner, Derrie Dryer, phoned Dan and said she could not let this happen and closed the article down. We then sent it to UPI, United Press International.

The next day, Dan's apartment was burnt to the ground. Luckily he and anything important had already been gone to another hideout. Friends of ours in the underworld kept us safe and private. Their money and power far overweighed that of the government. They said, "If you give the government enough noose, they will eventually hang themselves." The noose was tightening on governments worldwide.

My league friends were not bad people, they were just not of the government farce and created a different kingdom of their own. The power of the world banks over us never let a word of this out. The public globally was kept in the dark. Inbio did not exist. I know you, my readers at certain times throughout the book would like to hear more then I have written on a certain subject matter. Unfortunately I must for there are those people still working in the field that must be protected in order to continue their work.

Shortly afterwards the jurassic part was moved out of the country.

Years later Wolfensohn stepped down from office, his noose swung him to neverland, but I feel he will just be put into another position to throw off the pack of wolves.

La Marina 18

La Marina is a unique special treasure, from the dedicated families who own it to the wild animals who live in it. I loved discovering this place. It is a home of mine.

Jose had asked me if I could come out and see him. It had been a year since I last had visited.

It was great to be there. All the animals looked well and happy. A jaguar, Suzie, which nobody could get near, for she had come from the wilds to La Marina, fell in love with me. She responded to me immediately. I have a thing with jaguars. They are not afraid of me, nor I of them.

La Marina never bought any of these animals. They all found their way here either from Minae, lay people, or other zoos in the country. Everyone knew La Marina never turned a wild one away. One such was a beautiful female tiger . She came to La Marina in an unusual way. A Mexican circus was in town, San Jose. They just up and left one night and left the tigress in her cage right in the heart of the city. Minae called Jose and he rescued her. Sita was her name. I can not tell you how many circuses with magnificent animals passed through this country. I could not bear to see it. I always wanted to steal them all away.

Once I witnessed two polar bears sitting in a circus tent dying from the heat of the tropics. The upside is that not a year later Costa Rica passed a law banning all circuses with wild animals from performing in this country. Hallelujah!

La Marina has over three hundred and fifty species of wild animals. One of its best known and loved is the dante, or tapir. I had never known this animal and was amazed by them. They weigh over a thousand pounds, are solid black in color, and have coarse, short, thick hair. Their bodies are like those of giant water pigs with miniature elephant-like snouts, hoofed feet, rounded ears and small, cute dark eyes. They make a whistling type sound that is charming to the ear.

La Marina is a series of fresh flowing rivers guided to moving pools and creating a natural habitat for the tapir. They loved it here and thrived naturally.

Jose told me he desperately needed some money. His mother Alba had to make a decision. He then told me something I didn't know. One of the tapirs Chepa, was pregnant, and to the best of his knowledge there was no record in any documentary of a tapir birth in captivity. I had a friend with me that day, Mario Araya, who was a film photographer. He said he would look into it. This footage could bring necessary funds to La Marina. We drove back to the city late that night, coming up with ideas on how to help the zoological park.

La Marina is located in a city called Cuidad Quesada, which is a two and a half hour drive from San Jose, with winding beautiful mountain roads the whole drive. Mario is an excellent driver with racing as his hobby. We made it in record time back to the city.

We were exhausted by the time we got home. He dropped me off, then drove home. The next morning Mario called me at 8:00 AM to inform me, no zoo to date had ever been able to successfully breed tapirs. La Marina was going to be a first. This was exciting news. I began to contact wildlife shows to see where to go with our story.

Filming In The Jungle 19

Mario and I put the whole thing together. I rang him on the phone and we met over dinner. He was quite excited about the new work. Bertram Van Munster, owner of the American network show, Wild Things and the Discovery Network, contacted us. The Central American film company was also interested. We decided to let the three companies film. Two weeks prior to the birth, the film teams would arrive to prepare. Mario was hired to film the segment for Wild Things. The weather was going to be rainy and Chepa, the new movie star, would be birthing outdoors in her natural environment. Tapirs need large bodies of water. They submerge themselves to cool off, relax, mate and protect themselves from predators.

They can hold their breaths for a long time underwater. They also have a great sense of smell. It is a delight to watch them twitch their short, snout-like nose up and down, testing the air. They are so sensitive to all they observe. The crews put up tents and lean-tos, trying not to distract Chepa too much. She was not used to this kind of attention. The new sights and sounds might make her nervous. I told the crews to minimize their equipment and their lights.

I met with all the crews upon their arrival in San Jose. We went over everything and decided we would shoot some other animals in Costa Rica first. The networks would love it and we had some time to kill before Chepa was anywhere near to her birthing day.

I took the guys out to Tarcoles, a river heading out to the pacific side. This was the perfect spot to see caymans and crocodiles. A huge bridge spans the river there and groups of these reptiles hang out all day long. This spot of the riverbed is a series of small grassy islands that connect to the bordering cattle fields. The cows always come down to the river to drink and are surrounded by crocs yet they never have been attacked. In fact it looks like they are good friends.

The film crew was interesting. We talked and laughed a lot and had good fun. They were interested in everything. So we went on a safari. The guys wanted to get really close to the reptiles. A local Tica women with a four year boy told us her son could make them eat of his hand.

We wanted to see this but I thought, What if something goes wrong? But I knew Costarican children had an instinct to danger like no other children I have seen in the States. So we went with it. The little boy went into the little shack he lived in and got a few chicken hotdogs out of the refrigerator. He then proceeded, with no fear or hesitation. He was barefoot and shirtless.

We followed him to the river's edge and watched as these mighty giants, ten to twenty feet long, came up and gently, like babies, took the hotdogs out of the boys hand. He turned around and flashed a Hollywood smile for the camera man. I laughed and hugged him. The guys gave the mother some money and took a picture of them with the film crew. They promised to sent a copy of the photo to me so that I could give it to them.

After Tarcoles we drove to the Osa peninsula. National Geographic named it the most biologically diverse area on the planet. There we stayed at Sierra's place, Delfin Amor, dolphin love. She is a friend of mine who runs a dolphin research program and dolphin/whale tours. The place is teaming with scarlet macaws, monkeys, pumas and the nearby jungle is a paradise with everything else you want to see in the tropics.

This tip of the peninsula is breathtaking. It is verdant in every way. Very remote, most travel is by boat. Marine life here is so thick and diverse that Sierra was petitioning the government to make this a marine sanctuary. Tucked into the Osa Peninsula is a gulf named *Golfo Dulce*, meaning sweet gulf. A secret is hidden here. It is one of the deepest gulfs in the world. Divers have been sent down to measure its depths and do not reach bottom. It is a dark chasm. This is the hiding place for whales during birthing. Whales look for a quiet bay for their birth and the deeper it is the easier it is on the mother. We all hoped this would remain their private kingdom. We told no one of what we had discovered. Some things are not meant to be found.

The crews shot footage of incredible marine life.

Sierra knew dolphins. She has that sense with them. She communicates with them and whenever she goes out on the boats, the dolphins come. I meet her marvelous captain, Jerry, who told quite a story of his participation and assistance with a humpback and her newborn. He proudly wore a tattoo of the saga on his leg. On this trip we discovered a new species of dolphins. It was exciting for all of us to be some of the first people to welcome a new species. We filmed all day. The sunset was magnificent, and a rainbow came with it. It had been a perfect day. We ate like pigs and slept like logs. Later in the year, discovery network brought its ship, the Quest, down for three months. So much life waited there to be filmed.

The next morning we were up bright and early. We had a long trip in front of us back to San Jose. We thanked Sierra over and over, kissed and hugged, and were on our way. It took the whole day to get back. We went to bed early. Tomorrow we would be on our way to La Marina.

The next day came to fast. I wanted to sleep more, but I went with Mario Araya and his wife Tatiana. We got along great and became like sisters. By the end of the trip we all were like family. The drive was beautiful. In all my years of work in this country I never tired of the many miles I had to drive because the jungle is so enchanting and every time you are near, it shows you another splendor.

I was always up at 5:30 and in bed by 10:00 PM. Never needed an alarm clock either. The birds did that. We stopped for breakfast at a local little restaurant. Had gallo pinto, a staple of the country, which is rice and beans, coffee and fruits. Our view was a volcano, rolling valleys and rainforest mountain ranges.

Throughout the drive, one experiences several different types of weather. It will be cold, it will be brisk, it will be dry, then damp, then hot and humid. You always have to have a change of clothes and rain gear. You just never know...

We got to La Marina at around 11:00 AM. The weather was damp, humid, not too hot yet, with overcast skies. We set about with introductions. Three men were with each film crew and Mario with Tatiana. Nine of us in total. Jose's wife Marta and their three children were going to be our hosts for the duration. Dona Alba offered me a room in her house which is on the property of La Marina. It is a beautiful Spanish style home with an enclosed open porch looking into the park. The rest of the group slept in tents or inside Jose's house. Most of the time, we stayed outside with Chepa. Nobody wanted to miss anything. I took one nap in Alba's house, and one night Mario and Tati sleep in Jose's. That was our only time of luxury. The tents were set up, and we connected cables for electricity. Chepa was in another area, eating, so we could work. It took the rest of the day. Everything was set. Marta had cooked us a typical Costarican dinner. We all ate and talked with Jose, long into the night.

Every now and then one of us went to check on Chepa. After dinner we all went out for an evening walk around La Marina. By the end of our filming, we knew this zoological park like the back of our hands.

The animals come alive at night. The pack of coyotes started the first songs, then the tigress began to roar, the jaguars paced back and forth hungrily, growling. The whistling ducks perched for the night, their sounds are one of my favorite in the world. Evening is when the carnivores are fed. Sitting there listening to all of this made us feel what it must be like to be in their kingdom.

The Rojas family owns a huge dairy farm adjacent to the park. Their milk is rich, thick and sweet. The best. I drank gallons of it while I was there. They sell to Dos Pinos, the largest company in the country. This helps keep the zoological park going. What Jose really wants is to turn all the felines existing cages into large natural habitats. He just needed the money to do it.

It did not rain that night. We made up shifts and turned in for the night.

The next morning we were introduced to the zoo's vet. He came out to check on Chepa. I didn't like him from the start. He was a dorky, doughty type of man. Small, bald and fat. Unlike in the States, men in Costa Rica seldom go bald. This one was a rare sight. Mind you, I wasn't judging him by his appearance. He was one of those types that was a know-it-all and show off for the camera. In realty this vet was for cows and horses and pigs. He knew nothing but guesswork about wildlife. Jose told me he was the only one he could get out in these parts. The ones from San Jose were too expensive. I knew how tough Jose had it, so I made the best of it. I just stayed clear of the man.

When the exam was over, the vet said Chepa should birth within four days. He left and we took up vigil again.

On my breaks, I couldn't sleep. I would go around and visit the animals. I spent a lot of time with Suzie. She still went crazy over me and I had brought along a small home movie video camera which had yet to be used since I received it from my friend Mark. I asked Mario to tape some footage of me with Suzie.

I also spent a great deal of time with Seta, the tigress. Even though she was well cared for at La Marina, I could tell she wanted something different. She paced all the time. I wished there was some way to exercise her, but she wasn't getting close to anyone. The circus had left her because the handler had passed away and she never responded to anyone else. I wished I had the time to work on her. I knew I could change her, but I could not stay and live at the park for the duration of time it would take and of course it would take funds we all did not have.

I had to look for means to keep myself from despair. I filled the felines' concrete floored cages with grasses. All cats, domestic or wild, eat grasses. It scours their stomachs, cleans the intestines and naturally removes hairballs. There are certain grasses, of course, that are right for them. Here in the jungle there are many different types.

Further down the zoo's path, I came upon a giant crocodile in another water pen. Jose told me he was the largest on record. Thirty-two feet long. A river turtle was his friend and would sun with him. I even saw the turtle climb on the croc's head for a nap one day.

Mario called to me, from across the river. He, too, was walking around, getting footage of different things. I went over and he showed me the footage he had just shot through the screen. It was the back of another tapir, the father to be. He was halfway submerged in the lake. As I looked closer, I saw what Mario was so excited about. On the tapirs back was a frog. A golden one. Costa Rica has the most colorful frogs I have ever seen. Poison arrow ones and tree frogs are my favorite. The golden frog, which was thought to be extinct, was there right in front of us. The Columbians revered this frog, and priceless museum pieces were carved of the golden monarch. He was also the symbol on coins. He was considered the bearer of good fortune.

We told Jose, and he got excited.

I said, "There must be more and this is the perfect habitat for them."

We searched, but didn't see another one. A beautiful blue morpho butterfly sailed softly by. Time to go back to our watches. We all showered in a makeshift shower with ice cold mountain water. I showered and no sooner finished than it started to rain. We double checked all the equipment to make sure the plastic tarps of the roofs were good, then we settled in for a long, wet night.

We got drunk on guarro, our type of tequila. Chepa just looked at us with a silly look on her face. We sweetly sang to her. I think she was laughing at us.

Morning dawned bright and clear. We went into the neighboring town of Cuidad Quesada. Tatiana and I were getting some food supplies. We wanted to make dinner. Marta had her hands full and we didn't want to make her cook for us, too. The local townspeople had heard about our movie set and were full of stares and curiosity. Everyone talked to us. The local restaurant gave us a complimentary lunch. We also picked up a deck of cards. We got back just before the rain started again. It stopped after four hours and the night sky was full of stars. We all spent the night stargazing.

We talked about aliens and I couldn't believe how many of us had seen something alien. One of the film guys for the central American documentary told us that people in Costa Rica saw aliens and their space crafts all the time. So many people had experiences with them. Many people believed that extraterrestrials had hundreds of years ago left these huge round spheres in different parts of the country. How and why they showed up nobody knew. I had seen three in my travels throughout the country to date. Someone wrote a small book on how these aliens got here and what the spheres were for, but nobody believed much of it. The writer strongly defended the theory of the aliens using them as power fields.

Once on one of my drives I came across one of these giant spheres. I stretched out and laid on one and felt a very unusual energy coming through me. It was hard to explain. It took over your whole body and left you tingling but not on the surface, the tingling was inside of you. You felt your insides like you couldn't before.

Later that year at the beach along with Mitch and our friend Mark, we saw our first UFO. It came over the ocean, a sphere hurling through the sky at lightning speed. The glow of light it threw was eerie. Golden white light. People had seen it in San Jose also and the phones were ringing off the hook to the newspaper from everyone. It is still a vivid picture in my mind.

Day six of our vigil. Chepa looked exactly the same, but she was eating more. Her favorite food is a plant covered in spines, called ortega. You have to wear gloves as you cut it with a machete. It grew abundantly throughout the park. The crew was getting a little restless by now. I told them I thought the vet had misjudged the due date. Her belly had not dropped yet, nor was she dilated. The film crew went into town to take a break.

We left all cameras in position in case something should happen, and we were all instructed as to how to flick them on. We played cards well into the wee hours. We had become friends with the wild white-collared pigs in the pen besides us. All except Macho, the king of the herd. In the jungles of Costa Rica this wild pig is the most dangerous animal. It will charge at you for no reason. Their tusks are lethal. Their long hairs are more like spines than hair.

Jose told us a story about a man walking in the jungle who came upon a group of these wild pigs, and they chased down. You can't outrun them, so don't waste your breath. The man climbed up a tree. The herd began to ram the tree with their trunks. They knocked the tree down and ripped the man apart with their tusks. If you were able to climb a big tree you might make it, unless the tree had the infamous giant ant nests on them. Then the ants would bite you to death.

Jose's herd of wild pigs numbered thirty-eight. They all went about their business except for Macho, who would ram and charge the fence whenever we got close. He also had a squeal that made you cringe. His snort was like the sound of a locomotive engine running right over you. Their pen was located right next to our campsite. He became our nightly entertainment. But when the winds shifted so did we. We did not appreciate their smell.

One day, Jose told us a story of Macho's breakout with the herd. He said it was the roughest capture by far in his life. He showed us the long angry scars on his leg from the encounter. But he did manage to round them all up again and get them safely back inside the pen.

By the next day the vet was summoned again. He checked Chepa. She was very friendly and docile. Tati and I touched her, along with Jose who she knew. She liked being scratched and rubbed and massaged.

We all wanted that by now. A good massage. I could see Jose was tired. He was non-stop all the time. He worked harder than ten men and took little time to sleep. He was up at 4:30 every morning, taking care of the dairy farm and the milkings of over two hundred cows, then working in the zoo,and trying to spend time with his family. On top of that, he stayed with us every extra minute he had. He loved his tapirs, they were his favorite animals in the park.

Dona Alba also checked on the expectant mother every chance she got. She was there for the vets visit this time. The vet decided to do an exam of her cervix to see how far along she had come and whether she was dilated.

I asked him how he proposed to do this.

He said he would insert a piece of hollowed bamboo into her vagina and then with a flashlight at the other end see what was going on.

I turned to Jose and said " he has got to be kidding." I told Jose this was out of the question. Not only would it hurt and scare her, it could easily puncture her inside.

Jose and Alba agreed with me and told him they would not allow it.

I gave him a dirty look and felt like saying, "Why don't you do it to yourself first and see how it feels."

Jose did not ask the vet back. We simply waited for the birth to occur as nature intended. There was nothing wrong with Chepa so we just had to wait.

That night I found a treasure. It was to become the greatest treasure I had every discovered in Costa Rica. It was shortly after dinner, about 7:00 PM. The night was hot and sticky. It would become damp and cold as it did every night but not until much later. I was restless. I wanted to go walking.

I went to an area I had only gone by once before. It was the far backside of the park, where grains and equipment were stored. The door always had a lock on it, but this time it didn't. Maybe one of the workers had forgotten to lock it when he left. I looked around, saw no one, and turned the handle. I was greeted by scurrying rats. They lived in here and ate through the sacks of grains. I could not find the light switch and didn't want to enter. I also did not have a flashlight with me. But I heard something, a wild animal of some sort, a baby it sounded like, but I couldn't place what kind it was. I went back to the campsite for a flashlight. I did not tell the others what I was up to. I wanted to be alone.

As I hurried back, I saw Jose with his family in the main house. Good, no one around so I could investigate. I opened the door again, no rats this time, and flashed the light on. I listened to hear the sound again. There was so much stuff in there. It was hard to find something, especially if you really did not know what you were looking for.

Then I heard a hiss like little growl and I looked down to find tucked in a big box a baby mountain lion. It was so scared and angry. It could not get up and as I bent down to get closer to it, it hissed and spat and tried to claw at me. This was a very wild little thing. I feel in love with it instantly. Every motherly instinct in me came to life. I thought her to be female.

She did not look well and I thought why on earth would Jose not tell me about her and leave her here in this box. I spoke softly and soothingly to her. I hummed *"Rock-A- Bye Baby"* to her. She calmed down just a little bit. I told her I would be back and went off to find Jose. I waited anxiously for Jose to come out of the house. When he came out, he didn't see me right away and I startled him.

"What are you doing here?" he asked.

I looked into his eyes and said, "Jose what is that in your storage shed?" "Oh oh," he said as he rolled his eyes back and let out a great breath of air. We liked each other to much to mince words.

"I was hoping you wouldn't hear about her." "Why, whats wrong?" I asked.

"Well," Jose started, "Yesterday morning I went out to open the front gates of the park like I always do at 5am. There on the other side was a big box, shut with ropes. Through the small air holes I could see it was some type of wild cat."

He lifted the box up and took it inside. When he opened it he found two baby puma cubs.

"Quite often," he said, "People drop off animals without leaving a note. They always have some secret to hide."

These were two little sisters and they were very ill. Jose asked the same vet who had been by that morning to see Chepa to take a look at the cubs.

The vet said they had a bacterial or viral infection. Jose needed to quarantine them against the other animals. The vet said he would return the next day with some antibiotics.

Jose tried to feed them, but they would not take anything. He put them in the shed to keep them safe. Early the next morning as he went to check on them, one of the little ones had died.

"I thought the other one was going to die too so I didn't want to get you upset over them. "

I said, "Jose, this is what I am here for. Let me see what I can do." He said it looked pretty hopeless to him.

I told him, "At least let me try."

He told me the vet would be by in the morning with antibiotics.

I told him I didn't want them. I had my own natural antibiotics which were also a food source for this undernourished cub.

He finally consented. "Go on. Do what you must, but I don't want to see you crying if she doesn't make it."

"Agreed!" I shouted as I raced by him back to the shed.

It was late by now and the little lioness looked like she needed some sleep. But I wanted to get down her at least one dosage of an herbal formula I had with me.

I went into the house and got some fresh milk, warmed it a little, added the formula and went back to her. It was quite a struggle getting her to take it. She scratched, she squirmed, she wanted nothing to do with me. I persisted. She ripped my shirt to ribbons. I got half of it on her and half of it down her throat. It was better than nothing.

I had two pair of pants on. Sweatpants and rainpants. I took off my sweats, which were nice and warm from my body and laid them in her box for her to cuddle up against. I would have to put something better together for her in the morning.

I left and went back to the others. My shift was on and I took it with Tatiana and Mario. I told them all about the little puma. They couldn't wait to see her.

As my shift ended for the night I went back again to check on her. I did not want to shine any light on her so I just checked her by the light of the moon coming through the open door. She was sleeping, so I left without further ministering.

I wanted to hold her tight so badly. But first things first. I had to make her better. I knew that night that she would make it. I knew she would become mine. I wasn't taking no for an answer. I went to sleep that night and dreamed of being a mother lioness.

The following day was gray and overcast. It looked like it was going to rain buckets. I woke at 5:30 and immediately went out to the shed. Jose was there, with a big smile on his face.

"Are these yours?" he said, holding up my sweatpants.

I almost didn't recognize them. They had been torn to shreds. I laughed out loud. "They were."

"What happened to them?" Jose asked. "Looks like she wanted to tear you up."

We both knelt to get a better look at her. For the first time I really saw her. Puma cubs are born with beautiful markings, spotted dark markings on a velvet tawny coat. She had a fat round face and I swore I never saw anything so adorable in my life. She was still angry and afraid.

Jose told me some news he had received from an anonymous hunter. These two cubs were supposed to be sold to a zoo in another country. The poachers had shot the mother, probably right in front of the cubs, then proceeded to steal the little ones. However, little wild cubs are born with an instinct for natural self protection. Handling wild cubs is often times more dangerous than handling the adults. They never stop fighting.

The hunter had broken the legs of the cubs in the fight. They were then thrown into a crate which caused two more fractures to occur in the femurs. These little ones were still very young and their bones very soft. This was the reason, Jose said, that the one we still had could not move. I realized then she must be in such pain. Poor little thing! My heart went out to her.

Three months later Jose and I went into the jungle to find this poacher. We found him, and gave him two choices, A) be bodily tied up in a tree, to be used as bait and then dinner to whatever predator found him, and we got to watch, or B) leave this country and never return.

He left immediately and was personally escorted out of the country and all border patrols were told, he had no entrance back, ever.

Well, we got a reputation, but this one helped us in more ways than we knew. Poaching in the jungles of Jose's borders was cut in half.

We liked scaring people. It kept them away from us...

All of a sudden from the other end of the park, Jose and I were brought back to Chepa. We both heard a great deal of shouting and tapir grunts. When they grunt they are mad. We ran up just in time to see Ronghee, the father to be, running away from the film crew. It looked so comical. Ronghee had busted his way into the birthing pen to see Chepa. At first no one did anything. Then as Ronghee started to get rough in a

playful manner with Chepa, the film crew decided Ronghee
had to go. Nobody wanted Chepa to be hurt in any way.

But getting him out was tougher then they thought. Tapirs
dart at high sprint runs, catching you completely off guard,
and no one wants to get run over by a thousand pound tapir.
Jose finally got him out and I noticed for the first time that
Chepa's stomach was hanging lower. She had dropped.

This means the uterus has dropped lower, readying itself
for the birth canal. But this too could take days. We settled
Chepa down and then I suggested taking her for a slow walk
to stretch her legs a little and relax. Jose walked in front of her
nose with her favorite spiny grass and she followed. I could
see she felt better.

I left to work on the puma. Mario and Tati wanted to come.
But I asked them to first let me get better acquainted with her
before I brought any other people around. I now knew why
she hated people and I related the story to them. Mario and
Tati couldn't believe it. They asked if there was anything they
could do to help. I asked them to go into town and buy fresh
ground-up chicken.

I then searched the park area for a better place to put the
puma cub. I found the perfect nest, tucked under a beautiful tree with a canopy of leaves shading it. It had a large old
enclosure, made out of wood. It was close enough for me still
to be with Chepa, yet far from anyone passing by. The little
puma, would not hear any human voices either.

I washed the enclosure with lime juice. This is a great natural disinfectant. Chemical cleaners such as bleach destroy the
olfactory system and the keen sense of smell animals have. I
let it dry in the sun. It had turned into a lovely, sunny day. I
took gloves, a big blanket and a net bag to carry the lioness

to her new place. With the gloves I was able to work quickly and effectively. The blanket and net bag were for her safety. I did not want her to wiggle around much and hurt her broken bones. It was a short walk, and I walked along a jungle trail. The enclosure, when dry, was covered with fresh fallen leaves and a bed of moss. I wanted her to lay on softness. I gently laid her down. I will never forget the great courage this little girl had. She had big brown eyes you could drown in, for they were so deep. She had a tough little girl face on. She was determined to fight for her life. I made little sounds to her like her mother would. She still was not taking to me. I was in no rush. I let her smell the surroundings. She wanted to stay hidden.

Then I forced some more formula down her and left to see Chepa. Jose was there. He asked where the puma was. I told him I moved her.

He said, "Where?"

I said I would show him later, right now she was getting accustomed to her new hospital in the jungle. He knew I was taking over this one. He just looked up to the sky and shook his head in defeat.

Chepa was resting. Jose and I went to see her. He talked to her. She liked his voice. She had known it through her whole life. He spoke in a very deep low baritone to all the animals.

It had a soothing effect on all who heard it. I massaged Chepa with a circular motion, which aids in the ease of birthing. I slowly and gently touched her teats. They were warm and soft. I squeezed just a little bit of milk out of them. It felt like silk water. I tasted my finger, it was strong and rich.

Jose had to go back to work, and I stayed with Chepa . For the first time since meeting her, I felt that she wanted to communicate with me. I held and rubbed her head and looked right into her eyes. Chepa told me she was afraid of her body. She felt different inside. Things were moving on their own in places she had never felt before. A warm knowing smile came over me.

I tried to tell her all females feel that way. I massaged her belly and let her feel that everything was fine.

The film crew started to believe she was never going to birth. I laughed at their despair.

"C'mon," I said, "She is going to have the little one very soon."

They all told me, I had lived in Costa Rica too long and had adapted to the "Manana" attitude. In Costa Rica when they tell you they will do it, or get it, or call you, manana, (tomorrow), what they are really saying is when we feel like it.

We lay in our tents with Chepa and took a siesta. We woke to a cool wind., briskly blowing. It was taking the humidity away. It promised to be a beautiful night. The camera crew wanted to eat in town. They wanted some outside human contact. They were a good lot. I did not blame them. Mario and Tati had the late afternoon watch, they had just returned from town with the meat I requested.

I went to check on the puma. I mixed some more herbs into the chicken which I heated up. Warming up raw meat for wild feline babies, and most carnivores for that matter, is essential to absorption. A wild mother has already begun the digestive process in her stomach while regurgitating meat to her young. A fresh kill is also always warm.

As I brought the meal to her, she hissed and then made a hungry noise. That was different. I laid the plate in front of her; she still would not let me get near her. I knew she wanted the food but also did not want me there. I left and hid in a nearby bush.

She went to eat immediately. She was so hungry. I was tickled pink. She was getting better. The herbs were working. She ate half of what I brought her which was great. Just then like a cat himself, out of the trees stepped Jose.

"So this is what you did with her," he said.

I could tell he was amazed she was doing so well. "I guess your herbs work."

I said, "I guess I just got my first compliment from you." He told me to carry on and just stay out of trouble.

I giggled as he walked away. For the first time I felt that this puma cub really was to become mine. I was elated. I was jumping for joy inside.

I had to prepare for work on the puma's back legs which were fractured. An excellent remedy was the mud source from the volcano. This mud is infused by the heat of hot lava with jungle botanicals. It is high in sulfur and very healing. I wanted to soak her whole back area in this as it needed to work the lower spine also. Then I had to somehow get some comfrey root tea down her. This tastes awful but works like a miracle every time. Comfrey joins all non unions in the body, repairs torn ligaments and accelerates the healing process. It is great for skin, circulation and swelling in the body. It also works on the pain as it reduces the fluids swelling up in the breaks. Wrapping her legs with the fresh comfrey leaves, which are big and round, helps too. But I thought I had a fat chance in hell of doing that to her. But I was going to work on it. I liked these types of challenges. I learn a lot of the minds of animals through these simple tasks.

I found a fresh comfrey plant, dug up the roots, and boiled them down. The resulting tea has an orange color. I diluted her bowl of drinking water with this and prepared her for bed. I left the other portion of meat with her. If she didn't finish it by my first night watch, I would remove it. I didn't want to tempt any other stray animals that might to come for it and scare her or have ants scurrying about and biting her.

The next morning I promised Tati and Mario I would let them see my new baby. Jose and I did the first watch together. The crew was in town and Mario and Tati were in the main house with Marta and the kids. We watched the moon rise. It was enormous.

Jose was exhausted. He asked me if he could catch some shut eye.

I told him, sure. He looked so funny with his long giant like body lying in the tent. The tent only managed to cover half of him and his legs were out in the open. He reminded me of the story, Gulliver's Travels, of the giant and the little people tying him down.

I too was tired so I sang to Chepa to keep myself awake. Then it happened...

No sooner had Jose started to snore than I saw Chepa get into an odd position. It was sort of a squat. I froze for a split second, then grabbed Jose's legs and yanked him awake.

"Jose, Jose," I shouted, "get up."

He jolted awake. At first I thought he thought I was joking, then he looked around. We were the only ones there. No time to alert anyone. We needed to turn on the cameras. Out of all the people in our group Jose and I were the least likely candidates to be shooting film. We knew nothing about it. The crews cameras were ready to go, we just had to switch them on. Oh, oh, they wouldn't go on. The power had shut off. It was weird how at precisely that moment all the cameras were down. There was only one that worked, my little home video camera. I shoved it at Jose.

"You do the filming."

He was a champ. He got right in there and filmed the whole thing. We spoke not a word. We were in awe. Chepa was great. The baby came out quickly, and then Chepa laid down to lick the protective placenta sack off.

I never knew baby tapirs were so cute. They are incredible soft with spots and stripes running all over their coats. Their newborn hooves are as soft as a infant child's fingernails.

It was a boy. His little snout nose was wiggling up and down, sniffing all the new smells. His cute little ears were going back and forth listening to our whispers as we owwed and awwed at the new arrival. I touched him only a little and gave him back to mom. Both mother and son were perfect. Jose and I filmed for another ten minutes. We both looked at each other and wondered if Chepa had purposely waited till everyone else was gone and privileged us with her birth.

Jose looked like a proud papa.

Jose and I had a moment where deep inside of us we became one. It was like our souls touched. We looked into each other's eyes in a moment of something else felt. Something we both wanted.

Then Mario and Tati and Marta came by. They were speechless when they saw the new tapir. It was maddening to them to have waited this long and then missed the event.

Mario asked, "Did you catch it on film?"

Jose and I looked sheepishly at each other. "Well, we did the best we could." We explained the problem with the cameras to

Mario and he immediately got his going and started to continue shooting Chepa and the newborn. He inspected the footage we got and said it was pretty good for amateurs. At least the footage was clear and showed the whole birthing process. But now we owned the rights to the film.

We turned around to see the crews' truck coming back. Alba was walking up too. Everyone was full of questions. The crew was bummed they missed it, but they got over it quickly as they joined the celebration of the baby tapir. We made Discovery history. We were the first in the world to breed tapirs in captivity.

Alba choose a name for the new baby. He would be registered in her books as she had done with every animal that ever came to La Marina. She had the most accurate book work in the country.

We all slept our last night together. We talked into the wee hours of the morning, exchanged telephone numbers and promised to keep in touch and work together again on future projects.

Mario, Tati and I went to see the puma. They couldn't believe it. Another adorable baby. We stayed for hours with her. She ate, she spit, she hissed, she tried to get up. Finally, with the help of Tati, I got her in my arms with the blanket as sort of a protective barrier. I held her tight. It felt so right holding her. She was my little tesoro, which means treasure. I carried her around and showed her lots of things. Monkeys in the trees, flowers and jungle.

She was giving in to me just a little bit. I sang "Rock-A-Bye Baby" to her. It became my song with her. It soothed her like no other. I have a little girl singing voice and she enjoyed listening to it.

I then took her back for her afternoon nap. Mario, Tati, and I were staying for another night. Mario wanted to get more footage of the tapirs and I had to figure out a plan for my new little cub. I needed to take her with me to properly work with her. It would take some time to work on her and I wanted to have the chance to release her back to the wilds.

This was going to be a great favor to ask of Jose. I wanted to time it just right when I breached the question. I got my chance later in the evening as he was doing his rounds with the animals.

I asked him if he had ever considered working on releasing wildlife back to the wilds.

He said he had never done this and was not sure how to go about it.

I told him I wanted to make a deal with him. If I could successfully cure this feline of her ills and broken legs, would he give me the chance to return her to the wilds in the name of La Marina.

He said it was not up to him. He was not in charge, his mother was. I petitioned him to speak to her in my behalf.

He spoke with her that night.

In the morning she would make her decision. She called the vet to come by again. His diagnosis, though incorrect, served to save me. He told Alba he saw no chance of this puma fully recovering and life as a cripple would be too much of a strain on her, here at the zoo. She would not be able to mate and she could not survive in the jungle. She was useless in his eyes.

I said not a word.

Alba consented. The zoo was struggling with the animals they already had. Every ounce of energy and monies they expended was crucial. If I wanted to work on the puma that badly, Alba wished me well and nodded towards her son.

Later, Jose told me that we would have to move her on our own. Meaning, if we got stopped by the police, they would confiscate her and I could not get help from La Marina as it goes against all laws to release a wild animal into the custody of a lay person. He suggested that even though I was doing a good thing with the puma, I would get trouble from Minae. It was better to keep her existence a secret.

That night Tati, Mario and I came up with a plan to smuggle her to San Jose. She would stay with me at a friend's house, Christine Crawford, who had a heart of gold. She was an animal advocate, big time. Her help those first few months was immeasurable to me.

The next day we waited until dusk to begin our journey. Tatiana and I named the puma Juliana, after me and her. We were her new adopted mothers.

As Papa Jose said his goodbyes and wished us luck, I knew we had all shared something we would remember for the rest of our lives. I sat in the back of the cab of the truck alongside Juliana. I had her blanket to throw over her if we got stopped. We smoked a joint in the truck to calm her for the ride. She slept peacefully the whole way and nobody stopped us.

We arrived at Christina's late. She was up waiting. She had prepared a cozy little peaceful haven in one of her rooms for me. I kissed and squeezed her hard. I thanked Tati and Mario from the bottom of my heart and we all went to sleep in a real bed for the first time in two weeks. Ohhh how good the hot shower and cozy bed felt to me.

Juliana and I slept in late. A new chapter was beginning in both of our lives.

Juliana   20

I had gone through many doors in my journey here in Costa Rica. I had experienced many of my curiosities. I was more alive. I used my senses, all of them, day in, day out and was getting in touch with animals' minds. I knew them in their way, through their movements, the language of the body, and through the feelings they would send out to me. I was seeing in very physical, scientific sense and simultaneously I was seeing in a mystic sense. Nor one was more or less important. It was as it is. A given. A balance of how to do a trick that life throws out at us. This puma never lost her sense, her wild spirit. Instead she instilled this lost sense to all that knew her.

The city.

I woke the next morning to see Juliana curled up on her blanket by my bed on the floor. She was content with me. Christina called into the room. I had a phone call from Jose.

I took the phone and let out a long sleepy yawn. He wanted to make sure we had made it safely. I groaned and plopped back down in bed. Juliana just stared up at me with those beautiful big saucy-like eyes, not wanting to move off her bed either. Jose and I talked. I told him we made it safe and sound. Tomorrow I was going to the vets for x- rays of her legs. Jose told me he had some news. Carlos Manuel Rodriguez had re-signed from office. He disagreed with Odio on a lot. Too much shit was coming out about the government.

Jose said, "Looks like you won quite a victory."

I was happy. Staying out at La Marina all this time, I had lost touch with what was going on in the city. I called Dan. He already knew. Then Barbara Beck called me and the news spread like wildfire. I spent the day in bed. Juliana ate well, took her herbs and slept with me on her blanket by the bedside. The room had been converted into a den of sorts with a big bay window overlooking a yard full of trees.

The next day I took her outside in the back yard and laid her in a soft grassy patch. She stretched and tried to use her legs. She growled when her legs wouldn't respond. I massaged them a little. She was allowing me to touch her somewhat. She took in all the new sights and sounds and scents here in the city. Christine's place was on the outskirts of the city in a beautiful wooded development with only a few homes peppered around the woods. Nevertheless, it was not the jungle.

I didn't want to keep her here long. I was on a mission with this one. she would go with me and start her life at the ocean jungle place in Dominical. I was leaving the city and going back out to the beach. It had been a long time. Mitch and I were going to work together on her. He was coming in to the city the next day. He would stay with us until it was time to go.

I gave Juliana a stuffed animal to snuggle against. It was a reindeer and she loved it. She played with it, yet never tore it up. She was so loving to it. The next morning, I was a little nervous. I so wanted the outcome of the vet's visit to be good. Alex Valverde is one of the finest veterinarian's I have ever met. His office and hospital were impeccable. He was the president of the veterinarian's association.

He knew who I was and I knew of his reputation. When we met, we didn't have to say anything. And gratefully he asked no questions. He did a series of x-rays on her back legs. He had the examination room darkened and quiet for her. He touched her very professionally and Juliana did great.

The x-rays showed fractures in both legs in four points. Her viral infection was also a concern. Her blood work showed it was a lethal bacteria and hard to kill. He also said she was doing remarkable well under the circumstances. I told him she was on alternative natural medicines. I wanted to show him how effective my herbs were. I told him I was going to work on her for two weeks and then let him see her again. He said o.k. He was familiar with many different types of healing remedies and formulas. He wished me well and told me to call if I needed anything. He also was keeping her a private matter to everyone. It was to remain a secret that I had this cat.

Juliana swished her long tail back and forth, indicating she wanted to go. I wrapped her back into the blanket I carried her in and walked out to the truck. We drove slowly back to the house. She was having a new problem. She was not defecating. When cats can not defecate they refuse to eat. I think that when her legs were broken they were grabbed from behind and broken inwards, out. This could have caused the opening of the intestinal track to have become blocked.

My husband was waiting for me when we arrived. He was anxious to meet Juliana.

When I had phoned him to inform him of my new charge, I simply said "Guess what I have honey?" to which he answered, knowing my voice and its elation that it could only be a feline of some sort.

"You got a new baby."

Mitch and I worked on her for hours. Mitch was a master healer with his hands. He ran energy work, the Shen method on her. Finally she did have a bowel motion. It had hurt her but she was o.k. After that, by using a warm wet cloth to clean her and move it over her stomach I was also demonstrating what her mother would do, which helps in stimulation of the intestines.

I added olive oil to her meals to ease the movements. I prepared the wraps for her legs and with the help of Christine and Mitch, got them on her and let out a sigh of relief. Let the healing begin. She did not fuss over the wraps and slept contently through the night.

The next morning I called Jose. Alba was with him. I told them the outcome of the vet's visit. Alba stated to me that she spoke to Valverde last night and the chances for this little puma to ever be normal were slim.

Even though I knew they were wrong, I held my tongue. This was my way of getting her to stay with me for good. She would be too much work for anyone else. Alba again consented for her to stay with me. As I hung up the phone I was wearing the biggest smile in the world.

I called Mario and Tatiana. We got together and celebrated.

Juliana was remarkable. She healed quickly, grew, and began using her legs after only one week. By the end of the next week I brought Juliana back to Alex. He was really surprised. He was also very proud of me. He saw her improvement, and he saw my dedication. He gave me the green light to take her out of the city.

We prepared to leave the next day. We left at 4:00 AM to avoid any police on the road and drove the little one to her new home.

We arrived at 8:00 AM at our beach property. It was now called a reserve. For the duration of Juliana's stay here, the ocean jungle reserve was off limits to anyone but friends. Juliana's new habitat was set back into the jungle along a river embedded in huge rocks and thick lush rainforest. It was safe from humans, hidden and relatively cool for most of the day. We constructed a new jungle house near her enclosure. Mitch would meet everyone up top at the other house, this new spot was my private nursery with her. She stayed in a small room until the training pen was finished. It was large with a tree inside, a rock pool, lots of ledges for her to lie on and a nice big box with a covered entrance. Inside was clean straw hay, mosses and bamboo leaves. The box was on a platform high up off the ground with a fallen tree trunk acting as a ladder.

I constantly added jungle stuff to her lair. She loved her new home. My dogs were to become her new family, and I was to explore a new form of interspecies connection. I believe that every successful wild animal contact is to be done on their level.

We thus learn far more about the species for we see through their eyes. A bond between animal and human begins immediately. At the moment we meet with our animal, our mind has already made a first impression, prior to our brain making it verbal, even to ourselves. This first impression is instinct. The animal knew before you did what you felt. Man fears this phenomenal sense, yet we also posses it. But man doesn't live in it. From this first greetings of the minds that occur, animals draw a conclusion regarding the person in front of them. They do this in the blink of an eye. It scares us to know that something else knows something about our self, before we do, yes?

Step by step I went with this puma as one. I learned her walk, her jumps, her growl, her purr, her stretches, her face. From the moment she knew she was in charge of the teaching, she accepted me completely into her world. The indigenous people tell that when one who is wild walks in the jungle, the ground which they walk gives them the information they need to live in it. Every wild baby remembers how to live in the wilds from which they came. Again it is instinct.

I walked her every day on a harness leash. Through the rainforest, through rivers and up mountain hills. She loved to run. She had incredible bursts of energy and then she would suddenly lay down, spent, completely sprawled out, pant and rest. I learned about reserves of energy and how to use them. What was a shortcut to her, never was to me. She turned or leapt on a dime, over a log, over a river or straight up over a mountain. I was always panting.

I loved to watch the way she moved her body. It was fluid motion. She never lost her balance. There were but two times when she was young that she was caught off balance. She never forgot a mistake, or a move.

Her trust in me and Mitch was starting to grow. The painful memory in which she had her first encounter with man and lost her mother and sister, needed to be worked on slowly. First we try, then we trust. I treated her with a lot of respect and love, yet I did not step over the boundary. I knew she would do this return to her world alone. She would learn this side by side with the human factor in her life. I let her explore her world, always on her own. I was there for guardianship. We knew where we stood with each other very early in our lives together. There was no fear and no judgment. This led to an easy openness of communication.

The dogs were always with us. When she got loose from her harness or just broke away, she never strayed far from the dogs. The dogs knew they were to keep an eye on this little one. They knew she was a wild thing. She was always rough and tough on them. She had this ability to switch instantly from a mean, wild cat to a purring warm, loving kitten. But that was her nature and I liked it. I wanted her wilds to come back strong, actually, it really never left her.

She knew things. For instance, she always defecated in water. This throws off her scent when she is hunting. This habit never left her. She always checked her food before feasting, and she drank only running water. Still water in a bowel made her turn her noise up in disgust.

She didn't like anyone pulling her tail. A cat's tail communicates much to a trained observer. She taught me everyday. I watched as her skin rippled and twitched in anticipation. Her body became strung like a fine bow, waiting to ignite into action. Juliana had a beautiful face. It never changed or got hard with age. It remained a beautiful soft round baby face that housed the eyes of eternity.

She liked it when I pulled on her whiskers. They were long and tight. She liked me to touch her in different ways and different places. I handled her much like her mother would handle her. She felt my love for her and I hers.

Her life at the ocean jungles was routine. Every morning, while it was still cool, she walked with Mitch and me to discover the jungle. She encountered different animals and different challenges. She was in excellent condition. Her legs had healed perfectly, and she exercised them daily and hard. She was a beautiful jumper. She leapt great distances, in an effortless bound. She didn't like to get wet.

She was four months old now and had never been down to the ocean. I knew she heard it, smelled it, and tasted it on her coat, for the ocean breezes ran through our land every evening. We decided to take her down to a secluded beach cove when the evening came in. It was a beautiful dusk, my favorite part of a day.

We put her in a travel kennel in the back of the truck with the dogs and drove very slowly down. The dogs jumped out as soon as we stopped. They love to run the beach. Juliana was very hesitant. She was scared and in shock at the same time. The endless ocean blew her mind. There is a stream running from the jungle onto this beach. I took her over there and she sharpened her claws on a piece of driftwood. We always put ocean driftwood into her habitat. The salt and minerals from the sea are very beneficial, and as she licks herself constantly she is taking it in internally. This also disinfects and strengthens her nails naturally.

The waves crashed on the rocks, and Juliana wanted to go home. We stayed a little longer, tried to get the dogs to make her play, but she wanted nothing of this. She did not like the ocean. Costa Rica has many pumas in the beach areas. Then there were the pumas of the high mountains. Juliana seemed to be one of those. The heat of the jungles by the sea is very humid, and she panted a lot and was inactive during the heat of the day. The area of Dominical was not a good spot to release her anyway. It was just her nursery. It was becoming time to search for a place where we could work with her and release her.

I wanted the place to be high in the Cerros. This mountain chain is majestic. It is a corridor which passes through five countries. Pumas live up there. I decided to go "Hunting magic"........

At the end of the month, Alex Valverde came out for the final analysis of her health and ability to be released back into the wilds. It was great to see him.

He was very impressed by my work and said, "I have never given out a letter of recommendation to anyone. I don't believe in them. But you just changed my mind."

The following letter is what he wrote about my work with the puma.

LA URUCA Hospital Veterinarian

A QUIEN INTERESE

Hago constar que el felino, puma, fue valorado inicialmente el 3 de noviembre de 1998, en esta Clinica Veterinaria, y presentaba un cuadro de desnutricio'n, con fracturas en ambos femures.

El pronostico para la recuperacion del felino fue reservado, por su condicion y complicaciones presentes. Hoy, 15 mese despues, la recuperacion de la puma,

bajo la supervision de Julie Bindas ha sido impresionante. Los cuidados brindados consistieron principalmente de medicina natural, dieta adecuada, mantenerla en

un ambiente silvestre, y mucho carino.

Actualmente la puma se moviliza con normalidad y es capaz de cazar por si sola. La evolucion presente ha entusiasmado a Julie a preparar la eventual liberacion de

La puma a su ambiente natural

Alexander Valverde R Colegiado 424

The English translation of this letter is as follows.......

To Whom This May Concern

I declare upon the visit of the feline, puma on the 3rd of November 1998 in my veterinarian's clinic was with serious malnutrition and fractured femurs in both limbs.

The prognosis for the recovery of this feline was reserved because of the conditions and complications present.

After fifteen months, the recovery of the puma, under the supervision of Julie Bindas, was impressive. The care consisted primarily of natural medicines, proper diet, maintaining her in a natural environment and much love.

The puma moves normally and will be able to hunt on her own without problems. We look forward with enthusiasm as Julie prepares to return the puma to freedom in her natural environment.

Alexander Valverde R   Code 424

Hunting Magic 21

Jose and I were constantly in touch. He helped me to keep her. The information back to his mother was always the same. A deal was a deal. Since I had cured her, I was now given the opportunity to return her to the wilds. Jose's mind was changing. He was all for releasing wildlife back into the jungle. He was entering a new stage in his life also. He was learning from me and I from him. He was always busy and it was hard for him to get away and visit my reserve. We worked on turning La Marina into a rescue/release center. Alba was also going to retire and hand over the zoo to Jose.

That was good news. I knew Jose would do great things. He was on his way.

Costa Rica was now the most popular place to vacation in, and most of its visitors decided to stay. Thus the country's population was growing fast. Development, housing projects, investments and hotels were booming. Within the next five years, the growth of this country was insane. Almost as many foreigners as natives lived in Costa Rica. Eco tourism was on the rise and people took a bigger interest in the enviornment. Groups from all over the world set up projects to protect the nature of this land. The government became more aware of the gold of its country. I watched organizations being formed that would make a difference.

Costa Rica's gold was its beauty. It was this that drew the people in. The revenue collected in yearly tourism dollars prompted the government to take better care of what they had. For those of us that had been at the forfront of this time, it was a time of peace. Our efforts had been for something we could be proud of.

I went hunting. It was time to find that place in which Juliana would be released. One early morning I took the truck up the mountain road to the pass of the Cerro De La Muerte. Mountains of death. They were named this from the many deaths that occurred from the bitter cold and precarious rocks which took many road workers' lives during the building of the road that cut through this country. The indigenous people tell another story about its name. They say it houses the spirits of the dead. This place was sacred to them.

Such pristine beauty envelopes this area. The drive from the beach is about one and a half hours. Upon reaching San Isidro Del General, midway point, the weather begins to change. You start out in shorts and end up in sweatpants and jackets. The air is crisp, cold and fresh. The highest mountain peak is the Chirripo mountain. It has a dry, brush type vegetation. Very rocky, very barren. It gets freezing up here in the dry season. The icicles that hang off the mountain are endless. There are points on this drive where one can see both oceans on a clear day, the Atlantic and the Pacific. One early evening I saw the sun set and the moon rise with both oceans in front of me. It was magical. It was moving.

The Talamanca mountain range is the wilderness area with the greatest biological diversity in the country. It is also the largest natural forest in Costa Rica. Six national parks come together in this area. Los Santos, La Amistad, an international park, Chirripo, Hitoy-Cerere Tapanti and Rio Macho. La Amistad in 1983 became a world heritage site, a biosphere reserve of 193.920 hectares. Tapanti 5.113 hectares, Chirripo 50.150 hectares soaring 3819 meters above sea level, Hitoy-Cerere 9.154 hectares.

The diversity of each of them make this area a wonderland of nature. You see dry forest, rain forest, cloud forests and a multitude of inner micro climates. Majestic rivers, carve into the mountains and hot springs with thermal waters add to the beauty. It is the everlasting land of waterfalls. They cascade in every corner that meets the eye. The road is winding and dangerous, yet no matter how many times you cross it, it will never cease to amaze you. White lipped peccaries, snakes coiled around moss covered branches. The forest darkens, the sky lost behind an impenetrable mosaic of green leaves of every shape and size.

The bird life here is different than in the lowlands. The resplendent *Quetzal* lives here. It is one of the most beautiful birds in the world. It is highly revered by Mayan shamans as a sacred bird and an omen of power. It has a small, fussy round head and long flowing emerald green tail feathers. The prisms of light hitting the feathers bring out this exotic color. I had never seen this bird before. Today I was to become one of the lucky few that did.

I had just turned a sharp precarious curve in the road. A giant semi truck was barreling around the corner at the same time. And then out of the corner of my eye, I saw a flash of emerald that in that instant made me pull off to the side. There in the trees was a pair of quetzals.

My mouth dropped open. They stayed for a series of flights, tree to tree and then as if to call to me, sang their calling song which one never forgets and will always recognize. It was a flute melody, long and whistle like, the chimes of winds...

They flew down a dirt road off the main highway. I got in my truck and followed them. The road cut through the mountain top and then down into the valley. Only a small group of houses dotted this area. The quetzals lived in the parks. Cows grazed verdant green grasses, thick lush massive jungle around them, and rivers teemed with rainbow trout. The water was the sweetest tasting water in the world. The birds led me somewhere, I felt it. The road went for eight kilometers. It ended at the edge of a crescendo of mountains. It took me through the most mystical forest I have ever seen. The whole forest was a glow in red/gold. It was as if wizards and war-locks had created it.

Amistad is an internationally protected park because of this rare forest. Only in one other place in the world does another forest of red/gold exist. The moss that grows year round on the trees creates a carpet of golden splendor. When the sun hits it as it rises and falls, the colors it creates on this forest are a painter's delight. No photo that I have ever seen has ever truly captured the magic this place holds. You couldn't take it with you.

I collected some of the moss to add to my treasure chest of nature's phenomena. The quetzals had taken light on a branch of the aguacita tree. This small fruit is their main diet. There was a gate. A fence made of wood had a sign that said, "Cu-erici station." A small cabin amongst the tall pines and cedar trees was in the clearing ahead.

It smelled so good here. The air was thin, but I became ac-customed to it quickly. Walking up here took my breath away in more ways than one. The quetzals had lead me to the place I so searched for. I was looking at my new home with Juliana. A man and his son walked up the road from inside the gate. I flagged them down and in my best Spanish, which was still not so good, I tried to explain what I wanted to do here. They listened, barely understanding, but with such warm and welcoming looks towards me. I sensed these were special, rare people. I told them I would return with my husband as he spoke Spanish.

Carlos, the father, without understanding, understood me. He found it odd, I could tell, that a young, foreigner woman would want so much to return a puma back to the wilds. He had never heard of such a thing in these mountain forest. He shook my hand goodbye. It was strong, firm and warm. I liked him right away. He had indigenous blood in his Spanish lineage. He knew the wilds. He had a great spirit.

I left for my journey home in high hopes. I couldn't wait to get back and tell Mitch the great find. It had been a good day.

The drive home was tranquil and gorgeous. A rainbow followed me all the way down. That night Mitch and I talked into the wee hours of the morning.

Two days passed and we returned to Cuerici. We met with Carlos Solano and his son Alexander. As Mitch translated our story, I read the guys' expressions. They looked proudly at my undertaking and said they would be honored to be a part of this project.

Their family had a house down below and they were the caretakers of an enormous piece of land, smack in the middle of the park. Carlos's family had initially owned the land and sold it to another man, named Juan Carlos Crispos. Land was not for sale in international or national parks.

The grandfather law of the country allowed families with pieces to remain and only to sell back to the parks' system or as a private reserve. This is what Juan Carlos Crispos was doing. He was president of a foundation called *Fundacion Neotropical*. It was a worthy organization and Juan Carlos had a lot of respect for the jungles. He was an adventurous man and would bike ride from coast to coast, run marathons, climb impossible mountains and kayak every river cut. He organized a lot of functions and raised funding for nature.

He built a lodge on the reserve in Amistad which housed international students which came to learn about the jungles. Carlos Solano told Mitch and me that he would have to talk this over with Juan Carlos first. But he also told me that he would make sure it became possible.

The small cabin located at the main gate entrance was not in use. It was now just simply used as a storage place for the collection of the mora berries, a type of tropical blackberry, which grew like crazy up here. This area produced more moras than anywhere in the country. Many of the people up here made their living picking mora berries. The briar patches were visibly intertwined with the forest for as far as the eye could see.

Carlos said we could convert the cabin to suit our needs. Some fallen lumber could be made into posts for the puma's training pen which we could built alongside the cabin. The cabin had two rooms, hard wooden floors and sweet little windows. We would need to insulate one of the rooms as there were gaps between the wood. When the winds blew it would chill one to the bone. The cabin also needed a bathroom. But all in all it was lovely. It had a wonderful energy about it and to me it was perfect. I would use a wood burning stove for heat and cooking food.

There was no electricity here and Carlos family used a hydro system for the energy down at the lodge. But where we would be, we would not get any power.

Mitch and I drove home and planned out how we would come up with the money necessary to make the move. I created a website project of my work with this puma. I called it,

Hunting Magic. It became one of the most popular websites coming out of Costa Rica.

By the weekend we had our answer. Crispos agreed to our project. I raced down to Juliana's pen to tell her. She wondered why I was so excited. Little did she know, we had found heaven on earth for her.

It took us two more months before everything was ready for her to move. A small group of men from Amistad, friends of Carlos, put together her training pen. We kept the pumas existence quiet for as long as we could. I wanted to gradually get the townsfolk here used to the idea that there was a puma in their midst. People were afraid of pumas. Juan Jose had talked with Carlos almost every day. He approved of my choice, even though at first he had suggested releasing her back at his place, from where she came. However, too many hunters hunted there. Poaching was less in Amistad because it was harder to get in and out of these jungles. But nevertheless, we had poaching, too.

Jaguars did not live here in these high altitudes, but tapirs were aplenty in these parts, and they were hunted, along with anything else which could be sport to the hunters. If a puma was in their path, death was certain. The hunters feared Pumas the most.

The mountain lion was king of the beasts. So the time had come. A princess was entering this new domain.

Home Sweet Home 22

The move with Juliana was a special moment in all of our lives. The day was warm and sunny. We left at the crack of dawn. Juliana was in her kennel in the back of the truck with the dogs. She had grown and had dangerous claws now. The dogs played less and less with her. Even though she just wanted to play, her play was not the same with dogs which did not have the advantage of wild cat retractable claws.

They were all excited to go for a ride. We smoked a joint and blew the smoke on her. It worked like a charm. She was ready for the drive.

We encountered no other drivers on the road. As we climbed the mountains, frost covered the grasses. It was cold up here. We stopped once to check on Juliana. She was fine, she liked the cold. As we turned off the highway onto the road of Cuerici, our animals were getting excited. We drove the dirt road very slowly. The singing of the morning birds was inviting, happy. It reminded me of a fairy tale story.

We reached the cabin. We could see the Pacific ocean from up here. The view was as clear as can be. I seemed to be on top of the world. I breathed deeply. I loved this place. The Solano gang was there to greet us. What a dear family.

The cabin had a fire going. Fresh trout, blackberries, coffee and homemade biscuits waited for us. Inside the cabin, a small enclosure for Juliana was built into my bedroom, for when I wanted her with me. It was filled with sweet smelling straw hay. An exotic rare jungle orchid sat on the kitchen table.

I didn't know what to say. I had never felt so welcome anywhere in my life. I felt like I had just come home.

We took Juliana out of the truck. I had her on her leash. She was enchanted by the place. She cautiously checked out everything. The brisk climate agreed with her. She was active and playful. She was going to stay in the cabin with me for the first few days to get used to the new sights, sounds and smells. She sniffed the air longingly and threw back her head. As she did, I knew she liked what she smelled.

All the townsfolk were curious about us. Carlos had told them we were biologists studying the wildlife of Amistad. Only a special few knew we had a puma. They were told she was just a baby and not to be afraid, she was tame. The children were not fearful, rather seriously curious, the adults were cautious and a bit afraid. We did not let anyone see her. Not yet anyway. Her pen was positioned in such a way that no one could see her from any view unless they came through the house.

Her pens always had a lock on them. Not to keep Juliana in but rather to keep her safe from someone accidentally opening it. We spend two glorious weeks up there, living a simple life that was more fulfilling than anything else I had ever done. Alex, his brother Luis, and Carlos got to see Juliana. Alex wanted the job of overseeing her. I started to get her accustomed to him. He had a knack with her. He was so pure in his mind, I knew she read him like a book and liked what she read. Alex is one of the warmest, gentlest creatures I have ever met.

The Solano family is what we all should be. The simplicity of living amongst nature in joyful abandonment, never taking more than needed. Their lives were one of the richest I ever encountered in life. They taught me how to quiet the noisy mind. They taught me how to stop and smell the roses of life. They showed me what it was like to exist and what it was like to live. I was changing again, shedding my old self and becoming renewed.

Mitch and I had arranged a schedule with this new home. He could not stay up here all the time. He had too much work to do in Dominical. I was to remain up here the majority of the time. It was going to be hard but I had set my mind to it. Anything I set my mind to has always come to fruition.

The first month at Amistad got me acquainted with the locals. I was now a familiar face to them and they always went out of their way, both young and old, to greet me. However it came time for me to go to California to visit my daughter.

I had to take a week off from Juliana and help Mitch at the beach. He would have to take over for the two weeks I was gone. Alex was doing well at caring for Juliana in our absence.

Radio and or telephone contact was limited in Amistad, so our communications were brief. I said my goodbyes and wrote a list of what I could bring the family back. Camping gear, compass, and adventure gadgets were on the top of the list. For the women and children it was clothes.

My friends in the States always showered me with gifts. They knew I helped a lot of people. They were generous with whatever I needed to bring back. I collected so many clothes for the families of Amistad that I had to purchase two more suitcases and beg the customs people to let me on the plane with so much. But when the airline staff heard that I was bringing this down for the needy of their country; they put the bags on with pleasure.

I called Mitch every other day. He reported that everything was going fine. I told Island all about Juliana, and she was dying to meet her. For her summer school vacation she would come to Costa Rica and visit. I stocked up on medicinal herbs, books on mountain lions and things for myself this time. Before I knew it

I was on my way back to the jungles. When I flew into San Jose Mitch could not come and get me. I took a bus to Amistad and then Carlos brought me to the cabin. Mitch came out late that evening when he was done working. There had been a problem with pecaristas, which is a term used for squatters. Precaristas were infamous in Costa Rica. Overnight they took over any land they found, and put up makeshift bamboo structures to make it look like it was their land. They always planted corn on it. It was their symbol of takeover. Mitch told me that twelve families had decided to move into the far east corner of our property.

I remember the first encounter I had with precaristas. I was alone on the beach property, Mitch was in San Jose for the next two days. I came across three families of women and a bunch of children. They had already set up a bamboo structure using the rare exotic bamboo we were growing.

The men of this family were thieves, and I was furious that they were on my land. It mattered little to me that it was just women and children. These people would play this game with foreigners, acting out of pity. They thought surely no one would kick out women and children.

Well, they picked the wrong person to play with. I marched back into the house, grabbed the rifle off the wall and took my long matches. As I approached the squatters, the mothers started to scream and cry.

I gave them one warning.

They acted dumb. I then lit a match to the bamboo hut and cocked the rifle and aimed it right at the fat momma's head. It wasn't loaded. You never saw people run so fast in your life.

I got another reputation that day, but I never cared what people said about me. They always talked about me, and I just got used to it. Good, bad, or indifferent, it never meant that much to me. Nothing is good or bad, everything just is.... The precaristas were never seen in these parts again.

Mitch couldn't believe I did that. He simply said nothing. He said I was turning wild. Maybe I was...

I raced out of the bus with my bags, to wait at the top of the road for Carlos. He came shortly afterwards and drove me to the cabin. Then he and his family were taking a trip into San Isidro for supplies. They would not be back till late evening. I said I would be fine.

The family was waiting by the cabin. I kissed and hugged them all and told them to hurry back so we could open all their gifts. They left in a flurry. I opened the cabin door and put my bags in. I missed Juliana so much, I didn't want to do anything else, and ran out back to her.

There was a certain sound, a quick greeting call which we made to each other. It was to alert her that I was near. If she did not hear this sound I taught her to remain hidden to see who the intruder might be. It was important for her to learn caution with human beings. Once released they would become her only enemy.

The sound was a mixture of cat and bird put together in a squeak. As she heard my call, she answered back with such force and urgency. She really had missed me. I was so touched I threw caution to the wind. I flung open the door to her pen and was caught off guard as she leapt onto me. It was as if she wanted to give me a great big hug.

With quick precision one claw caught my lip and proceeded to perfectly slice the right side of my mouth completely open.

It happened so fast we both were startled. I felt the warm blood going into my mouth. I felt little pain; I guess I was in shock. The door behind me was wide open; she could have run out had she wanted to. But she didn't. Instead, a look, exactly like that of a child's, came over her face. She knew she had hurt me and she was worried and scared.

She leaped onto her bed box and stared at me. I felt her emotion and knew that her mind had registered exactly what she had done. I was amazed by this reaction. I felt for her. I slowly turned around and left the pen. As I locked the door I spoke to her with my mind. I told her I had been foolish to forget she was a lioness.

It was my mistake, not hers. I told her I would be back. I knew she felt like she was being punished when I left her after such a brief visit. I could feel the blood turning into a big clot on my face. I went into the cabin. I had forgotten we still had no mirror in the cabin. The only way I could see my wound was through the reflection in the glass pane of the window.

It didn't look good. I could tell I would need stitches. I did not clean the blood off my face. A wound is better left alone. The blood naturally cleans it, coagulates the blood flow and makes a protective coat around the area until it is ready to be worked on.

No one was around. I walked back up to the highway eight kilometers. Even though I was dying for a lift, I dared not draw any attention to myself as I looked pretty scary. I also did not want anyone asking questions about how I had received my wound.

When I finally reached the top it started raining hard. It was almost dark. I was exhausted and a little dizzy. I was completely out of breath and just sat down on the grass for a while. I was planning on flagging a car going by to help me get to San Isidro.

I knew there were other ways of healing this wound but I was on my own. I had no supplies on me nor at the cabin, to deal with this.

A car finally went by and I flagged it down. A foreign gentleman was driving alone.

He took one look at my face and I thought, oh, oh, he will probably scream and drive off. But he didn't. He made a joke of me coming out of nowhere with this face and introduced himself.

I could not talk much, my lip was not working.

He pulled his car off the road and went into the backseat for a black bag. Come to find out, this guy was a plastic surgeon from Switzerland here on vacation. He gently cleaned my face and stitched me up with silk thread.

"This way it will heal nicely on that pretty face of yours," he said. I never felt the sewing. My lip was numb.

Just as he finished, Mitch drove up and so did the Solano family. They could not believe their eyes. We all went to the local truckstop resturant on the road for a drink and the story.

I wished I had a camera with me because the faces of the people surrounding me were comical at best. Carlos told me that the Cuerici Indians use the cobwebs of spiders to close wounds that need stitching. The enzyme a spider uses when creating their web is one of Mother Nature's secrets. It will preserve perfectly whatever it traps and has a natural disinfectant property which keeps it germ free.

I told Carlos I would have to meet this group of indigenous people. "Good luck," he said. "They do not speak to white people."

But one was a friend of the family and he would see what he could do.

We started on our way back down. I thanked the doctor and asked him what I owed him. He said, "Stay pretty," and left.

The next morning Jose called. I told him what had happened. He told me to put fresh raw cow's milk cream on the wound and it would heal without a scar.

You know, this really worked. Everyone thought I would have a hideous scar on me for life. With the help of the cow's cream, it healed to a mere fraction of what it was. I still today wear this mark on my face. But I do not mind. It is my puma face. Juliana licked my wound every chance she got. I had to be careful because her tongue is like sandpaper, and it could open the stitches fast. But I loved her caring for me.

I know she liked the milk too. Every now and then I would give her fresh raw cow's milk. It was her comfort food. I went into San Isidro that week and ran into Ziggy and Sabine from Pro-Felis. He had heard about my puma project and told me what I was attempting to do was impossible. Bonding with a wild animal and then trying to release it back into the wilds just did not work. He stated that even the ever famous Elsa from Born Free movie fame had to depend on George to shoot game for her till the end. Conventional scientific wisdom said it couldn't be done.

Ziggy saw my face and said, "She will scar you worse than this. You best heed my warning." He said I should do it his way.

I replied to him of his own releases and success.

He glared at me for a moment. "I'm telling you, cat woman, what you are planning is impossible."

I glared back at him and said, "Impossible is nothing," and walked away.

Ziggy left Costa Rica the next year. He had really tried to do his work, but Minae was impossible, funding was always short and he made a statement which rang so true. "Why release animals back into jungles when they are being destroyed anyway? The jungles are disappearing. There is no more room for the animals anymore. And who wants to spend the rest of their life in a cage?"

I never got to say good bye to him. I may have disagreed with him at times but I always respected him.

Wherever you are Ziggy, thanks...for everything...

Juliana Part II 23

It was the year 2000. Mitch and I were separating. We would still work together on the puma project, but we were to live apart. I was to take an apartment in San Jose and commute every morning. Weekends I would stay at the cabin. As I packed up my things from the beach, the rains began to pour.

I loved the rain. It always renewed me. I am a double Pisces. I can't live without water. I named my S.A. Corporation *LLU-VIA SALVAJE*, which means wild rains. In fact I started this logo just one day before the no name hurricane hit the coast years ago. Our friend, Mark Mackay, made the comment after the storm. "Powerful name you picked. I think Mother Nature was telling you something!"

Today the rains were freeing me. By the time we were done packing it was already getting dark. It was treacherous driving the Cerro at night but we had done it a thousand times. Mitch's truck was falling to pieces. Money was hard coming in. I would have to find a truck for myself. We reached the highest peak on the drive and could not see the paved road in front of us. It was raining in sheets. I saw it rain sideways. I had to ride with my head stuck out of the window, directing Mitch as to where the road was. When I brought my head back in, the water poured off me into my lap. If you went off the sides, you fell off never ending cliffs. There were no guard rails nor lights on this lonely, long stretch at night. It was three hours to San Jose.

All of a sudden the windshield wipers just snapped and broke off. We pulled over. Mitch stepped out of the truck for two seconds and was completely soaked. He pulled an onion out of the back of the truck where we had a few provisions. He cut it in half and rubbed it on the windshield. He was a *Mac*

Gyver type of guy. It worked like Rain Ex in repelling the rain. One had to"know other ways" in the jungle. We reached San Jose five hours later, alive. Ha ha!

The next few days I worked on finding a place. I have always been lucky about getting just the right spot for my needs. I found a great apartment, one of just three on a beautiful mountain top overlooking the valley. The town was called Escazu, and it was the same area I had first lived in when I set foot on Costarican ground. My daughter's first school in Costa Rica, Country Day School, was located just down the road. I felt good about my choice.

Mitch and I made a schedule for the next months. He didn't want me to just end it like this. We would take our time. I would come sometimes, I promised, and stay at the beach with him. We loved each other, we simply wanted to choose different paths for our lives. His love for the land in Dominical, its simple life and surfing, was all this man needed.

I admired him for knowing this was his place in life and never faulted him that. He always gave me my free will. I am eternally grateful for that, for I knew my wings to fly started with him. I would always love him and he me, we just needed to go on our own way. We believed in spirit, not marriage vows, which are always broken.

Soul mates never break, not now, not into forever. I know that now, and somehow became a better person for it. It is this desire and need of free will in me which pushed me every day to free the wilds ones. For it is they that taught us spirit and free will in the very beginning of life.

Man is the only creature that has the need to possess, to capture, to take. The animals don't have this need, for they know instinctively that they always had everything and that in reality man owns nothing. It was given to him freely in the beginning of time. If only he could go back to this, he would free himself and the world from all its torment and rage.

We are all one. The beasts and the birds, man and his kind. There are no such things as boundaries or borders. We simply made them up. The minds of animals are brilliant. They see that which we do not. They are not lost. They don't take more than they need. They know how to let go and let their young grow in ways mankind cannot.

For man fears. He fears the unknown, and the animals are part of this unknown. To see clearly into their minds would make us see our own minds. This is part of our evolution.

The next week I went to set up house in the cabin at Amistad. The quetzals came; a rainbow of emeralds and rubies on a carpet of clouds. They danced a ballet in the air, and looked into my eyes, etching a new horizon to broaden my eyes and crossing realms of time. I loved this place more and more.

My new neighbors greeted me with small gifts from the mountains. A famous artist, Robert Jennings, whom I was dating now and then from the city painted my walls. A beautiful mural of bursting morning flowers in shades of pastels. Mitch put in a bathroom with shower, even though there was no way to make the water hot and the mountain water was frigid. We would shower only during the heat of the day, which was never that hot. I even bought a giant blue plastic container and would heat water over the stove and squeeze myself into it for a bath. This you had to see. None the less the weather was beautiful. Even in it's extreme.

When I First Walked the Jungles of Amistad International Park...

There is so much that enchants me in this silent world of the wilds, that I move ever so softly as not to break the spell cast around me.

Haunting, beautiful moss closes in on you.

Up to this point in my life, I knew only domesticated animals, man's animals. The wild ones I had known were one by one on their own in a world of our making...

I was now meeting the world's animals. The kingdom .....

What a difference in the wild ones, free, without boundaries in their lives, without man.

The uncontrol of no control, the release of ownership, interference.

No cutting of wings, or de-fingering of claws, nor to deform their talons.

Our biggest fear is to lose control...over anything and everything in our lives. These animals were symbols of man's free spirit.

How contagious this moment was...

Why does man feel that when controlled, it is more intelligent, "For it can follow a command."

We do this every day of our lives.

Take a wild beast, teach it to do commands...yes, possible, proven so...

Yet you never have control over them. They are free spirits, no one owns that, these are the gifts....

Wild - what a mimilludged word

Wild means free to me.For those animals caged against their free will, is it their spirit that sleeps, that dies? No.. Not in this lifetime. For this is eternal.

Spirit never dies, the shell of an animal, which remains while they are caged, is what we too are in society today.

With love and respect I will tell you how one can live in this kingdom and rather then lose control, man will learn to let go of it.

My puma showed me this and I in turn lived with her in this kingdom come.....

Rain and Ranas 24

It started to rain. Rain here is a phenomenon of nature herself. Just before the skies spring open with this life-giving tempest, the air grows hot, humid, heavy with anticipation. Leaves close, others unfold, in wanton desire of each single droplet. The frogs croak, each one a prince waiting for that first wet kiss. The cicadas begin a cascade of sound, growing in intensity, simply by rubbing their multitude of legs in an urgent love maker's rhythm. Birdlife swarms to shelter, while the ground opens up.

Alluring.

You left your head up, you smile to the sky, to catch the first liquid beads upon your face is pure ecstasy.

These are the wild rains......

Gone Fishing 25

Behind the cabin at Amistad, in a grassy area, grasses the kind you want to lay in, was a watering trough for the animals. It looked more like a bathtub to me, one that could easily fit three people for a decadent bath.

This is where I gave Juliana her first lessons on catching fish. The neighboring streams teamed with fat, juicy trout. Their meat was so pink, with the kind of juice that dripped slowly down your chin and along your neck while you feasted.

From the first time I gave her a fresh trout to eat, she loved it more than any other food. After, she licked and cleaned herself for a hour. The scent of a wild cat is intoxicating. It is warm fur, the smell of softness.

We made a run-off for her, of running water from a stream into a trough. This was her drinking water and where she defecated. At different ends, of course. One day while I was cleaning up her playground, I dropped, more like it slipped right out of my hands, a live trout into her trough. It started jumping around and around.

She looked at me and said, "go get it for me." I told her, "you go."

She started using her paw to swoosh around to catch it. She managed to grab it, flew it through the air and finally landed on the ground before her. She pounced on it, gave her growl, which she does when she has food in her mouth and leaped into her den to eat in private. She always ate out of our sight. We never watched. We gave her due respect while dining.

I worked with a series of cat sounds with her, each one indicating a different message. When I left her to eat, I let out a call which let her know I was going, but which also meant I would always return. She would become quite content and ate in peace.

I taught her skills back. After one week of lessons in the bathtub, we moved on to the streams. Taking her out there was distracting, for there is so much to see.

She pounced on birds, jumped back at geckos, and ran a zig zag pattern through the jungle. She was on a collar leash (she had graduated from her harness) for she did not yet know her boundaries, and we were too new to the area in case she should decide to wander off. Needless to say I became quite an acrobat following her walk.

The stream was cold and beautiful. Wild orchids formed a curtain of splendor, rare to behold. She wasn't in the mood for jumping around in the stream and she was a little timid about it. There was so much movement in it...

Instead, she crouched down on the banks and pawed at the trout swimming by. I laughed at her, "You're going to have to work harder than that," I said.

She ignored me. She was having too much fun and knew I would give her dinner anyway. So I didn't give her dinner that night.

She screamed at me and I told her she had to return to the stream and catch a fish. At 5:00 AM the next morning I took her back to the stream. She smelled the air for a long time. I too smelled it. It was heavily, laden with the scent of fresh dew drenched mosses and bouquets of flowers, so very delicate in their fragrance. How heavenly.... Magnolia trees were everywhere, a slightly different type than those of North America or Europe, the scent of the flower more delicate. It is my most favorite perfume. Each morning, I slipped a flower into my blouse, inhaling its fragrance throughout the day.

Juliana twitched. I knew she wanted to eat, she looked but one time at me to help her, then with a serious look on her face as she read my mind, she entered the stream and began the hunt. A cat's paws are an amazingly accurate, fast tool. She knew hers well. She had a fish in under two minutes and growled loudly as she sat down to eat it.

I laughed at her, and she growled lowly at me to knock it off. I couldn't help myself. This time I was being childish and cute with her. But I was also very proud of my little hunter. Juliana was simply clever in everything she did.

I looked away for the remainder of her meal. Afterwards I asked her to catch me one for lunch. Then it was her turn to laugh at me, and she took off so suddenly with me on the other end of the leash that I fell right into the stream. Brrrrr so cold. We walked slowly back to the cabin. I put her in her habitat where she groomed herself silly for the next hour.

I did the same. I looked out my window and saw her cuddle up in the fresh straw hay which made her bed. So I too, cuddled up in my down comforter and slept with her. This was one of my greatest pleasures, to sleep with her. At times I would bring her into the cabin and alongside my bed, which was on the floor, I made a pen for her to sleep.

As we slept, I always felt her paw come through the pen and touch me, gently somewhere, whether my arm or my leg, and she purred. One of life's simple pleasures.

The Diary 26

For the next year I kept a diary of my work with Juliana and my life. This time formed the base of everything Juliana and I did from this day forward.

New Year's Eve 2000

After a night of celebration with friends, I went to the beaches of Jaco on the Pacific coast.

I ended a relationship with a lover I had taken. He was the artist I spoke of who painted the cabin wall. I had met him by posing as a nude model for his canvas. The show of the artwork and paintings I had posed for brought in enough dollars so I could buy myself a truck and create a website which told my story of Juliana to the world. I wasn't ready for a serious relationship though with anyone. I didn't have the time either. That night I pitched a small tent on the beach shore at Playa Hermosa, just a little ways south of Jaco. I wanted to be alone.

I slept to the sounds of the crashing waves. Upon awakening I was astounded to see that in the dark of the night, I had pitched my tent right on top of a sea turtle's nest. While I slept, they hatched, for I woke to broken soft skinned egg shells all around me. I smiled brightly at the morning sun. This would be a good year.

I decided to drive further south along the coast to a beach area called Manuel Antonio, and go out in a fisherman friend's boat for a morning cruise. We came across a pod of dolphins and their babies. I asked him to stop the boat and turn off the engines so as to not scare them away. The dolphins were curious and playful this morning and I decided to join in.

I dove into the water. The temperature was perfect, warm, safe feeling. At first the mothers formed a protective circle around the young, but yet they did not leave. I was as still as

I could be. I pretended to be a mermaid. Dolphins will swim with you if you don't use your hands and reach out too suddenly. They have no arms, so ours are a bit of a question to them. I surfaced for air, and then remained treading water for a few minutes. I talked to them, mentally, then cooed to them while I treaded water, using only my legs in a ballet motion.

They relaxed and began to play again. So I swam with the dolphins. I loved every minute of it. I was content. Animals and humans can communicate. Unfolding this existence of interspecies communication was fascinating to me. Each animal has a totem power they hold within themselves. We are joined by them in every day occurrences and each gives us a certain link. The indigenous people have animal medicine cards which depict every animal and its totem power. I worked with these cards at times. They always rang true.

January 3 through the 15th

Every January Costa Rica becomes covered with rainbows. Every day one witnesses the most beautiful types of rainbows, one after another. The central valley is famous for this. One of my most favorite types of rainbows is called Caligula, a rainbow that appears in the rain. It is a soft rain, or as the people in the Caribbean calls it, "women's rain." During this rain the sun still shines.

Each morning I saw a rainbow. My drives from the city to the cabin were always incredulous. I never tired of this drive. This month the rainbows took me there and waited in the central valley for my return. There were wide ones, full spectrum colors. There were double rainbows and those that went on forever. Some even followed me up into the mountains. The colors were always so bright. It was our summer and a more beautiful one I had yet ever to see.

One morning I was driving along the high mountain road to Juliana's and there in the center of the road was something so black, it stood out so much.

What was it? I stopped the truck. A very proud, very big, very intimidating tarantula. He was perfect and regal in his walk. He took his time walking across the road and I was so close I could see every curtain hung hair on his long dark legs. They appeared to be so soft and velvety. Mother Nature found beautiful ways to express herself in all her creatures.

I would spend the mornings with the puma and return in the afternoons. I had a small practice working with animals and people dispensing herbal remedies. I worked with vets, wildlife centers, the common folk and their animals. So my afternoons were work time.

Juliana was growing. She was happy and healthy. We were ready to build a large enclosure for her deep into the jungles. I wanted my time apart from her to be a time when she got to learn her jungle. There was a routine I kept to with her. I arrived and fed her. Usually it was a live kill, such as guinea pig, rabbit or a rodent type animal common to the mountains. Trout was always in her diet too. At times I would go to the local butcher, who had become a friend of mine and get lamb for her at a good price. The butcher knew I was feeding a puma and gave me all I needed. She also liked eggs so sometimes I put down about six eggs and let her break them up and suck the juice out.

I communicated with her about everything I was thinking. She knew me well, my moods, my emotions, my good days and my bad. I was handling her less now, also. She was getting too strong to play with, and at times had to be reminded I was not another puma, which she could roughhouse with.

Every other day, Mitch joined me to walk her. It was better to walk her with his help as she had the strength to get away from me if she wanted to. But she did pretty well about her walks with us.

Our dogs helped greatly in this. They stayed close so she would too. She always wanted to go where they were going. It was like a gang going exploring for something to get into. Juliana discovered a lot on these walks and so did we. To see the jungle through her eyes was enchanting. She saw better and faster than I, thus showing me things me would never have seen without her. Her keen sense of smell and hearing also opened up a new world to me. To see the jungle through a puma's eyes is an experience of a lifetime.

She was becoming the time of my life. My ability to communicate with her was to be put to the test. One morning when I needed to sleep in a little later than 5:00 AM, which was a rare treat for me. I arrived at 8:30 at Carlos's house, first passing my cabin. His house was the end of the road and beyond was the magnificent mountain chain of Chirripo, Amistad and the five park corridor link which trailed across the whole country and linked to others.

Their place was always warm and cozy, a simple log cabin, but very comfortable. The trout streams flowed past their yard and Carlos and his son Alex farmed the trout for restaurants and the town of San Isidro. Mora berry picking was their main stay though, and I would come and always find Alex picking berries through the fields. Alex's mom, Magela, made scrumptious biscuit out of the berries and she greeted me with a glass of freshly milked cow's milk still warm from the tits and a plate of her treats.

This morning we had no time for this. Alex and Carlos greeted me by the door and I could tell something was up. They told me Juliana got out of her pen and had been out all morning. They looked and called for her but she did not come. I ran out the door and drove my truck up the road, an in-between part of where her pen was located.

I stopped and thought, I know her, where would she go? and then as a million different spots raced through my mind, I couldn't possible cover all that territory so I simply choose to call her to me.

I stopped the truck, climbed up the bank of the road, then weaved my way up the short distance to this small mountain top and sat on a tree stump. I closed my eyes and sent her a message, I am here, come.

Alex had taken off in the opposite direction, and I heard him calling to her. Mitch, who arrived on the scene just a few minutes ago, went off in another direction.

I slowly opened my eyes, and she jumped right in front of me, silent as a cat. She cried out her baby squeal at seeing me. This had been a new experience for her. She had run on her own. She was excited, nervous, and tingling scared.

She was so happy to see me. She talked her baby talk to me for a time then the boys came and we got her safely back in the truck and back inside her pen. I always knew when she felt safe, lonely, what ran through her mind, what she thought of me, so many things I knew about her. When animals communicate with us they are unlocking what we have already stored in our minds. They are solely accessing it for us. Even when I was great distances from her, no matter where in the world for that matter, I had a sense with her, about her. I wonder if she too had this type of sense of me, in her?

January 15

Eduardo Teran was a dear friend of mine. I met him when I first moved to Costa Rica. He came from an affluent up-standing family. That Christmas, he gave me a wonderful gift, a photo session with his sister Diana. She would do a photo session of me and my puma. Diana was a master photographer. She was greatly admired and had quite a reputation. Her work was unique and surreal, and reached the four corners of the globe.

I was honored to have her shoot me and Juliana. That morning a group of Diana's friends and I, set out for the session. We piled into Diana's SUV and drove the mountain road. What a majestic morning and a double rainbow covering us the whole day. It was wonderful. One could feel magic in the air. This place held an aura of mystic imaginings.

This was a new experience for the puma. First she would be with new people. Second she would have to be docile with me and behave, and third she was to be on camera. Animals sense a great deal of things we as humans take for granted. The camera was something she sensed immediately. The group was instructed to stay a good distance from us. I took Juliana out of her pen and walked her around the jungle side for a bit. I felt her nervousness, and she kept quite close to me. She would rub and stare back, push to me and then move again. I let her know the whole time, this was an o.k. thing. It was going to be fun. As long as she had me and was able to touch me in her comfort zone, she was accepting the process. Her movements, ever so slight, were as fast as a blink.

The guests took up watch in the distance. Diana set up a tripod with a long zoom lens as far away as possible to ease into the shoot. We had by this time built a new natural area situated amongst the thick dense forest about a mile from the cabin. Her favorite tree stump was close to her new enclosure, a throw's distance away. She leaped up on this first whenever she was taken out of her pen. She could see a great distance from here and liked to be on the top. Unlike the jaguars, which prefer to be hidden in the jungle undergrowth, pumas love mountain tops. They blend in perfectly with the rocks and their matching colors . They are kings and queens on a throne. Juliana listened to my Diana's movements and let the camera click.

Immediately I sensed her unease, she did not like the click of the camera, nor its eye. I wondered if she was mistaking this apparatus for the click of the gun which shot her mother.

I kept her on a short leash, but the minute we turned our backs on her, she bounded full force to attack the camera. Eyes, especially where cats are concerned, are a breach of confidence. If eyes stare at her unblinkingly, she doesn't trust them. The direction of one's eyes allow the animals to tell much of what is before them. They see right through them and sense the one behind the veil.

When encountering a wild one, the eyes should be down, not on them, until given consent by the animal itself. Perhaps she somehow knew that many other eyes would see her from this thing, the camera, which would bring her out into the world.

Diana handled the attack of the puma like a pro. Juliana did not hurt or reach for Diana, just the tripod and camera set-up. It all tumbled to the ground, and I was one leap behind her, grabbed the leash and drew her back.

Diana took a deep breath and continued. Diana was great about it all and the photo session was one of the best I had ever done. Juliana somehow knew this was all for her. I even saw her reach a point where she hammed up a few poses for me. It was evident she liked the people, just not the camera. The group was amazed by her. She was such a beautiful animal with a character bewitching to all who came to know her. They spoke of how perfectly she had adapted to her life with me. She fit in with us and yet still retained her wild spirit, which was exactly how I wanted it to be.

The day drew to a close, the star was put back into her enclosure and as we all headed back to the city the rainbows were still with us.

January 18

Wolves full moon tonight.

Juliana had been moved to her new enclosure, nestled in the jungles amongst a small pasture of cows belonging to the Solano family and covered with mora bushes. The view was tremendous. We made a box above ground and filled it with hay for her and also dug a den under the ground. She liked to go there when she got frightened of things. One thing she was frightened of at first was the cows. Every animal was new to her, and watching her expressions told me a good deal about her moods. A little stream ran through her pen and a fat strong tree which was closed off midway up the side. Wild bamboo and several different plants grew inside the pen. She liked to eat the green bamboo leaves. Greens are important to all carnivores.

She loved her new place. She was constantly running around in it. She had plenty of places to hide and would crouch down low to the ground and ambush whatever went by. It was one of her games.

January 19 to the 30th

I went to met Jose in Puntarenas. We spent the day together talking of animals. I always enjoyed my visits with this man. I was changing him and his thoughts on animals. He had a good heart and a sound conscience, rare to find. He was truly an animal man and would make a great leader of men. We talked of a dream to open an animal park, a kingdom which was theirs, and where man went only with invitation. Ahhh, we had grand thoughts, he and I. I kissed him good bye and went home.

Alex Solano was to have a new job. He was to become the full time caretaker and guardian of the puma. He truly liked her. He understood animals ways from his life of living in the jungle mountains. His father was also a great role model. He had a respect for life which was refreshing. Alex was nineteen years old and cute as a button. He was kind, soft spoken and good-humored. His family became my family. I loved them dearly and would do anything for them.

Juliana loved Alex. She could tell by instinct he was one of the good ones. The bond that grew between them was simply magical. She looked forward to seeing him everyday, and after a time she trusted him with everything. Her bond with me was that of a mother and child, Alex was the human she had for everything else. She would gently jump up on him as he entered her cage and make cooing sounds. Juliana was cautious as she always is at first with new people, but within minutes would be jumping around her pen showing off.

When I brought someone to her she knew they were alright; when someone would come and I was not present, she was different. She held to the wild ways of caution and distance, which was good. She had to learn not all humans were there for a good purpose. Unfortunately I had to teach her this lessons for when the day came to release her back to the wilds, her greatest enemy would be hunters.

Alex and I headed to the Solano's house for a lunch feast of trout and biscuits and corn and rice, and talked of our future plans for the puma. As the sun set we drove back to the central valley. It had been a good day.

The following morning I awoke in the wee hours to a strong earthquake tremor. I had been working a lot, not only with the puma but also with other clients and patients. Derrie Dryer also asked me to write a series of articles on animals for the Tico Times newspaper. I always had a lot of energy, but I wanted ocean energy now and planned a trip out to our beach land.

On my way the next morning Mitch rang me and told me to meet him and Mark Mackay up at Juliana's. I took my time, I wanted to relax. By the time I arrived, Mark had already shot some footage of Juliana. I was a little annoyed with Mitch at first for not running this by me first, but I knew Mark had great experience with wildlife on film. He was an avid lover of nature. He had a production company in Canada and filmed remarkable documentaries around the world. Still I knew Juliana didn't like cameras. Both Mark and Mitch told me she had reacted the same disdainful way to the camera eye. It was a video, so at least there had been no, click!, sound for her to handle.

Mark and his production company wanted to shoot our story. I agreed, it needed to be documented. But as I found out at the end of my journey with her, my greatest footage of her was inside my mind. There were Kodak moments like I had not seen before and always without a camera. It seemed certain, perfect experiences were only for a few of us.

I was again witnessing more of the animals' mentality. Juliana's reaction to different humans was so precise. The surrounding energy of the people around her made her mimic what they were putting out, even if it wasn't being put for on her. She picked up on every little nuance of every living thing she encountered.

Today, she did a new thing. We all sat around the stump by her enclosure for about an hour and talked. Juliana, at first merely sat back contently and listened. I knew she liked the sound of my voice. After a half hour or so, she joined in our conversation. I heard her emit sounds which were a first to my ears. I realized she mimicked our voices and words, and she did pretty damn good. I walked away from the guys, to her, and gave her all my attention. Watching her made me get that urge that comes over you when you just want to squeeze someone to death.

February 2000

The beach day. Warm ocean breezes, waves, birds, monkeys and all, were out for the summer time. A huge male coyote was running alongside the road down at the beach. We had a lot of coyotes but they mostly stay up on higher ground. We heard their howls on full moon nights up in Platanillo. There, they were aplenty. Once, I encountered one digging up iguana eggs.

I found Mitch at a local bar talking with some of the folk. One of them was a fisherman who sold fresh fish and shrimp. While Mitch bought some for us, I went for a walk on the beach out in front. This stretch was called Roca's Hermancio, after a wonderful man and his family who had taken over this point of land many years ago. In the early days of living here, Hermancio was my eager dance partner at the local disco spot.

He taught me the dances of romance. Many a night we would Fred Astaire and Ginger Rogers the night away. Mitch did not dance. I loved to.

I climbed one of the rock formations surrounded by the ocean. The tide was way out, so it was easy. I climbed to the very top and felt like Juliana. There I came upon a nest of vulture eggs. They were big and long and a greywhite in color. I climbed down and ran to get Mitch to see.

The fisherman told me he thought the mother had died, for he saw an adult vulture the other day, wedged in the rocks against the point wall. This was unusual. I gathered perhaps the high surf of the day before might have caught her of guard and smashed her against the rocks. I stayed until dark and saw no mother return, or other vultures. The eggs needed warmth, so I went up to fetch them. I carried the nest down with the eggs. Mitch thought I was nuts, but said nothing.

I took the four eggs to the house and warmed them for the night. The next morning they had hatched. The little vultures were the ugliest things you had ever seen and ever so hungry. Oh, oh. I had no idea what to give them. So I made a gruel of worms, grain, milk and meat pieces. I ground them up, slightly warmed the mess, and dribbled it down their necks. They cried the whole time, and once again I came up with a language of sounds to mimic what I thought would be their mother's response.

They communicated with me instantly. I cared for them for two weeks. Alex was taking good care of Juliana, so I stayed at the beach. The vultures were very intelligent. They would watch every move I made. They also knew where every movement would lead to before I did, even though I was the one making the movement. Their eyesight was keen. They spotted me coming miles away at times.

A couple of times wild vultures flew over, listening to their cries. They were growing quickly. They liked to eat liver. I fed them all kinds of wild stuff. What a menu. They ate it all.

There was something eerie about this animal. They see things we can not. They were very psychic. How do they know death? To all that see them, they are the grim bearers of approaching death. When one sees a vulture, one knows something is at death's door.

They fascinated me. Their dark ebony eyes were deep, bottomless. When with them, I sensed a dimension of seeing which was uncanny. They lead me to a different space and time. They were timeless. Out of every species, they are chosen to ring in the bells that toll, which turn us to a different space and a different time. Death, the unknown door. To be able to speak with this creature would enable us to see our deaths and the reason for it.

At this time I wished I had a laboratory, for I was overwhelmed by the ability these birds had to eat the rot of carrion in any condition and never get sick themselves. I truly believe their saliva their digestive juices must carry a great antibody, which would cure disease.

Mitch took over the babies, and I returned to the city for a few days. I met Alycia Ibarra, my school teacher friend, and her daughter and friend at Juliana's. All three were animal communicators. It was good to bond with the women in my life. My life was always surrounded by men.

Juliana was happy to see me after this separation. She made her insistent call, rer, rer, rerrrr. She liked the women and we all had quite a time with her. Juliana spoke to all of us. It was as if the greater the numbers of those who open up to the minds of animals, so to a greater force of communication came through. We spoke to her of her future in the wilds. She questioned it. She knew not what to think. It would come with time.

No matter where I went, animals always came to me. Each knew something about myself I was yet to learn. Sometimes I would try to hard to understand, other times I just let it go. I was open to it. I had a knowing. That was enough for now.

I returned to the city to greet a friend from San Francisco. My daughter had her first job with this man. He had a motorcycle dealership Golden Gate Harley Davidson and had driven to Central America on a special military Harley, which was very cool. His name was Dean, and he was waiting for me with a bottle of french champagne. Mmm what a treat.

I took a little fun time off and went riding with him. The bike went anywhere, through anything, and I had a blast. All to soon it came to an end.

Time to go back to the beach to check on the vultures, and Dean went on his way. His journey took him to the tip of South America. We wished each other luck in our endeavors and took off.

When I arrived at the beach, the vultures ran to me like chickens. I was a little taken aback at this welcome, but I was a mother again.

I could see they would be trying to fly soon. By month's end, they were ready to go. They used things as tools now, sticks and rocks for opening crevices of things that piked their curiosity. They foraged and keenly smelled out food carrion. Their beaks were growing strong, and they made short flights all around me, always following me.

I looked up at them and thought, I have a flock of vultures circling me and I'm not dying. I laughed. There was so much to learn from the animals. And I was one who was hungry for more, all the time…

I liked to be with these guys, I felt spooky, I was a black ghost . Was it that they had such a unappealing appearance and lifestyle which kept man from wanting to get close to them? When in reality, may they be angels. I think them somber and respectable in their presentation.

I took them to the same stretch of beach where I had found them and walked with them. People stared at us, They really thought I was a witch now. Yes, the people of Costa Rica have their superstitions too. Superstitions have their place. These feelings are our senses awakening. Might they not open too fast, for I think we would not know what to do with them. Slowly we begin to feel from them and slowly they begin to feel us. They are a transmission of perceptive frequencies which form the landmine area in our minds, a different part of our brains.

As I walked the beach with my vultures, I sensed they were ready. A group of adult vultures had been observing me and my flock of vultures the whole time. I told them to take the little ones back to their place. The little ones flew to greet them. They cautiously circled each other, and then would fly back and forth from me to the flock.

We slept on the beach that night with sleeping bags. In the morning my little ones had a new family. They were gone. About six months later I walked a beach at a river mouth a few miles from Roca's Hermancio. As I lay on a tree limb, soaking up sun, four vultures landed around me. It was my flock. They had grown. I thought them beautiful. They cried to me. I cried back to them. They stayed with me and even allowed Mitch to snap off a few pictures. Then they were off.

March 2000

A male puma was coming around. We spotted his tracks not far from Juliana's pen. She was coming into heat. We took her out for a walk. She rubbed against us and purred deeply. Her breathing became a slow controlled rhythm. She had so much passion. Wild cats hold a sexual prowess equal to none. I felt her every wave of heat. You lose all control. The savage beast inside of us wants to mate. Nothing will stop it.....

For the next three days the male visited her. He sprayed her area. She rolled in every spot. Moaning purrs came out of her. She then did what cats do in acceptance to another. She squatted down and urinated on his wet scented spot.

I thought of releasing her. If she went with the male, he would show her the way. Pumas are solitary animals, and the males only stay with the females during mating, so we decided to try in the next few days to let her go. I mentally prepared myself. I was very attached to this puma. I went through mental anguish and then I got ready.

That night I spoke with my friends who had seen me through my time with the puma. They knew I needed support from them now. This release was to be a trial run. My so-called witch friends, Kattia, and Alycia knew she would be free someday. It was written all over her.

Letting go of anything in our lives is hard. When we have loved it, it is torture. But with love comes the desire to never take away the free will. I so loved Juliana, that her freedom would be my ultimate show of love to her.

I dreamed of all my animals that night. Spirit, my white wolf, was running to me, Kaiser the tiger roared in splendor, a whale breached the crests of the waves and a mighty jaguar dressed in shaman garbs beckoned to me. Each dream was so clear. In the morning I felt like I had been running all night long. I was tired, but then I wasn't

As I was getting ready for the drive up the mountains, Iala telephoned me. She knew what I was about to attempt. She told me she was making a spirit wheel to guide Juliana's passage to the wilds. She told me to call in the blue flame to protect her and the violet light to guide her. As I drove, I did this. And then there it was, an incredible rainbow with the violet color predominant. I smiled and threw Iala a kiss from above. Signs come to us in many ways and forms. I had asked to see a quetzal this morning. I wanted my sign too.

I brought Juliana a big fat guinea pig to eat before her release. She played with it for a long time, which she always did with a live kill. She would handle it much as a child handles a stuffed animal. She would cuddle it, lick it, push it to run, and make sweet sounds to it. Then when she was ready a sound would come quick and throaty, a victory growl as she killed it swift and silent. I never really watched this part of her life. I sent off the spirit of the animal she was about to take and thanked it for being her food.

Not far from her habitat was a tall tree with a long thick trunk, in which quetzals had made a nest. Quetzals make a hole in the trunk of a hollowed tree and lay the eggs down deep. My sign had come. The quetzals were here. I spent the day up there; we would wait until evening to release her. Today, the gold of the forest was rich in color. Though often photographed, these trees created a special glow which could not be seen by a camera. It is for your eyes only, for those fortunate enough to enter into this forest and take nothing, only the illusion.

Mitch arrived with my dogs. We took watches with Juliana. We parked the truck as close to the jungle as we could, and we would just be there for her, in case anything went wrong. The dogs would also help in the process. She would have us all around her. It was time. I took her from her pen, spoke to her lovingly and told her to have a good time with her lover. I told her not to be afraid, I was here for her. Then I took off her leash and collar. She looked at me and was shocked. This was a first. No leash.

She ran off then came back and told me to follow her. I sent her out. This is the excerpt taken from my diary website story.

Jungle Rescue: *A Puma's Tale*

This is an account of the three day and three night vigil and rescue of Kirichimayua, the puma, her Indian given name. Her first release attempt was quite incredible. It was such a learning, fear releasing and eye-opening moment.

The event began at 7:00 PM. three days after the full moon of Febuary 2000. It was possible the male puma who had been coming around to see Kiri was still in the vicinity so I decided to let her roam at will for the night.

She bounded into the jungles and I took up my vigil in the truck for the night, letting her know where I would be in case she needed me.

At first, she came back and checked on me every ten to fifteen minutes.

Mitch, my partner on the project, was with me as well. At 11:00 PM, I no longer heard her rustling about or her call when I called out to her periodically.

No answer.

Mitch and Lobo, one of my german shepherds went to check on her. All of a sudden she returned my call. It was faint and coming not far, not close.

Mitch came back and said he thought she was up in a tree, but because of the

darkness of the jungle could not see.

We don't use flashlights as they bother the animals' vision, and in case the male was around did not want to frighten him off.

We decided to let her stay for the night. She might come down or we might have been wrong as to where she was. We went up the short walk to the cabin and settled in for the night.

The following morning at sunrise, I found her ninety feet up in a tall, fat, one- hundred-year-old beautiful oak tree. It had a strong, thick trunk and a large comfortable nook in its center with mature majestic branches. They formed a perfect bed for the night.

I talked to her and tried to coax her down. She was excited to see me,. She seemed to enjoy the view, the multitude of birds, singing away. After an hour of this, Mitch and I realized she wouldn't come down on her own, we would have to bring her down.

In the past on her jungle walks with us she frequently pushed to go higher up trees. We always had to pull her down, which in every case just made her jump down, not climb down. Thus it dawned on me she does not know how to climb down a tree. We went to employ the help of the family who cares for the jungle and Juliana in our absences.

Alex, her overseer, had a friend up at the biological station volunteering. His name was Joel. He was from Venezuela and quite prepared and skilled at climbing.

Joel went with us. First, we tried again to coax her down. She wouldn't come, but told me she was thirsty. It is very cold in this bosque, a forest type jungle, at an altitude of 9000 feet.

It is very windy at night. It didn't rain, yet a small sprinkle occurred and Kiri licked the raindrops off her coat and the branch limbs.

Joel began his ascent. Midway up the trunk, Juliana, not knowing Joel, got weary of him and jumped into the next tree, which unfortunately was a dry, dead, very dangerous tree. She went higher up, to the top branch which was a very skinny, not very secure, small branch at hundred and twenty feet.

So our challenge was upon us. This was going to be difficult. My neck hurt from looking up so long. As I turned around, there on a tree branch only a few feet away was the magnificent shaman bird the quetzal. Earlier, I had seen the female fly over me. She too, has beautiful, breathtaking colors.

This is very rare that humans get to see this bird, and I took it as a good omen.

The male stayed, watched us, and made his calls, which caused his long emerald- like tail to dance as a harem dancer's scarves do. They have a nest in the area and were probably worried about the big cat in the tree tops of their nursery.

In the mean time Joel descended the oak and got ready to climb up the dead tree. It was quite dangerous and slow to get up the tree. Midway up, he had to come down as the safety factor with this tree was too risky. Juliana was curious about our activities, yet seemed content and made her little baby noises to me when I talked to her. She enjoyed this outing even though we had our questions about it.

Late afternoon fell. We took a break and had black coffee, lots of sugar and sweet rolls.

Alex's father, Carlos Solano, is an excellent climber and basic all around jungle Indian man. He was gone for the day, so help from him was not coming today.

Kiri was getting tired, hungry and finally wanted to come down, but let me know that she just couldn't, she wasn't afraid of her situation, just not knowing what to do.

We attempted one last try before dark. I went up to see if being ninety feet up, the safest distance to climb, would make her come. It didn't, and the guys thought it was unsafe for me to continue. All we had to work with was a line and one harness, and a sling shot for getting the lines across, and that was it.

As we prepared for another night in the jungle with Kiri, ideas went through my head. Great ones, but without proper equipment not feasible. All we could do would be to contact Carlos as soon as possible for help.

I sent a message to Victor Gallo, an extraordinary experienced climbing man with all the equipment and know-how anyone needs to make it through anything. He was not around, off on his own adventures.

The night passed uneventfully. I checked on her through the night and just let her know I was there. She was content and slept.

Day Two

Much the same with results at times and backups at others. I was getting concerned about her, but Carlos was on his way. He arrived shortly before dark and I almost dragged him to see the situation. He came to see her, quickly assessed the problem and told me in is warm, knowing way that at first light tomorrow he would rescue my cat.....

I barely slept, anxious for morning to dawn.

It was a beautiful peaceful night and dawn brought the singing of some of the best singers I have ever heard.

Carlos was ready, equipment and all, and our little pack went out. Carlos talked to Juliana and then ascended the big oak. This was the only way we were going to get close to her. He got up to the crook of the oak and Kiri was getting excited. We had Carlos try to tempt her to jump back into the oak tree where we could harness her and send her down, but even with her favorite food, a trout, we still could not make her move. Funny, she was hungry and did try to eat the trout, as we finally just threw it up to her. But on such a slim branch it was too difficult to hold the trout and hang on at the same time. It hung in her mouth for just a brief second. She did get one morsel down and then the remainder of it fell to the ground.

By midday Carlos decided to make a guard rail of tree trunks cut to form a platform below her about fifteen feet in case she fell. By this time she was weary and looking at all the activity a little wobbly, and the winds were picking up, swaying the dead limb.

We decided to lasso her and swing her onto the oak where Carlos was. It was quite something to see, the perfect throws that made their mark every time by this man and the equally throw for throw paw of Juliana's catching it and throwing it back. She had such precision and balance. She was a true acrobat.

Finally Carlos told me that we had to make a desperate move.

While we created a diversion down below, he did, in one mighty attempt, throw the loop around her. It worked nicely, but, as she began to fall, she hit against the oak, lightly breaking some momentum. Quickly, Carlos let the line holding her go. She was free falling right towards me. My heart was in my throat. I couldn't breathe, it seemed her flight was eternal. She brushed the safety line which slowed her speed, came down on all fours and landed perfectly in front of me.

I ran to pick her up. The commotion and everybody's emotions were high, and I just wanted to be alone with her for a minute. She was in shock and a little woozy from such a long time up and then back down, what a rush for her. She purred as I carried her to a grassy spot and laid her down to ground.

Tears of joy rolled down my face. Until that moment I never realized what she really meant to me. She is my baby....

I took her to her habitat cage, checked on her legs and fed and watered her. Then I let her get some rest. I asked Mitch to come and watch her while I went back to thank my hero.

The guys were elated that everything was o.k. And Carlos didn't want to come down from the tree either. He said, "It is so peaceful up here, it is how it should be....."

We all were exhausted and excited and had much to tell the next day after we go some well deserved rest. I slept like a log that night with enchanted forest scenes coming into my dreams.

To celebrate we ate at the Georgiana, a truck stop restaurant which tasted gourmet this evening.

And so the saga continues. I learned how to climb with the help of Victor Gallo and Carlos. We all challenged our fears. The best magic of that day were the strong, completely formed legs of my puma. I had worked with her legs every now and then, using the method called the Tellington Touch by Linda Tellington Jones. Now I saw how various types of alternative healings worked. To be able to jump from such a height is a feat in itself, and to land perfectly with no limp or strain and just minutes after the jump to run around and use her legs like nothing happened, is a miracle.

This was a test I needed to know regardless how it came into play. May this experience open our eyes to the wonderful healing of our teachers in life and the medicinal herbs which abound in our jungles. May the hand of man help protect this important rainforest and realize its worth.

I would like to extend a special thanks to Solano family for their wisdom, help, spirit and strength. To be like these people in every way is to really become the true human race. Carlos is an amazing man from whom we can only try to learn to become as strong in body, mind and soul.

P.S.: After this episode, we decided to school Juliana in tree climbing and a second release attempt will occur around March's full moon, since the male puma will be back from his twenty-eight day trek through his domain by this time. Soon Juliana would come into heat again, and this will help greatly in releasing her.

I was back in the city. I had a ton of work to do. I was asked to come teach students at the Simon Bolivar Zoo and help treat a little margay. I had gotten such a reputation with my animal work that the phone never stopped ringing. I had an exhausting schedule, but I never faltered. Of course there were times I wanted to give up. Our self worth comes to us only after a time. The words of Alycia came to me at those times.

She said, "If just one person benefits, learns or changes because of me, that is a gift I have bestowed on this earth."

I knew I was changing many. The animals were coming to me one by one. I had encounters with every species. I was being sent out to all points of Costa Rica. Driving hundreds of miles, I was starting to feel like my truck was part of my body. Besides all this work, I started mountain/rock climbing lessons at Victor Gallo's, and Mitch took over teaching Juliana about climbing up and down trees.

One group I was neglecting for lack of time were my domestic partners. Mitch and I shared our pets, however my dog, Lobo, and my cat, Africa , were dedicated to me. Africa was a beautiful black cat with long fur on her tail like a snow leopard. She had green eyes and a precious love for me. Each night she curled up beside my neck and gently used her paws to knead me and suckle me to sleep. She talked to me in a series of purrs. She was a great comfort to me.

The only thing she didn't like was my relationship with the puma. She did not like her because Juliana tried to catch her every chance she got. Africa was quick and knew before it happened to run up and jump onto the roof top.

She also guarded me at night. One evening while I slept a scorpion crawled on the blankets and Africa woke me up to shoo it away. Then there was Lobo, my protector. No matter what the situation was, he never let anyone come to close to me. When I had a disagreement with Mitch, Lobo put himself between us. He did the same with the puma, when she plaid too roughly with me. He always showed me the way when I would get lost in the jungles. Lobo is a book in himself. He saved my life countless times. He is my best dog, and he knew me better than any animal. Our communication was solid.

California

It was time for me to take a trip Stateside. I needed to see Island. I had also been invited to make a presentation of my project to several organizations in the United States, who had been following my story on my website. I could only go for ten days, so I prepared myself for another run. My project had touched the heart of many people. I met with Penelope Smith, author of Animal Talk. What a interesting character she was. We talked of animal communication and the broadening of its scope to the many people who were interested. Penelope wanted to come to Costa Rica. We made plans. I squeezed in as much time as I could with Island. I loved hearing about everything that happened in her life. We missed each other terribly and worked on perhaps being able to see each other more. Towards the end of my trip I was invited to come out and met Tippy Hedren. She was the owner of Shambala. Shambala was a wild cat reserve where Ms. Hedren rescued tigers and lions from private ownership which had gone wrong. Her place was set in the canyons of the Los Angeles forest. It was an oasis. The animals were happy and she loved them. Her place was very welcoming. It truly looked like the African plains with its canyons and openess.

An area with a large swimming hole housed a gentle giant, the elephant whom she cherished. I liked Ms. Hedren immediately. She was so little and made quite a picture amongst her big cats. They loved and respected her. I met a misfit, another one of man's experiments. A cross between a lion and a tiger stood right in front of me. It was strange to say the least. We took tea on the veranda of her African style home, and talked of our animals. As the sun set, the roaring of the big cats soothed me. This was their active time. Playtime.

Tippy gave me a great ball for Juliana. It is what her cats played with. It was made of a material they could not puncture.

Tippy and I made plans to throw a benefit to help both our projects. Tippy was getting ready to present a bill to congress which would put a stop to private ownership of wild animals in the United States. I agreed wholeheartedly with her. She was leaving for Washington D. C. the next day with her daughter Melanie Griffin.

I took the bill with me to Costa Rica and got thousands of signatures. This bill was a long time in coming. I wished her well, thanked her for the gift and looked forward to her arrival in Costa Rica.

She was elated, she too, just needed to find the time from her busy schedule to get away from it all, as she put it. I also visited Martine Colette, owner of the Waystation, another wild animal refuge. Martine was also very welcoming. She was the first of the contacts I had organized to come to Costa Rica and see the projects which so desperately needed funding.

Martine came down shortly after my return to Costa Rica. And of course, the first stop was to Jose's place. She loved La Marina. A veterinarian friend, Dr. Raymond Kray, who accompanied her, fell in love with the country and decided to retire in Costa Rica. He was a bird man and Costa Rica was as such a paradise to him. Ray did a lot to help the birdlife and teach those involved around the country. He even treated the macaw belonging to the president.

All to soon it was time to go home. My visit had been profitable. I had renewed hope again. It was hard leaving my daughter. We so missed each other. Island was always great about my life's work, she supported me in every way, which helped me get through the long good byes. Though I know she wished things were different, she understood the driving desire I had for animals. She is my rock.

I received one more gift from a natural heating company in Santa Barbara, California. They sent me a huge gas heater for my cabin in Amistad. I was touched. I pictured the waves of heat it would produce. I was on my way...

April 2000

Mitch picked me up at the airport. We spent the night in the city and left for Amistad at dawn. I was anxious to see Juliana. Mitch said everything was going well. He had taken her back to the tree which she got stuck in, and she looked up it for a long time, but did not want to climb it. He had worked with her a lot on her climbing skills and he told me she now knew what to do.

Juliana went crazy when she saw me. I always call to her before I am in sight of the cage. It was a quick high pitched, short cat sound. She always answered back. Today she screamed it back again and again. She was so excited. I held her close, I rarely got to do this with her anymore. We purred to and caressed each other. It was so good to see her.

She loved her ball and spent hours playing with it. The heater worked great and was a blessing against the cold nights. I could only spend a few nights in Amistad, then I had to go back to the city. The work had piled up in my absence, and I had to do everything by myself. It made me tired just to think about it. Easter was coming and the country shuts down for the whole week of Semana Santa.

The next week flew by. Then, as I was planning my next day with the puma, Alex called me. He told me Juliana was sick. She had eaten a set of worker's gloves made of suede and leather. I asked no questions, I wasted no time. I grabbed what I needed and ran out the door.

I told him I was on my way. I drove like lightning. When I arrived, Alex told me the whole story. Two days before, Alex was cleaning out her pen. He forgot to take his gloves out and Juliana ate them. At first Alex did not know she ate the gloves, he merely thought he had misplaced them.

The following morning he told me she would not eat. When he went back in the evening to check on her, he could not find her. He got worried and unlocked her pen. He then saw her in the corner of her box. She was not breathing. Alex's quick thinking saved her life. He didn't know what was wrong, but he saw her abdomen so extended that he push hard on it. He then pounded her chest to get her to breathe. She vomited heavily twice and brought up some of the pieces of gloves. The glove pieces had swollen with the fluids inside her body, working against the foreign matter, and pieces still stuck in her esophagus had slowly worked their way to cutting off her breath. He said he rested with her for a bit and gave her some water. She drank very little and went out to try to defecate. She couldn't. She went back sickly to her box and lay down.

I rushed over to her. She came out of her box to greet me. I could tell she wasn't feeling good. Her stomach ached. I went in to check her. She did not want her stomach touched. She was curled up in a ball protecting the stomach area which pained her. Her eyes were a little red. She still wouldn't eat. Cats do not eat if they have something stuck inside them. If they cannot defecate they take no more into their bodies.

I knew there was more of the gloves inside her and had to get them out soon. I put together a remedy, using sasgrada, a plant for fast bowel movement. It was hard getting it down her, but she took it. I stayed for four hours waiting to see if anything would happen. It didn't. At that point I knew the gloves had not made it into the intestines yet and that they were not being properly digested in her stomach.

We moved her into the cabin. I gave her a tea which eased her discomfort. She let me do whatever I asked of her. She seemed cold, I heated the cabin, and I lay down with her. By next morning I knew I would have to get help. She was in so much pain. She was telling me to please help her. I had to get a vet to help me. I called Carlos Villalobos, but he told me to bring her into the city. I didn't want to do this. She would hate the drive in her condition and the city would be to much for her.

I went to San Isidro and looked up some vets I had heard of from a reliable source, who had opened a new clinic in town. People said they were really good guys. Guillermo and Adrian were their names. They were very understanding and both sensed my urgency. They closed the clinic and followed me to the puma.

Mitch was waiting with her, doing energy work on her. Guillermo and Adrian were very quiet in their work with her. Juliana looked at me and at them and read my mind. I told her to just trust these men. She did.

They needed to feel her belly. I told them this would be hard. We had to try. She didn't like this, she really was trying to cooperate but under such pain it was too hard on her. I also had the lives of these vets in my hands. So I gave the o.k. to tranquilize her. She had never been sedated before. I asked them to start on a low dosage at first. They were using katamine. I didn't like this tranquilizer but had no choice. Katamine is a hallucinogen. It stays in the animal long after they have come awake. If the animal is in the wilds, nature helps release it toxic effects quickly, for those in captivity the side effects can stay in their conscience for months sometimes years. Much like a recurring horrible nightmare. And we don't even know it is there... They stuck her with the needle as gently as possible, I held her tight, constantly reassuring her. She was showing a supreme trust in me. I stroked her. She nestled close, the drug was taking effect. I had a moment of total control with her as the dosage took over and she started to sway.

I told Guillermo now was his chance. He reached in quickly to her bed and felt the abdomen. The look on his face was grave.

"We have to take her in now," he said.

He administered the rest of the dosage for the ride. I kept her eyes moist with tepid chamomile tea. When tranquilized, cats eyes do not close and it is always necessary to keep them moist and covered. Cats have a mirror like membrane in the backs of their eyes that let them hunt and move in almost complete darkness, called a tapetum lucidum. The membrane reflects light after it has already traveled through the retina giving the eyes another chance to nab the photons as they make their second trip. I sat in the truck with the vets and held her in my arms. I hated seeing her like this. It was evening when we arrived, which was good. No people about, no cars on the road.

The clinic was immaculate. We headed for the surgery room. The guys asked me if I wanted to assist. I nodded most certainly. As we scrubbed up I kept my eye on Juliana. Her breathing was even. I talked to her even then, in soft gentle tones. Even on the unconscious level of sub conscience, animals hear us.

As I watched them cut open her stomach, I was amazed at how beautiful she is inside. The organs, the blood; it was not gruesome. To watch her body silently like this, her muscles, their form, everything about her was perfect. Both men worked two hours, piece by piece, removing small particles of wet soaked, expanded leather. Their hope was that the gloves had not entered into the intestines.

I told them I thought not. We opened a small entry part of the intestines to be sure and thank god, none was there. It was four in the morning by the time we were done. They wanted her to stay at the clinic to keep a watch over her. I told her she was in good hands with me. I wanted to drive her back to the cabin before she awoke from the anesthesia. I wanted her to awake in her bed and surroundings to ease the pain of her experience.

They gave me some medicine to help the acid build-up in her stomach, and antibiotics. I politely refused and told them I had natural antibiotics for her and that chamomile tea was the best thing for her stomach. This relaxes the stomach, thus slowing down the formation of acids. They wished me luck and thanked me for the experience they had been part of. This was the first time for them too. I thanked them for their work and understanding. We tiredly said good bye.

Mitch and I slowly drove the truck up to the cabin. The sun was rising when we reached it. Juliana was waking. She smelled deeply. She liked that she was home. I tucked her into bed, sang "Rock-A-Bye Baby" to her and passed out with her. We slept away the morning, then she woke me with a soft purr.

Mitch went to get some fresh creamy cow's milk for her, still warm. I opened a capsule of my antibiotics and mixed in the green golden powder. I was using goldenseal root. This aids in alkalizing the stomach against the acidic. It is strong smelling and tasting. Therefore it needs to be disguised in order for her to accept it. She drank all of it. I could tell she was still thirsty. I brewed chamomile, let it cool and gave her to drink. I can't believe it, she loved it. Again animals know what they need. Give them their medicine and they know what to do every time. On many of my walks I witnessed wildlife use and know different plants to cure themselves.

We slept again. I knew she was hungry that night, but I wanted to wait until morning to get something else down her. She drank gallons of tea. The next morning I gave her eggs with milk again and her herbs. She looked a lot better. We took her out for a very short walk to let her pee. She had urinated a little in the cabin but she didn't feel comfortable doing this, I could tell. Outdoors she peed for a long time. She looked around her jungle and just sat for a spell on a grassy knoll with me. I knew she was going to be all right. I was so glad. It had been a harrowing experience.

Alex came to visit her. The whole family was very worried. I knew Alex felt alittle at fault, so I took some time with him to let him know that he did nothing wrong. She shouldn't have eaten the gloves. She had to learn. And if it wasn't for his quick thinking in making her vomit she would have died that day. So I told him he was her angel and to never doubt his ways again. Our eyes moistened. He hugged me for a long time.

Juliana healed quickly. She had a cough and a sneeze for a day, which is one of the after effects of the anesthesia. She ate some fresh trout. Mitch came back from the beach to relieve me and brought some fresh tuna. She devoured it. It was her first ocean fish.

I covered her wounds with honey. This is a very effective healer with antiseptic properties in it. When she licked her wounds she also got the internal benefits of honey. By the fourth day the hair was growing back on her belly. The incisions were not so red anymore and she was moving around a lot.

We kept her in the cabin for ten days to make sure the stitches had done their work. Juliana was stitched after the surgery with the stitches inside her. This way she would not lick herself too much and accidentally open it up. She remained on a supplemented diet of bee pollen, pipa aqua and herbs. By the time the vets came to check on her, she was healed. They were astonished and asked me to give a seminar on my medicines in San Isidro. I told them I would love to.

I finally had to go back to work. Alex was ready and eager to take over the care of Juliana. I told him to call if he needed anything, then I was off.

Victor and Derek were waiting for me when I got back to my apartment. They asked if I would lead a group of visitors through an adventure weekend. The pay was good and I needed some different form of adrenaline. I consented. I went bungee jumping, hang gliding and river rafting. I climbed mountains I never knew. I had a great time. I needed it.

A week after my adventures, I found some quiet time to read. A relaxing, much welcomed pleasure. I was reading the book The Horse Whisperer, by Monty Roberts. I liked his ways. He too knew animals. I loved the book and even wrote to him of my work with the puma. He answered me back and told me to always believe in my instincts no matter what man says.

I went to see Juliana. The sun was setting throwing warm colors all around me, as I lay on the grass by her pen. The night wanderers of the jungle animals were waking. The sunset was magnificent. The colors of fire. Then blues and greens of the waters. As I turned my head I saw each and every animal watching the sunset too. They too knew how to enjoy the beauty they lived in. They are as we are in more ways then one knows. We all sighed.

The puma was fully recovered, but she had a new habit after this experience which she kept doing for as long as I can remember. She would pull hair out of her tail. I saw patches of hair missing from her tail at different times. I put different offensive smelling natural oils on it to deter her from chewing it. But this was hard to do and she would do this often. I ran with her in the wilds a lot this trip.

I was working with what I had learned from Monty Roberts on the body language of animals. Juliana got the message every time. She told me I would make a very good puma myself. She loved to mimic me. She only needed to see something one time and she never forgot it. For instance, I had a padlock on her cage which I opened with a key I always wore around my neck. Alex had a duplicate. No one else. As she watched me one day unlock her pen, she had a mischievous look on her face. Sure enough, the next time her cage was locked I watched her, hidden from sight, using her claw and placing it directly into the keyhole. She could have easily opened it up. She was one smart girl........

It was a few days before Easter. I was going away for the holidays. I had been invited to Puntarenas a port town on the

Pacific, by a group of guys I had met. I had known the one brother for some time now and had just recently met the oldest one. I liked him. They were called the Cartago boys and had a family cartel background. This was a group of my underworld friends.

I didn't know yet but I was to fall in love with the big brother, Memo. I spent the weekend in his boat going around and seeing some of the islands. We got along great and even Mitch who knew Memo told me we made a good match. It felt good to have a lover again. We both had crazy schedules so we didn't see each other much, but we did a lot together when we were. He helped me make money which I desperately needed to keep my project going.

I spent a lot of time in Cartago during this period. It was the capitol of Costa Rica until an earthquake tumbled it down. The city was beautiful and there is a church there that I loved. Memo's need for adreneline came from motor cross running. Whenever we could we would ride the backlands of Cartago. He also helped me a great deal with my truck. I drove a 89 Toyota black hi-lux pick up. Its name was Black Puppy. I loved this truck. It was a good luck charm. It never gave me any trouble and I turned over the mileage meter three times. My truck was illegal, which meant the paperwork and taxes needed to be taken care of. I didn't have the money. Taxes on vehicles were one hundred percent the value. Memo helped me with paperwork which would suffice only in a dire situation, but better than nothing, and I spent the next year driving at insane times to outsmart the traffic police. I saw a different side of Costa Rica, its power people and its play. But this is how it was. I had to do whatever it took to keep my projects going.

At this time during my Easter break with Memo, I met one of his friends, George from Puntarenas. His family were the Tesoro Mar heirs. Tesoro mar means ocean treasure and it was the largest tuna company in central America. They had a fleet of boats. They were the first tuna company to go dolphin safe with their netting. Later that year I helped him put together a dolphin protection project which was a first for our country.

My vacation ended with a message on my phone. Minae had contacted me. In Amistad they had a lodge which was built to hold meetings about the fortress of parks. They finally found out about my puma. They wanted to know more about the project. I met with them. It seemed that a new law had come into effect dealing with releasing animals back to the wilds in this park system. I was told I needed permits to do so. I took in the information and the next day passed it along to Carlos.

Basically Carlos felt as I. What we do, we do our way. The concern of the park officials was that since the park was now opening up to tourists, any animal could prove dangerous. They assumed that a domesticated wild animal would not fear man and thus possible harm the tourist.

We would approach that step when needed. For now the project continued on the same path. Carlos took me to meet an indigenous friend of his who had just come down the mountain for his yearly trip to white man's land. The journey was a walk of fifteen days and many tribes of indigenous people came on this yearly pilgrimage. When I met this friend of Carlos', he handed me a prayer he had come across in our world from a great Indian chief. He knew all about my story with the puma. He said I should keep it. His eyes held mine for a long moment. He smiled at what he saw in me "Your work has not yet begun, let the wilds teach you"...

An Indian's Prayer

Dear God, I come to you as one of your many children.

I am small and weak. Give me your strength and wisdom

Make my ears strong that I may hear you

My eyes sharp to see your beautiful sunsets

That my hands respect the things that you make

Wisdom to learn the many lessons hidden in every leaf and rock Make me strong, not to be superior to my brothers, but to fight my worst enemy, myself......

So I will come to you with straight eyes and my soul comes to you without shame.

(I shook his warm, strong hand and he was gone)

May 2000

On May first, many strange ceremonies came into my life. Totem animals crossed my roads. Spirit, my wolf came to me. We spoke to the masters. The next night a gathering of woman lead by one American Indian on a full moon night took us all away. The ritual took place at Diana Teran's, the photographers', house. We moved outdoors as the moon lit up the sky. Her house was on the outskirts of the city with a beautiful great tree which had survived lightning strikes in the center. We formed a circle around the tree. We smoked a peace pipe, burned myrrh, cobalt and sage. After the initial ceremony I remember raising up off my knees and found on the ground on which I had knelt a snake totem. A smooth wooden carving of a small snake. The leader simply looked at me and then smiled. I then meditated. I was looking for answers. I had questions in all aspects of my life. Answers began to flow. More came to me that I knew what to do with. It was a time for renewing the spirit.

On May 5th of that year the planets aligned in a formation not seen since 6000 years ago. Egypt was overthrown at this time. The door of the opening of the universe was closed. On this night of the year 2000 it would open again. A new consciencness would come into effect. Seven planets aligned in a row for the first time in 300,000 years........

Carlos came to me that night and told me of a place deep beneath the mountains' breath, hidden from man. A corridor, which was the border stronghold of the indigenous people. Only a handful of men had ever been there. Carlos was one of them. He told me it was an animal kingdom. It was time to take Juliana up there.

It would be a six day walk with her into the passage. Carlos had a plan and in two days we would have to be ready. Carlos, Mitch, Alex and Joel would set off with her. Upon reaching the place, Carlos and Alex would stay for a day and then return home. They would walk home a different way to throw off Juliana. Mitch and Joel would stay the week. Then they would choose the right time to come back. And Juliana was to stay.......

If all went as planned, I would then return with Carlos in three weeks time and see her. We prepared in those two days. The men were excited; this would be some journey for all of them. This busy time helped me through the emotions running inside me. I knew the experiences we had with the puma were a training ground for both sides. Whatever would happen, it showed us what she still lacked and showed her what she was to become.

I talked with her often. We had seen puma tracks again. Every twenty-eight days this male seemed to end here with her on his roamings through his territory. She also came into heat each month. She knew something was about to happen. She had all the expressions of an anxious young girl about to leave home for the first time. She was very affectionate with me.

I cried into her soft, warm furs. I wanted to go along of course, but I knew she would follow me back for sure. She would look at it as an outing. I wasn't ready to force her. I just wanted to show her something. A place where she could go, if she wanted to. This was to be a good test for all of us on how we were doing raising a puma.

May 7

Mario and Tati came out this morning to see her. They couldn't believe how much she had grown. I guess we all still thought of her as our baby. I was touched by their sweetness to her and I know she remembered them. It took her a minute but when Mario and Tatiana started to talk amongst themselves Juliana's ears lifted a funny way. It was like she was tilting her head to hear with her inner ear the memory of these familiar voices. We were with her for about an hour. Mario shot some film of her. He was very discreet about it and since there was no clicking sound as with a camera, Juliana, who was quite occupied with all the new people and smells, seemed almost not to notice.

They went up to the house while I spent a little alone time with her. I took Juliana out on the leash by myself. She kissed me, then pulled me to a tree two hundred feet away. I had not noticed until she showed it to me, but there on the tree's trunk were long claw mark scratches and the bark and the ground had been sprayed by the male. Juliana rolled and purred on every part she could touch which her lover used much like a love letter to her.

Reluctantly, I put her back. I was sad about her leaving and a deep feeling of loneliness crept over me. But I held my emotions in check. This was to be a joyous time. I shook off my mood and went to join the others. We ate a family feast at the Solano's house that night. We talked of everything possible to be prepared for. Really it was our emotions we were preparing to deal with, the rest of the stuff was ready. I watched Mitch transform into his Indian self. He is half Cherokee Indian by birth and the spiritual part of him was mutating. His dreams were spinning at him right now. This was to be a ritual for him.

His bond with Juliana was different from mine. She always showed him what he feared most about himself. She was bewitching in what she did to all of us.

May 8th

At 2:00 AM Mitch was up , pacing the floors.

At 4:00 AM we breakfasted together, simple, hearty fare.

I kissed them goodbye. We send bundles of luck, and four men walked a jungle princess to her destiny.

I drove back to the city with Mario and Tati. All I could do was wait, so I kept myself busy. I spent most of my time with our animals. I had them all to myself. It was nice.

May 20th

The night before, Magela had called me to tell me Carlos and Alex were but a day's walk from home. On the way back they had taken a different route which was shorter in time and distance. They had radioed her from some friend's cottage in the mountains. Their message was short and sweet. "So far, so good."

I was waiting with my dogs. It seems we were all wagging our tails at their arrival. Both men had smiles on their faces. Carlos and Alex loved their mountains and any chance they got to go romp in it was pure pleasure to them. They didn't look the least bit tired. They could walk jungles for days on end. They were incredible in their stamina and knowledge of the mountains.

We hugged and kissed and I was bursting at the seams with questions. I waited till they greeted their family. Anna, their daughter, had a warm meaty lunch prepared for them. Between mouthfuls we talked about the walk-in.

First, Alex said, they had to arrange a suitable walking line. Who went first, so to speak, for Juliana did not like people walking behind her. They also needed to do the first leg rather quickly and not take too much time with her desire to explore a spot or two. Since Juliana knew Joel the least and was still a little weary of him, he and Carlos took the lead, then it was Alex and Mitch with her by their side.

She did well, Alex said. She walked right alongside at their pace. She felt the intent demeanor in them and caused no fuss. Plus she loved walking in the jungle and as long as you didn't turn around and act like you were taking her back, she basically did fine. Carlos told me they all drank water together, puma style from the first river. As Juliana crouched on the banks to drink, so did they. Alex laughed at remembering the comical look on her face at the men, a little like we were crazy or something, he said.

When night came, the jungle came alive. Juliana listened intently to every sound. The third night it was evident to Carlos that they were being followed. Juliana

was acting differently too. The male puma was on their trail. Mitch had asked if there was any danger in being followed by the wild male. He had a worried look on his face.

Alex chuckled. "The male puma should love us for bringing him this beautiful playmate," he said.

Carlos also assured the group that the male would not bother them. Pumas did not charge and attack people in these mountains. They let them live, unlike what man does to them. In his youth Carlos had hunted puma for its meat. The muscle of this animal was extremely nutritional. They never hunted for sport. They were the indigenous people, not white man.

The group made it to the spot. It was magnificent. Alex said he had never seen such beauty in his life. The weather had held pretty good, only a few days of light rain. The nights were cold, but they had snow and high mountain sleeping bags and would light a small fire. Alex and Carlos spent one night at the site and then began the journey home. Only one thing didn't go as planned.

They had planned to keep Juliana on her leash for the first couple of days after arriving at the designated spot. Alex and Carlos then would have the chance to leave without her following. But the scene changed. No sooner had Juliana got to the place, and camp was being set up, that she made her move.

With such precision she in one touch, unclipped her collar with her claws and was free. She swooshed her tail at them all. As if to say, now I play, follow the leader...

She was gone into the brush in one silent bound. The group just nodded. Let her go. Let her play. More than likely, the male was calling to her. She stayed out all night. When Alex and Carlos were preparing their return, she came out of nowhere to check on the guys.

She was nervous and excited. She ran first to Alex, then to Mitch. He offered her some food. She didn't take it. She bounded back out. Carlos stated that she was most definitely involved with the male, for otherwise she would have stayed and eaten. He was calling her and yet their ears could not hear him.

Carlos told Alex this was a perfect time to leave. She was too busy falling in love to want to follow them back. And they immediately got on their way. So that was the report. Now we waited again. I left the family to themselves and went back to the city. I was giving a seminar to the Simon Bolivar Zoo the next day. I needed to do paperwork. Yuck, I loathed paperwork.

The seminar was interesting. I met many new faces and some old ones. Everyone was full of questions. I went over the whole zoo with the veterinarian and gave him ideas and warnings of the problems his animals were facing. He was very attentive. I had noticed that ever since the incident with Kaiser, the tiger, drinking pipa water, they were now giving pipas to all the carnivores.

The hard shell husk which housed the precious water, turned into a playing ball for them and also ripping it into pieces aided their teeth and gums. I smiled a little smile. One by one, little by little. There was also fresh cut grass in the cages. At the end of the day I met Yolanda Matamoris, the overseer of the zoo. She was a business lady, she cared little for the animals well being. I never liked her.

She asked me an odd question. "I need a fresh new wild specimen for my breeding program."

"What kind of animal?" I asked. "A puma, female," she said.

I told her I didn't know where she could find one. I also told her she was far from being ready or able to start a breeding program. She couldn't even take care of the animals she had.

She didn't like my tone. I didn't care. I had seen that a donation to her zoo from a foreigner, for building better enclosures for her cats, had gone to opening up a Mac Donalds franchise which never did any business anyway.

She informed me she was being given a huge tract of new land to move the zoo to. There she was planning on changing everything.

This never came to be. No one would give this woman money needed for a new zoo, solely based on the fact of how she had run this one into the ground and groups were petitioning her to close it down.

I went to see the jaguar cubs Agatha and Brutus. They remembered me and played hard with me. I had great difficulty getting away from them. They so wanted me to stay. Their paws and forefeet were beginning to show signs of deformation. This occurs when carnivores, especially cats, live and walk on concrete.

Cats need to exercise their claws and the movement which occurs on concrete limits many muscles and ligaments from properly functioning. They were becoming cripples and it is painful for them.

I immediately brought this to the attention of Danilo, the vet. I searched the zoo grounds for a better area to move them too. I found an old enclosure which was complete on earth's ground. It even had a nice tree growing in it. Not tall but with a good trunk, so the cats could sharpen and stretch their claws.

Danilo told me he would have to run it by Yolanda. I just gave him a look.

The good news is, by the end of the month Agatha and Brutus moved to this new enclosure. I suggested that because of lack of fund for several bigger natural areas, they might just create one giant playpen so to speak, and give each animal at least a couple of hours a day, or however they wanted to schedule it, to be in a natural area where they could stretch and run and feel earth beneath them. Danilo thought this a great idea. I spent the next full day writing everything that could be done to help the animals' welfare without spending too much money. It was brilliant. I sent it to Danilo. I had done the best I could.

It rained all that week. I thought of the jungle group. The dogs were asking me when Mitch would be home. I told them soon.

May 25th

I received a phone call from Mitch. It was 5:00 AM. I was first shocked then scared, did something go wrong, why were they back so soon?

Mitch told me everything was fine and to come out and get him. He would tell me everything when I arrived.

I loaded up the truck with the dogs, cancelled my appointments and drove up the mountain. When I arrived, the dogs jumped out of the truck to tackle Mitch. They barked and yelped at him. They had really missed him. I knew they had wanted to go too.

Mitch handed me a few sheets of paper where he had logged the day to day info on Juliana for me. It was a beautiful letter of sorts which told of his many trials and visions while up in this paradise. He told me that Joel had wanted to head back.

I was a little angry at this. This was to have taken its time, but Mitch said he couldn't stay out there alone. They also had not waited for Carlos to come and take them back a different way so by coming back the same trail, it would be easy for Juliana to pick up the scent.

I was disheartened by this, but I said nothing. I knew they were tired. Mitch told me Juliana was excellent. He had watched her hunt rabbit and she never did eat any of the food brought along, so this was a good sign. She knew how to hunt for herself. He saw

her at least once a day. She would come in and say hi. One day he was reading in a hammock and she scared him by jumping right into his lap. He wrote the following passage on his journey.

Mitch's Story

Even though I am not a writer, I want to share with you an experience which will remain forever in my mind. At the very beginning I received a phone call from Julie, who had been out at La Marina doing film work. She said, "Guess what honey, guess what I have?"

Knowing her as I do I knew it was an animal of some sorts.

I thought I am in for some big changes and surprises. What I didn't know was how much so...

In those early days, walking this puma in the different jungles, I received loads of scratches, and bleeding became second nature to my arms. My arms became her fangs' chew bone and her claws' scratching posts.

As she grew, so did her wild side. I was becoming more and more afraid of her. I never shared these fears with Julie. I was afraid she would laugh at me for she thought I was invincible. One day as I was walking Juliana, I felt a lot of fear of being mauled by her.

She sensed my fear. I knew this because about twenty minutes later, while stopping to rest, I was squatting down, and all of a sudden she jumped into my lap. I almost jumped out of my skin. But she purred loudly and rubbed her head against my stomach just like a house cat would.

Then I had my first experience of animal communication. It was so clear to hear inside my head. She told me that she loved me very much and would never harm me. She was working on my fears, all of them in a sense. She was returning me my powers, which is what the indigenous people believe this totem animal is in our lives. This is what puma represents. Each animal represents a different power. The healing she performed on me was so strong that in the next five years I only once feared her again.

This other time of fear occurred when I was walking her again in the jungle, close to the edge of the forest, when all of a sudden I heard another puma growl. Juliana's ears went back and her eyes changed color. They turned from golden brown to fiery green. This happened every time she got spooked or mad. All I could do was sit down and wait it out, wait for her to change back. Thirty minutes went by. Her eyes changed back, her ears came forward again and I quickly finished the distance between her cage and the forest and put her back in.

I remember the visit from the famous animal communicator, Penelope Smith, to our place with Juliana. Penelope told me the puma had come into my life because I needed to complete something from a past life.

As I began the walk this day with Carlos, Alex and Joel, all of this was going through my mind. We four walked where none had gone before us. Two chopped the whole way with machetes, because the thick forest was in our way, one marked trees for our trail back, and I walked Juliana on a leash quite a bit back as Juliana did not like being so close to people. She knew and trusted only myself, Julie and Alex.

The going was slow. I stopped often with the puma, but catching up to the others was not a problem for they were having great difficulty in cutting the paths ahead. It was very cold, we were at 10,000 feet elevation.

When the male puma came close again, I saw Juliana's eyes go green. I was tempted to release her right then and there but breathed to steady my nerves and moved on. Alex and Carlos shouted back not to worry.

As we nearer our destination, Juliana just laid down and would not budge. I tugged and pulled on the leash, to no avail. In a sudden, quick movement she took her claws and unleashed herself.

She then looked at me, and she seemed to say, "See you later," and took off running into the jungle.

At first I freaked out, then I realized she had waited till now to free herself, she must know what she is doing. Maybe the male was telling her something.

I caught up to the others and told them she was off. They got excited that she was free so deep in the jungle. We pitched a campsite and tent, ate and rested for a couple of hours.

Then Carlos and Alex took this chance to return. It did not look like Juliana would come back this night. Joel and I went to bed shortly afterwards and were up at the crack of dawn. As Joel and I talked, I sneezed, and Juliana meowed back at me. We didn't know it, but she was but a few meters away from us, hidden watching us. I called her and she came running to me like a little puppy. I reached down and gave her a big kiss. I had brought a kilo of meat with me to feed her, so I offered her some. She just looked at me and said, why would I eat that when I have a whole jungle of live game to eat.

She then looked at me and said, "Let's go."

She wanted me to follow her, so I did. She lead me through the jungles on trails made by the dantes tapirs. It was like little roads cut into the brush from these massive animals. I think she wanted to hunt one.

Too big for her, I thought. She was so excited throughout this walk, she ran ahead, yet always returned to check on my progress and make sure she wasn't losing me. Or she just stopped and waited for me to catch up. We did this for a couple of hours, then we returned to camp. I had cleared a spot in the brush the day before, to hang my hammock up. It was a little ways apart from the main encampment. So I grabbed my book and laid down to read. Juliana came and lay down next to me. After reading for about a half hour I fell asleep. Juliana slept too. We woke up together, she said goodbye once again and took off.

I went to the other side of the campsite where Joel was as Juliana would not be anywhere around him and told him what had happened.

As I finished the story, a great urge to lie down came over me. This was strange as I had just slept, but I went into the tent and fell instantly asleep. It was the deepest sleep I have ever been in.

I had heard of astral projection and astral travel, but I really did not understand it. I was about to find out. What took place next was the most intense experience of my life. I was amidst a deep dark space with no stars or moon. I had become a large dark wild south American pantherine and I was spinning somersaults when all of a sudden I was soaring above a Mayan Indian village cut out of the jungle. A large cone-shaped mountain with a huge flat top was draped in bright green jungle. At the base of the mountain, in the jungle, perfectly uniformed square rock shrines were connected by rock trails. I floated above and around this village. There was more but I forgot and awoke with a start.

I hurried to write the travel down. Years later Tom Sexton, an astral psychic who practices in California, told me the meaning of this walk with the puma. I had told him nothing of my experiences. He merely asked me to write down questions I wanted answered.

I wrote, "What was my walk with a puma in Costa Rica about?"

He immediately answered by describing the whole experi-
ence to me exactly how it had occurred. He repeated every-
thing I had written down three years ago. He told me I had
turned into a panterine, a South American panther. I was
returning a sacrifice to this prehistoric Indian nation.

It was almost too weird to share this story with Joel at the
time I awoke.

The remainder of my stay in the jungle went much the
same. Juliana came and went. The final day she did not come
at all.

Joel then said he wanted to go. He was going through some-
thing of his own but I never knew what it was.

The weather was changing. Dark, ominous clouds were
forming, and I agreed to head back. I was also a little scared
of having any further dreams. I knew each night I dreamt
something strange, for I would wake covered in sweat. There
was an eeriness about everything, a force I was not yet able to
understand nor face.

So we headed back. We followed the same trail out as we
had taken in. I hoped Juliana would not follow.

Eugene Mitchell

May 29th

Carlos called me and told me Juliana has come back. I was
shocked, stunned, happy and afraid. I was everything. She had
walked through farmland close to Carlos'. Walking through
this way was for the puma the most direct path to her habitat.

Carlos also told me the man who owned the farm was furious and scared. He said the puma had attacked his cow and
dog.

I told Carlos I was on my way.

He said he was going to go to the man's house to talk to him.

Carlos said, "I don't like this man much," and for him to say this of anyone was rare. I took this as a warning.

I knew Juliana would not attack his animals. I was furious now. I drove in record time to Amistad, and saw Carlos.

He spoke first, "Have not seen or heard Juliana."

I turned to call her and there she was, walking right up to me. She knew the sound of my truck when it was still on the main highway six kilometers on top of her valley.

She knew exactly when to walk out of the jungle to me.

She looked good. Her muscle tone had doubled. She had hunted and eaten well. Later in her habitat, she proved it by defecating wild rabbit fur. Carlos and I tried putting her in the truck immediately. She stood aback with Carlos. Then I simply held the truck door opened and sent her the message, "Get in, now." inside of me I was yelling the command at her.

She had to hurry before anyone else come around. We were in the middle of the main dirt road down the valley. She leaped right in. We took her to her home. She ran in and began to smell everything.

We were lucky to have gotten her so easily. Carlos didn't want the man to see her again. Carlos said, he told the man she had just gotten out a few hours ago.

The man had been petrified of her. The truth came from his wife's side of the story. She was reluctant to say anything in front of her husband. Finally, stepping aside with Carlos she told him, the puma had just walked through and it was the dog that attacked her and as for the cows, they just ran away scared. She even told him that her young son was playing not far away and the puma had paid him no mind. Carlos said this man was going to make a report to the police on the incident.

We had a problem on our hands.

I went to Juliana and just sat there. So many feelings rushed through me. She had done well. She had survived out there, even though she came back. And, she, was different now. One could see the maturity her adventure had brought out. Her senses were keener. She was listening to another world. She wanted to rest, she wanted me to stay. I lay down in the grass and stayed the day. She began at some point an intense communication with me. This is what came.... This animal is here for the higher awareness.

Thought focus - clear direct intention. Purest form of communication, to guide our thoughts. Blueprints - next level of dimensional words.

Animal is reading everything in your head space.

She was teaching me a deeper meditation. A way to read.

Many times in the past my communication with her lead to frustration for I was only touching the surface. With this new outlook and form I reached a level of knowing not only her mind but the minds of the "Others" in a single touch. What is it I am touching?

The minds of every living thing. This touch is not hidden, for it has been locked in the deepest recess of our minds a time long ago. We all hold the key to our own locks. Each of us, when ready, has the know-how to open it. This is but one part of the brain which we have yet to see inside of ourselves.

Carlos checked on us. He sat with me a while and just talked. He knew I was confused. He felt everything coming off me. He always had the gift of setting my mind straight.

We were very close to each other from the day we first met. I needed not to talk much and he always understood. His warm strong eyes were there to look upon for strength when I needed them. Carlos gave me courage, which to me is the greatest tool in life. He always told me, "Look into my eyes and hold my gaze,"

I did till my storms passed. Carlos was my spirit guide. He was a gift to me. If this puma lead me to met this man in my life, it was enough...

Alex and Mitch were on their way to see Juliana. I told them to leave her alone for a while. She needed to come down from her adventure and I wanted her to have time to ponder what she had been through. I needed to deal with some new steps in my project. I needed to go see Jose Rojas. I returned to the city while the boys took care of the puma.

May 31st

I was driving up to La Marina.

Word came that a man named Fernando, the neighbor up at Amistad, called Minae in San Isidro, and they wanted to come and inspect the puma project.

My project was not on paper. I had just gotten to Jose's when I received the news. Jose told me he stood behind me one hundred percent. It was time, he said, to make my project a documented branch of La Marina. We would thus still retain full power and no one including Yolanda from the zoo could take her away from me.

He spoke with Carlos on the phone over lunch and reassured him we would get some protection. Carlos said it was a good time to met Juan Carlos Crispo, the owner of the property in Amistad which my project was on.

Throughout all this time we were never at the mountain at the same time. He had purchased the piece of land to preserve and protect it. He was also doing biological research. Crespo had purchased it from Carlos Solano's family. Carlos, of course, was given his own piece and home.

He was the" heffa" of the place. Meaning, the main man. He oversaw everything that went on. Carlos ran the international student project and served as one of the guides. A beautiful lodge had been built to house the students which entered into the jungles on daily treks exploring its wonders.

I agreed it was be nice to meet the man who, without ever knowing me, had given his consent for me to do my puma project on his reserve. In respect of his acceptance to me I had to let him know exactly what we were up to. If police would come onto his land, he had the right to know everything. I felt he would understand. I had heard good things about this guy.

June 2000

The puma was physically well, but she was confused. I knew she wanted the wilds again, but she wanted us too. She also missed the male. I sensed a longing in her.

Mitch came to me with different news. He had a job offer in California, working with the exportation of tropical palms. It was one he could not refuse. He was leaving in two weeks. He said it would be a year of work.

What could I say. He needed my help in overseeing the land on the beach. It was going to be a hard year for me.

I spent the week with him at the beach. There was a lot to go over. It was so nice to spend time out there. I really missed this place. The toucans were always about. Flocks of them were constantly at the house. The howler monkeys were having a war this day and it seemed like the mountains would come down from their rolling thunder.

Lobo was not feeling well. He was getting thinner by the week, no matter how much he ate.

Jose called and let me know the paperwork I needed for the puma would be ready by week's end. Good news. He also asked if I thought the puma had gotten pregnant from her romp with the male.

I told him this had crossed my mind but I wasn't sure. Gestation for a puma is about a hundred days. We would have to wait and see over the next couple of weeks. Mitch left on June 7th, and Russia's president Gorbachev arrived in Costa Rica.

I was asked to assist in his visit for I still retained some of my knowledge of the Russian tongue as my father was a native of the Ukraine.

Gorbachev was visiting Earth College for its idealism. Earth College was an institution which helped change the face of the environment in Costa Rica.

I had worked with them some years back with Ian Ratowsky on the creation of banana paper. How this project got started was very interesting. Banana exportation is big business down here. Dole, the leading company, played havoc with human lives and the environment. I remember seeing a fleet of limousines coming down the road in the city one day. What a sight that was. Never before had I seen even one limo in the country. I was told they were the Dole company's party and they were heading to an annual meeting.

The Caribbean coast was home to their plantations. They employed many people and housed them in little more than rat shacks. The toxic chemicals they used to spray the plantations, dust cropping via small aircrafts, severely damaged the earth. The run-off of neighboring rivers polluted and choked the huge sources of water with the plastic waste and cut banana plants which were discarded into the rivers after picking. The people had many illnesses due to the constant exposure to toxic spraying. The men were stricken with infertility. They worked like slaves for pennies a day.

Earth College, along with Ian, did an experiment. They went out to the largest river on the Caribbean and began a clean up of the debris. They dried the discarded banana plant waste and turned it into beautiful paper.

This was a huge success and even today natural paper from coffee and banana waste are best-selling items amongst tourists.

Meeting Gorbachev was fascinating. He and his family were interested and curious about everything. Earth College had a few students from Russia. This sparked an interest in him to create a sister school in his country.

Gorbachev and his family loved the beach. They took an afternoon off to play there. There was a mishap. His daughter had gone for a swim, the ocean looked calm. I was not with them on this afternoon. Here in Costa Rica there are tremendous tides and rip currents, swinging and swaying constantly from right to left. She got caught up in one of them and knew not how to swim out.

There were but a few locals on this stretch of beach but luckily one of them, a young boy, realized she was in danger and jumped in to save her. It was a scare but ended safely.

Gorbachev and his family had a real passion for nature. They knew more about the jungles than any tourist I had ever met. They spoke of their homeland and the forests with their wild animals. I was fascinated by the Siberian tigers and let them know that someday I wished to travel to Russia and see this magnificent beast in its own kingdom.

Conservation needed a lot of work in Russia. Poaching from the people of China was horrendous. Most of the help which came into Russia for wildlife came from outsiders, international organizations.

There was too much fear of its mafia in this country, and few good efforts ever amounted to much. The Chinese used various parts of this great animal, the Siberian tiger, for fertility drugs. They were ever so wrong. To kill a tiger was the greatest show of strength a man could show. To me it was the greatest show of fear...

I was only with the family a few short days. My final night we dined at a gorgeous home which had a baby grand piano. This was a rare find. Few pianos of any type were in Costa Rica. I loved to play and had studied classical music. I played that night and received waves of applause. It felt good to touch the keys again. Music soothes the savage beast... I pictured myself playing piano in the Siberian Taiga.

Gorbachev returned to his place in San Francisco, California. He had heard me talk about my various projects and my passion for my work over the last couple of days, and stated, "You are their miracle."

I blushed at the compliment. He asked if this would ever come forth into a book. I said I did not know. If it did, he said, he would like it to be translated into Russian and brought to his homeland. I promised him I would make sure of it. My mother had always told me I should write books for my imagination and my life were always so interesting and wild. So with the Russian president's request, the first thoughts of writing a book were put into my mind. I figured it would probably happen when I was sixty or something, for I didn't know when I would ever have the time. Hmmm, it didn't take that long...

At dawn the next morning we all said our warm farewells.

It was a long drive home. Their driver took me in and it wasn't as bad as being behind the wheel, like usual.

When I reached the apartment, my neighbors who took care of my pets in my absence, told me Lobo was doing worse. I made an appointment with Villalobos to help me diagnose his problems. The next morning we both agreed on the possibility of an intestinal virus and severe ulcers in his stomach. He asked if I wanted to ultra-sound him.

I told him, Let's wait.

Lobo had eaten carrion left off of the puma, many times in the past, of course without us knowing. I felt a parasitic activity had started and was eating him away. Ulcers would occur in the stomach and the liver needed to be filtered. The process with my natural remedies would have to be taken in a series.

I took him home and worked with him. No matter how sick he was, he always watched over me. He made an effort not to weaken by my side. My heart went out to him. I loved him so much. Fury, my wild shepherd, was worried about him to. Mitch had taken She-Dog with him to the States. Those two were inseparable. Mitch called two times a week. Everything was going well with him. I was glad. I knew he needed this. He sent me money to cover bills, which helped a great deal.

I stayed with Lobo for four days. He was improving. I decided it was okay to leave him for two days and head out to the puma, then to the beach place. Time to make my rounds.

I pulled into my cabin at the pumas to a spectacular day. I decided to do some spring cleaning in the cabin. I washed everything and hung it out to dry in the fresh sunshine.

The birdlife in Amistad is wonderful. They sang to me the whole day. Costa Rica has the greatest variety of birdlife. More so then any other place in the world. It is a bird watchers paradise.

I picked berries and fell in love with the blooms of a wild magnolia which grows in these parts. Their petals were so soft. I chopped kindling then set upon cleaning Juliana's pen.

The puma was well but she was pulling tufts of hair out of her tail. I knew she wanted to go out again, but I told her she would have to wait some time for this.

Alex asked if I wanted her in the cabin with me this night.

I told him no. It was better for her not to be in my cabin too much. The umbilical cord between us needed to be severed. After her experience in the wilds those weeks ago, I decided I would baby her no more. It was time for her to grow up.

I walked up the hill to my cabin and saw a stranger opening my gate. This gate was the Cuerici biological station entrance and mine. It was right by my cabin.

The hairs on my back raised. How dare someone just come in. Alex had not told me they were expecting anyone.

I went to the driver and asked, "Who are you?"

He replied, "Juan Carlos, the owner of this place." "Who are you?"

It was a quick sensory moment for both of us. Sizing each other up. Then he extended the warmest smile and the friendliest handshake. I smiled back at him. I apologized for my intro. He threw his head back and laughed," I like seeing this kind of protection on my reserve. You must be the catwoman."

I laughed back and said yes, its time we get to know one another. We planned dinner at the lodge since he was spending a few nights.

He was climbing the Chirripo mountain with some friends of his. Introductions were made all around amidst raised eyebrows and chuckles. The defender jeep started up again and we went on our way.

I added some new plants and things to Juliana's habitat. Her constant running about ruined some of the vegetation and I constantly replaced things so that her home was always a jungle.

I was excited that Juan Carlos would finally meet her. Early in the evening he did, and he admired her so. We talked about everything. I told him everything that had happened up to this point, and said there might be some trouble for him because of her.

He simply replied, "Bring it on. No one is going to do a damn thing to jeopardize this puma's life."

I sighed a sigh of relief. This man had courage. I liked everything about him. He had a lot of power and the intelligence and experience to go with it. He was an advocate of the great outdoors. He had done things one sees on Adventure TV. He was presently getting in condition for the Eco Challenge in Borneo. It was quite a feat to be chosen out of thousands. First Costa Rican in history, he said. At dinner we went over our plans. Carlos agreed with it all. Finally, some of the worry I had been carrying around was off my shoulders. I slept soundly that night. At dawn, I started for the beach.

The area of Perez Zeldon is huge. Within it are some of the most beautiful waterfalls in the world. We had a property with a magnificent one on it. It was located next to the town of Platanillo and it was called *San Juan De Dios*. I bathed and relaxed in the rushing falls. I loved to be nude in the waterfalls. When I was living there, Mitch and I took every client that came to us to the waterfalls. It was part of our daily routine. I missed that. I took full advantage now and wasted away the afternoon. When I reached the beach, I jumped in the ocean too.

I ran into a friend of mine which had told me that the other day a whale had beached herself. Today, close to the same spot, a dolphin did the same. The locals had helped keeping them wet and safe. A marine biologist was on his way out from Puntarenas. Marine life specialists were hard to come by. I went out to take a look. My experience with sea animals was limited, but I knew one could diagnosis an illness through a saliva sample.

My professor of herbology did this type of diagnosis. Hair samples, feathers, scales, they all carry blueprints of every living species.

Both dolphin and whale were being well looked after. There were many locals helping to wet down the animals and shift them around so they didn't lay on one spot for to long. They were not physically hurt on the outside.

I gave one of the locals Sierra's telephone number. She might be able to help. I stayed until the group from Puntarenas arrived. The whale was very docile with me. It was a black pilot whale. I had often seen schools of them around.

The offshore island of Isla Cano came into my sight and the next day I suggested I would go out with a boat and see if there was anything similar happening out there. I left to go up to the house. The beach place was a mess. I spent the rest of the evening cleaning up. It still looked dirty. Finally I went to find the maid and tell her to come bright and early the next day.

Then it was dark. The full moon tonight was breathtaking. The moon and the sun are the yin and yang of our planet. Feminine energy is received through the moon, masculine through the sun. I asked the moon to cover me with her powers. I always received so much energy on the full moon. It was hard to sleep through those nights. I knew Juliana felt the same way.

I called Memo. I wanted him. He told me to come whenever I wanted. He would be waiting...

Next morning a small group of us boated out to Isla Cano. What original beauty this island has. We had snorkels and fins, and after covering the island banks and not finding any beached or dead animals, we went for a swim. The visibility was great, the sea life marvelous. On the other side of the island waves were breaking in perfect order. I wished I had brought my surfboard. It hadn't been ridden in a long time. We covered the short distance back to shore.

The marine biologists gave the dolphin and whale a dosage of something I do not recall. Then we used the boat to gently take them out to sea. Both swam off slowly at first but seemed to be doing alright. We stayed in the waters with them for an hour. Then they were gone.

The ride back over the Cerro was cold and rainy. I did not stop at the puma's. When I arrived at my apartment, Derek had left a beautiful box, a gift. My answering machine was full of messages left by my friends, all giving me such love and support.

They were all there to help. They knew I had quite a load these days. Lobo looked good. He jumped all over me and would not let me out of his sight.

Africa had brought me her new boyfriend, a street cat. I named him Emerald for his eyes matched the precious jewels. He was big. Not very handsome, just big. Here was an example of true love between animals. Even though Africa was spayed, Emerald was as affectionate as any lover could be. He wasn't interested in just sex. Emerald spent every moment he could with her while she was outside. He nuzzled her and always gave her the best seat on the ledge bordering the apartments. He was really in love with her. I smiled sweetly at them, then picked up the phone and went to see my own lover.....

Till month's end I had basically the same routine. Everything was going well. I went out one weekend to the Ark herb farm, owned by dear friends of mine, Tommy and Pat. They had a company of herbs and spices called Los Patitos. This couple was one of the original group that came to the jungles in the very beginning. They had a lovely place. Their gardens were enchanting. We went on a sniff, smell and taste tour of the herbs. They were green thumb experts. Tommy could make things grow no one could, and Pat knew more about plants and greens than any university library.

I loved their book collection. We spoke about making an herbal line of products. I was one of the first people to tell Tommy he should grow herbs, and he did. Echinacea was the first. It had become popular in the States for it boasted immune systems and had antibiotic properties. Tommy gave me some Valerian and told me to give it to the puma. It was kind of like catnip. The odor was pungent. Unfortunately, hunters used Valerian to attract wild cats.

I took a big batch home with me. I ran right into a red fox while I walked to my truck. He stopped and stared at me for the longest time. I told him don't be afraid, and he wasn't.

I went to see Alycia and Kattia. We girl talked and animal talked. The experiences

Alycia was going through with horses were incredulous. With her own powers she brought horses back to life. She was an experienced communicator. One would never believe what she had accomplished unless they had witnessed it.

My truck needed a paint job. Memo took the truck, said he would do it and gave me a brand new king-size purple Toyota Hi lux pick-up to drive. It was pure luxury.

I drove with the dogs to the puma. I dropped off six live rabbits for her. The dogs ran and played with Juliana. Lobo overdid it a bit and I had to put him back in the truck to rest. I put some of the valerian in Juliana's box, and she went crazy for it. She wouldn't stop rolling in it. The dogs could care less about it.

Alex came by with a group of students from Italy. He asked if he could show this particular group the puma. The puma was not part of any tour, but I loved the energy of the youth and shouted to bring them down. After getting high off the valerian, Juliana was ever so sweet and showy to the group. They stayed for hours and said it had been the highlight of their trip. They all wanted to know the website so they could take the memory home with them. The website and this project was called, Hunting Magic. It happened everyday in one way or another. It was an appropriate name.

I received the written form with all the seals, stamps and stars, which made Juliana officially mine under the protection of La Marina. No one from the beau racy could fuck with me now. The next morning before I left, Alex and I took Juliana out for a walk. Indio, his dog was with us. They played so hard together. They would chase each other, then give nips of love bites to back and forth. They got along so well. They were pals. Indio was the only animal I knew that really enjoyed his friendship with Juliana.

July 2000

On the first of the month Minae called Carlos and told him they were coming out to see the puma. Carlos said, he didn't know if the puma was here or not. He was good at being evasive. He never lied though. He told them it was possible I had gone into the jungles with her. They said, nonetheless, they would be out.

Even though we had all the permission in the world now, we still didn't want Minae ever to see her. Carlos told Alex to bring the puma to a secret spot he had, not far from his house but tucked away out of sight. Even if someone walked close by, they could not see her. It was an old, giant cage used for holding her favorite food, trout, as it was being prepared for delivery. It was a bit small and rusty, but it worked. She didn't mind it at all. Carlos thought it best that I was not around.

I had no desire to talk with these men. The ruse was pulled off. Carlos answered all the questions. He satisfied them. They left the same day. Alex waited till nightfall to be sure and then took the puma back to her home.

That weekend Memo and I went to see her. He had never seen her before. He was taken aback by her at first. A mixed feeling of awe and fear and wonder. He spoke not a word. She was mesmerizing him. He sure looked at me differently after that. He couldn't believe the trust she had with me. It was late night when we had arrived and Juliana was surprised to see me visit her at night. She wasn't pregnant and the male was back around for her. Memo and I made love in front of her that night and when spent, lay and listened to the callings of the male, not far away. It was time to leave them. We slept in the cabin.

At daybreak, Alex knocked on the door and said Juliana had escaped. I dressed, quickly, kissed Memo, and ran off. I guess the pumas had taken their cue from us. The male had not only tried to ripe the partial roofing off her pen, but had also dug a hole for her to come out the bottom. He really wanted her.

I told Alex, she might be gone for a day or two but that it was important to watch for her return so we wouldn't have another episode with Fernando. I took a stool sample of the puma with me, to check for parasites. I gave it to Villalobos and he told me she was clean. Because of her live diet and the ever presence of herbs I gave her, she carried nothing.

Derek called and asked if I wanted to enter an archery contest. He said he was competing also. I said sure. I loved a challenge. He and I practiced at Victor Gallo's place every night till the event. I took third place overall. The men were impressed. Another feather in my cap. Victor gave me a gift. He had just returned from the States and had bought me a climbing harness just like his. I was touched. We had a little crush on each other. I was not lacking for male companionship. That never was a problem of mine. I loved them all for one reason or another.

My project was, for the most part, unfolding differently than any biologist, zoologist or animal person would expect it to go.

Those people questioned my methods. Most felt I had made Juliana to much a part of human life. There was a time when I doubted myself. But this is not so now, nor at this turning point of my project. For me, it was as follows...

Don't lose yourself in what it is you're supposed to do with the animals

Let them show you what it is you need to do

Listen with your inner ear

Take every movement, breath and intention you have mechanically become part of....

And let go of it

Become a canvas on which they can paint the scene

The picture will be nothing you expected

Expect the unexpected

One will find feeling, longings and desires suppressed by our own selves

The smallest first steps, breathe differently, really breathe.. blink slower, close your eyes

blindfold yourself, smell everything in front of you

Find the other senses which sleep

Gently will they come

This is the balance of what we do everyday and what we've forgotten how to do everyday

Once we admit to the forgotten, we grow.....by leaps and bounds

People always ask me how I exercise, how I keep in such shape. I do exactly what she takes me to do, the balance which occurs in me, is the inner exercise bodies were made for. To move as an animal. Our racing minds begin to relax, we click into another brain wave. Why do we torment ourselves so?

This is the higher life which the animals show us...everyday

We are not going anywhere

We have to learn how to be here first

So, people, today pick any animal to mimic, become that animal in every way and see the difference which instantly occurs in you. You won't be so heavy, you won't be so stressed. You just won't be you, sometimes that is what we all need...

Enjoy the animals, for they are the coolest creation of our creators. The best gift I ever found on this earth...

Juliana brought back blueprinted info from the jungles she roamed in. Little by little, every leaf, every stone, every sight, every sound, each encounter with each animal taught her the domain of life which was hers by birthright. She in turn was teaching me. For every species learns something different. Every individual animal has a personality which enables it to learn one thing or another. We help them overcome their fears. It is only their kingdom we need to teach them in, introduce them to, little by little. Mother nature does the rest.

I was learning the wild ones ways. I was learning the jungle. I was working with Mother Nature. I never knew a more powerful professor than her.

I am feeling the puma now.

I stand in the jungle, alone. I close my eyes in order to see. I inhale a breath deeper than the deepest dive in the ocean I ever made. I begin to smell, to smell so ever fully, catching any faint nuance of changes. Each molecule of air carries different scents, ever so slightly. I walk, I smell moisture, moss dampness, I know the rocks, stones are there. They have that smell. I feel the weight of the air, from winds, sun, rain, dew on my face. The earth ground smells rich. Pungent, dark, wet, endless.... It is always warm.

I step differently, no pattern, no mindless thought control of limbs forced to a rhythm which never changes in our day. You feel every muscle in you body as you move. You move like you never moved. You accomplish what you never thought......

I drink from running streams, laden with the heavy rains which come from the neighboring cloud forests and down below, the rainforest. Water that runs is alive. One can taste the difference. Water has a taste and a scent. A liquid smell of fresh color, ever fluid upon its entry into your senses. Your sense of smell grows. You add information to every part of your body, with each step you take. The music of the birds, the rushing stream, the sway of the branches, the whispers of the wind, are an orchestra for the senses. My head clears. I quiet the noisy mind. That which I carry, which at times seems so hard, melts away. I look at everything I am doing differently, without despair. We have but moments like this to give new energy to our thoughts and bodies. A time of renewal. Time to put away the daily grind which imprisons us.

I walked out of the jungle and is it just me or is the jungle cheering me on, content with the moment it was able to give to another living thing. Such is its power. Put on this earth for all to pull from whenever they need it.

Juliana returned in three days time. Alex was out picking mora berries which was good for she went straight to him. He got her back into her enclosure with no trouble. She was tired and wanted to sleep.

Alex then called me and let me know all was well. There was not a mark on her. I wondered again if she had bred. There was the slight possibility that upon receiving her brutal treatment at the hands of the poachers when I first found her, it could have been overlooked that damage to her vaginal opening had occurred also. Only by x-raying her could we be sure. I put this off though. I wasn't ready to know and it scared me.

We returned to our routines. I put on a small benefit in the city, in a club in Escazu called *Cafe Urbano*. The owner, Ignacio Cantos, was helping me raise some desperate funds for the project. It went off well, and even the president of our country, Figueres, was there. The parking lot and the adjoining streets were full. Everyone was in their finery. Jose came from La Marina with Marta. He looked so handsome in a suit. I had never seen him so well attired.

I dressed in a simple black yet elegant dress which clung sensuously to my long curves. My hair shone in a cascade of curls down my back. I walked in alone. I was a head turner. It was an evening of dining and dancing and much talk on the future of Costa Rica's wildlife. Champagne and Johnny Walker Blue poured all night long.

I met with two different ambassadors. All agreed we needed to do more. We were running out of time as a country, as part of the world. The clock, to me, had already started many years ago. Ticking... I was given hope... And those I saw had hope as well.

The meeting ran into the wee hours of the morning. The president's guards hailed me a cab to get home and I was asleep before my head hit the pillow.

The next morning I awoke to a very strong, very long earthquake with three aftershocks. It shook everything in my place. As I drove up to see the puma, I noticed a dry, deep pool bed which for as long as I could remember was just that. Now, however, it was filling with thick, phosphorous green water. Fluid matter from the volcanoes.

Earthquakes were a regular thing here, but of late everybody speculated when the next big one would blow. I wondered what the animals thought when they felt the earth shake. Alex said Juliana had gone into her underground den when it had shook. Little rain had fallen, which was unusual for this time of year. The Costarican's had a saying, "When it rains the earth will not shake."

A quake only occurs when it is dry and still. I looked to the sky and asked it to rain. The next day it rained for a week.

The last day of July, Carlos told me upon my next visit with the puma he had heard her screaming like nothing he had ever heard before. It was a dark, early evening. He went out to check on her as Alex was away for a few days and found nothing out of the ordinary.

He told me she had been doing this for the last three nights. Sounded like pain, sounded like fury. I went to her and asked her to communicate with me. She did. She was showing me there was another puma. This one was not a male. It was another female. I dreaded her first encounter with a wild female. Her fighting skills were not so strong. A full grown, wild puma fighting territory or a male could tear her apart.

All I could do was work her harder, plenty of physical exercise and feeding her more. I would have to wait till the day came when she would have to fight and hope that I was close by to be there on her return to address her wounds. It was an experience she had to make. I tried not to think of it too much.

I spent the next few days in the cabin with the dogs. They were now getting to the point where none of them wanted to play with her anymore. Indio was the only dog that was her friend. Mine just stayed their distance and put up with her solely because of me.

August 2000

The yearly procession to the magnificent church in Cartago
was underway. People walked to it from all over the country.
Young, old, everyone came. A miracle had happened here
many years ago and the tradition of this pilgrimage continued
every year since. It was something to see. This church to me
was the most beautiful in the country. I always went to watch.

Mitch called and told me he was coming back for a couple
weeks. It would be nice to see him. I got everything ready for
his return, made sure the place at the beach was ship shape.
I fetched him from the airport. He was loaded with supplies.
It was a nice warm welcome for both of us. The dogs went
berserk. I told Mitch not to wear any nice clothes for the dogs
were going to tackle him to the ground. They did, we laughed
so hard. We talked about everything. We had a serious talk
about the puma project. The following morning we woke
early to start the drive. We would first stop at the puma's for a
couple hours then proceed down to the beach place.

Mitch was anxious to see his land. Juliana was happy to see
him, she meowed like a house cat and nuzzled up against him.
He was going to take her for a walk. I was going to leave them
alone. They needed some time together.

Upon their return later that morning Mitch told me, she
had smelled the scent left by the male again. She had peed
on his spot and got up on her hind legs to smell a trunk of a
tree where he had left his scent. She rubbed on it for a time.
Mitch also noticed claw marks scratched into the tree trunk
from him. She followed his scent for an hour. At one point
he told me she smelled something and put her ears back, her
eyes burned a bright green and she was afraid. She growled
and was upset for a full twenty minutes. Mitch just stayed

calmly with her and spoke to her in soft tones. He said it was a strange different reaction he had never experienced with her. It was hard for her coming back. She didn't want to, but yet in the end she did, reluctantly.

The quetzals were there on his return. He was happy to see them. He said he so missed Costa Rica. He didn't like the States. He couldn't wait to finish the work and come home. Costa Rica had been his home since he was sixteen years old. I knew this separation from his world must be hard. From the wild jungles to the concrete jungles. Quite a culture shock especially for a man who was more animal than human anyway.

People always called us Tarzan and Jane. Everyone was happy to see us. They all hoped we might get back together again. What they didn't realize is that we were always together, in spirit and in soul. Our paths were taking us in different direction. Our split was not a bad thing, it was a movement of time given to each of us. Our spirits take us on journeys. Some journeys must be done alone. I truly believe this for all relationships I see. Even our relationships with our children or our animals.

Another earthquake, there were many this month. No trouble came from any of them. Thank God. We made it to the beach while it was still light. Mitch jumped into the ocean for a surf and I walked the beaches. Something unusual was happening. Pink, violet coral fans were growing off of each rock at a regular spot of mine called Roca Verde. This had never happened before. I wondered if the warming of the earth, globally was having an effect on everything. The month ended quickly and Mitch returned to the States......

September 2000

Another huge earthquake shook the cabin. It was a freaky time for earthquakes to occur, in the middle of rainy season. I slipped into my clothes and went to check on the puma. As I started my descent I made my usual call to her, no response.

I ran up the hill, caught my breath and looked around. Something was wrong. I did not see her at all.

I half jumped half leaped the remainder of the downhill run to her pen. She most definitely was not in there. I walked around the enclosure looking for possible openings.

There it was. A huge dug out hole. She had again escaped. It wasn't the usual time for the male to be about. I wondered if the quake had anything to do with it. No, she wouldn't have dug out to go run and hide, she would have gone into her underground hideaway.

I went to Carlos' house. He told me he could help for a bit but that Alex had gone into San Isidro with his mother for supplies. They would be back late in the day. We didn't know if Juliana had been out all night. She was for sure going to something, otherwise she would have come to the cabin where I had been all night. The dogs were with me and they would have alerted me to her being about if she had come close to the cabin.

I was a little worried. Carlos went to check on the spot where Juliana usually came down from the mountain. I followed her trail from the pen. I picked up her tracks a short distance away. She had taken a different road this time. I called her. Nothing. I sat and sent her a message, then walked about. As I jumped across a stream, my tail, so to speak, twitched. A reaction to something around. I slowly turned and there she was.

Something was different about her, she was not so bouncy like she is when she comes upon me. She didn't even stalk me, which she does in play. She let out a soft whimper. She was hurt and then I saw where. A deep hole showed on her right leg just above the paw. It was red, bleeding and angry looking. I baby talked to her, she finally came close. I had no leash. Hoping she would follow, I walked back.

She limped severely. She followed me slowly back, stopping periodically to lick her wound. I got her into the pen and then Carlos showed back up. She didn't want to see him for some reason, more than likely it was the pain she was in. She just wanted me at those times, like a child wants only their mother when they have a boboo.

Carlos changed the hay in her bedding so it was fresh and clean. I stroked her gently. She was okay about me touching the paw. I needed some help but without Alex I would have to try and dress the wound on my own. Carlos went to the cabin and got my medicine bag.

I cleaned it with a liquid which was equal parts water and a 35% food grade hydrogen peroxide. This is a very strong brew. One must use care when administering so as not to burn the delicate ripped skin. As I poured, she was relatively still except for a few twitches with her paw as the water ran down it.

It did not look infected, but it was a huge hole. The opening would have to be closed. I remembered watching the indigenous people work with cobwebs to close a wound and act like a stitch. I found plenty of cobwebs. I never brushed them off. I liked spiders and thought their webs works of art. I created quite a bandage with them and remained with Juliana till she was quiet enough not to fuss with the dressing. She finally slept.

At first Carlos had wondered if the wound was from a gunshot. It was such a perfect hole. I told him it had not gone completely through. I guessed it to be a bite. But whether from the male or a fight with a female I knew not.

I received my answer a few days later. Her wound was healing nicely. I was adding more foliage to her pen and the wind blew the door open. Juliana noticed immediately and I watched, thinking she is going too bound out in a flash. She didn't. This was odd; she always took any chance to go out in the forest and play. I shut the door. When a week had gone by I decided to take her for a walk. She had been in, for the duration time so the paw could mend.

We made it to the outskirts of the mountain when she wanted to come back in. This was not like her. She growled, a territorial sound, letting some other animal know this was her domain. So that's what it had been. She had her first encounter with the female. I was just thankful the wounds were not worse.

Now I had to heal the fear in her. She had to go back and face the jungle. Alex and I both took her. She was better. After the second time she was her normal self again. Perhaps the female had moved on. Even though the mountains were full of pumas, they rarely came into the boundaries of the houses and farms in this area. They never attacked their domestic livestock

One day, a delightful girl named Morningstar visited us. She had lived her entire life with her family inside the mountains. They were about an hour's walk from our cabin. Her mother and father were originally from Canada. They had settled here and raised their two children.

Morningstar told me there were plenty of pumas around her area all the time. In fact they had a small herd of goats, twenty to be exact. She told us, one by one the pumas had taken them. All but two were left.

I asked if this angered her and her family.

She tossed back her strawberry blonde hair and said, "We love the wildlife. We look at it as sharing our food. The last two goats are now kept close to the house and not one puma comes to take them."

I was glad to hear this. This family were Carlos' friends and he later told me theywere extraordinary people. I planned a visit them with Carlos the next week. They knew the pumas better than anyone in these parts. Carlos, Alex, and I mended and fortified Juliana's pen. The entire perimeter had an under earth cover of mayo, a type of fence material to discourage further diggings.

At days' end I headed back to the city. I was working on a new type of healing for dolphins and whales. My mentor in life whom I met while I was living in Los Angeles, prior to moving to Costa Rica was helping me. His name was Oded. He did monumental things with body works. He is one of the most diverse healers I know. He is always searching the horizons. He had been working with vibrational frequencies for some years now.

As I was driving back to the city he called me. What a surprise, it had been so very long since I had spoken with him. He was presently in El Hod, Israel.

I pulled the truck over to have a long overdue chat with him. We swapped stories of our lives then he asked me if I had seen the work being done with frequency. I told him I had little knowledge of it but was aware of its existence. He sent me an amulet of ocean water vibrated with the frequency of a star. He had worn it around his neck for the past year. With it came vital information on the vibrational waters.

Everything in life has a frequency it lives on. Even bacteria and disease. The balance of any disease in the body can be eradicated by its positive frequency. This would be a remarkable way to work with sea life. The frequency of anything can be transmitted into water. Water is a carrier. Much the same as a homeopathic remedy is designed and formed. One can empower water. It heals what it comes in contact with.

This method was brilliant and years later was tested at a Caribbean marine life center. The results were highly successful. I created vibrational waters from the strong positive elements of the jungle. Those enlightened with the practice released healing waters all over the world. Oded took it one step further and worked with children that had aids. He made miracles.....

Another twist on the subject is that like the vibrational frequency boundary we wanted to set up for project jaguar, which would keep the cats away from cattle, I also knew that the same principal could ring true for dolphins, keeping them away from tuna nets. We have the ability to do this. Now we just need the will of the people.

I got a telephone call from Juan Carlos. He had just returned from the Borneo challenge. He came in 28th. It was a major accomplishment. I cheered gleefully and he modestly excepted the praise. It was a wow...We planned on meeting at the puma's next weekend.

That night I experienced my first tornado. I never knew we had them in Costa Rica. First a beautiful light shone through the clouds, then a fantastic storm of water erupted into a tornado of rain and wind. I felt the circle of energy coming from

this storm all through my body. It was electrifying. We lost a
few rooftops in the local vicinity but that was all.

Oded was sending me a teenage couple, friends from Isreal
who were interested in seeing Costa Rica. Their names were
Rory and Naama. I picked them up the next day. They were
carefree and easy. They brought me delicious olive oil, like
none I had ever tasted before. *Mmmm rico.* Rory's mother, who
was an artist working with silver, made me a beautiful bracelet
which I still wear today. I swear it protects me.

I decided to take them up to the puma. They were very excited. It would be nice for Juliana to met some beautiful children. The day was spectacular, the drive showed us all of the
weather patterns of our country, from rains to clouds to fog,
to radiant sunshine. The mountains were blue. As I rounded
a bend in the road, a beautiful sleek long black cat leaped the
entire breadth of the road. This type of panther in our country is very rarely seen. It was a seductive sight. I had always
wanted to work with this cat . Maybe some day I would get
my chance.

We got to the cabin and I suggested a walk in the jungle
with the puma. The kids were elated. I had never done this
with anyone else but I felt it would be just fine. These kids had
a great energy and perhaps they would take home a memory
of something beautiful that needed to be known by the whole
world.

Juliana loved Rory and Naama instantly. She had such a
way with people. She always left them breathless. Maybe I
thought her purpose in life was just that, to teach the people.
Maybe she wasn't meant to be free, and maybe there was a
way she could be both. The kids loved walking with her. Their
excitement was contagious. Just like one of them, Juliana was

playing along. At one point though we came upon a huge tree which had fallen from the high winds that blow through at this time of year.

Juliana forgot I was on the other end of the leash in her excitement of the walk. She made a giant leap and cleverly avoided the downslide hill on the other side of the fallen tree. I however, did not. I flew into the air and over the tree limb from her great force, then was dragged for a full five minutes before I could scream out to her to stop.

She stopped immediately and looked at me dumfounded. She honestly had forgotten I was on the other end. My right arm felt like it had been pulled completely out of its socket.

The kids laughed hysterically. They said that the expressions on both of our faces were truly a sight to behold.

They said, "Do you two know that you both read each other's mind in split second timing?"

I never looked at it that way. I let out a small groan as I unwrapped the leash from my arm. I never wrap the leash around my arm, thus if something like this happens which it has in the past, for a puma mores differently than a human, I could just let go of the leash and not get dragged or pulled. I was keeping a tighter rein on her this time just because we had the kids to think about.

When hearing my moan, Juliana came over to me with a look of worry. She cared about me. So cute I said. Then I felt the pain again and wanted to smack her. But I didn't. I just hugged her hard. She then did something she had not done in ages, not since she was a cub, she kissed me. She actually puts her mouth on mine and softly kisses. I taught her this just once and she never forgot. She not only knows what to do, but when to do it and for why, thus again proving the minds of animals are just like ours.

The kids helped me get her back . We fished for trout, then we all headed down to the beach. The kids stayed the remainder of the visit at our beach place. They couldn't stop talking about the puma.

It was nice being with them. I felt like they were my own. When it was time for them to go, we all cried and hugged. I sent treasures from the jungles for Oded.

Back in San Jose, I had a new worry. Lobo was not doing well again. I felt like I was missing something going on with him. I consented to have all tests and x-rays done of his insides. The results were terrible. He had cancer of the prostate and intestines. Villalobos said it was pretty extensive, he had to have had it for a long time. He was amazed Lobo wasn't dead or worse sick. I knew it was from the herbs I had him on.

So now I had to work with cancer. Joel Hyman had a proven formula for cancer, however, one needed to catch it in time. I sent off hair samples express mail and left Lobo at Villalobos clinic. He wanted to try some of his own medicines.

I didn't want to lose Lobo. I would try anything. Lobo howled every night for me. Villalobos said it would be easier on him if I stayed away this week. After the fifth day, I could take it no more. I had to go and see him. When I arrived I almost got sick. Lobo was laying in a bed of hay. He was so thin. You could count all his ribs. No muscle tone, labored breathing, his gums were white. As he tried to get up to greet me he toppled over. He was so weak he could not even let out a bark, a sound.

He had too many drugs in his body. I went to the ground with him. I held him tight and cried into his coat. I carried him to the truck and laid him in the front seat with me. I went back to the clinic and told the secretary to tell Villalobos I was taking him home. I left a note thanking him for trying and paid the bill. I slowly drove home. I set up a bed for him next to mine. I went out and bought him fresh ground meat mixed it with milk and honey. He devoured it, then slept. The herbs had come in from Joel. He told me to try, but he didn't know if it was too late. Now I had to deal with getting the herbs out of customs.

I needed them now and knew I would be in for the usual run-around for getting things out of the airport customs. I took a number and waited two hours for my turn. It was agony waiting. After filling out mountains of paperwork I was told I could come back tomorrow and fetch the package. I said I wasn't leaving. I asked for the head person in charge. It was a woman. I pleaded my case with her, I told her I would take her to my house to see how sick my dog was if she didn't believe me. She looked at me. I looked at her. She was a beautiful woman. She was from the Caribbean side. Her skin a mulatto color like a bronzed statue. She also had the most exquisite emeralds draped on her arms and neck. She stood up.

"We are closing in five minutes," she said. "Let me go get them for you."

My eyes softened and a sigh of relief escaped my lips. Minutes later I had the precious herbs in my hands. As she handed them to me she also handed me her card.

"If you ever need anything, you come straight to me," she said.

I kissed her and flew out the door. When I reached the apartment Lobo wanted to go out. I let him out. All the food I had just given him came out of him like water. I gave him the herbs and settled in for the night with him. I fed him small portions at half hour intervals. As it got time to go to bed I started to meditate. What was the answer to this?

Spirit my wolf came into my meditation. I don't know why, I could not tell. Then Lobo came over and gently nuzzled me. He communicated with me. He said that he felt I was angry and disappointed with him because he was not strong for me. His physical problems seem a burden on me. That's why I left him at the clinic. I wanted him no more.

I cried. I told him it was the farthest thing from the truth. I told him how sorry I was for making him feel this way. He had the strongest spirit and will to survive.

He knew he had to be my male in Mitch's absence. He told me he trusted me. He told me he had seen me do miracles on other animals and he knew I would cure him too. Or, he said, do you want me to go and I don't understand where I am going.

It took all my strength not to cry to the heavens just then. But I held the tears back. I needed to be strong for him now. I wrapped my arms around him and slept the whole night like this.

Mitch called the next night and talked with Lobo. Lobo's tail wagged at hearing his voice and he let out a weak bark. She-Dog came to the phone and barked at him too. I wished so much right now we were all together. I did shamanic healings on this brave animal. I saw him as a Indian warrior in past lives. I saw beautiful things about this one. Alycia, Kattia and Iala helped me through this time.

It took a long time for Lobo to get better. He was never one hundred percent, but the vet said it was a miracle he was at all. I could not put him down. I just couldn't. He needed a lot of care but I was o.k. with that. He was worth it.

Alex called and wondered when I would be back again. It had been two weeks. The puma was well. Only a small opening was left where her wound was, but she was licking it too much and kept opening it. She was also pulling her hair out again.

I had a meeting at the zoo the next day about jaguars and the upcoming convention which was hosted this year in Costa Rica. I told Alex I would come right after that. The meeting at the zoo went well. It seems like project jaguar was expanding its ideas to other countries. Brazil and Mexico were very interested in my ideas. I was to give a forum at the convention.

Memo called that evening and asked when we would be able to see each other again. He knew I had a busy schedule. I asked him to come up to the puma with me the next day.

He said yes. Good, I wouldn't have to drive. I was tired of driving. I recall a statement Christine Crawford had made one night when I had the puma at her house. I asked her if she won a million dollars tonight (we were playing the Florida state lottery at this time) what would she buy first?

She replied, "A chauffeur." She hated to drive.

I laugh to myself as I remember her comment. Now I knew how she felt. Memo picked me up and drove. I slept in his lap the whole time. I guess I was more tired than I realized.

When we arrived, Juliana called out to me even before I did. She so missed me. I put cajuput oil on her wound. This is a highly effective, rare to find oil. It comes from Indonesia. It heals and disinfects completely. It also does not have a good taste so the puma would not lick the area anymore. With the help of Alex, I put some on her tail. It was reddening from her constant licking.

She wasn't too happy with me at this. I rewarded her good behavior with a rabbit. I walked to the truck with Alex to go over some plans. Memo stayed by Juliana to watch her game with the rabbit. Afterwards I asked him if she said anything to him jokingly.

He said, "As a matter of fact she did." He said she was saying, "Watch this," as she pounced, attacked and plaid with the rabbit.

He took me then to the beach to check on the house. We spent the night, and then drove back at dawn to the city. Our relationship was odd, but we both understood each other and never asked anything of the other, the time we had with each other was the time we had.

At month's end, I met with Juan Carlos. We had a meeting about the puma. He wanted to incorporate her into a project with his students. If we were not going to release her, we could give her an enormous piece of land on which to roam and make treetop stations from which students could safely observe her. They wouldn't disturb her and night vision binoculars would be provided to see her at night. It would be just like observing in the wilds. The area would even be made so she could interact with the male.

We all needed to think on this plan. I wasn't fully ready to abandon my idea to release her. I knew she was capable of being free, it was just a matter of when. I knew it would be her decision. I knew one day she would tell me she was ready. In the meantime, maybe it was not a bad idea to give her to others to learn from. I could even set up seminars and teach animal communication. We decided to make the decision by the end of the rainy season. Everyone was in agreement and we would contact Jose Rojas.

Construction was better attempted without the rains and muds. I also had to come up with money. Juan Carlos had friends who were willing to help with the materials needed at wholesale price. Able manpower was also available.

The month ended on that note...

October 2000

Jose had some time to meet with me. He told me to take a break and come to Tabacon, where he was cutting and bailing hay for a farmer. Tabacon is a spa tourist lodge located at the Arenal volcano. It is one of my favorite spots in the country to unwind. It houses natural pools of hot springs set amongst the jungles, with a spectacular view of the volcano as it erupts every night. Sitting in those springs melts away every ache and pain. It's great stress therapy.

I cheerfully accepted. I met him at Lake Arenal. It is a beautiful lake and a favorite spot of windsurfers as it has wind all the time. I spotted Jose riding his new Holland tractor. I wanted to ride on the tractor. I parked out of sight and snuck up on him. Stalking him like a lioness out on the plains of the African bush I was ready to pounce. The loud noise of the tractor made it easy. I scared the shit out of him as I jumped up on the machine. I was laughing , as I kissed him on the cheek. We spent the next hours playing . We were kids again. We both needed it. Tumbling through the straw cut grasses we rolled into each other and found ourselves in a compromising position. We should have held back but we didn't. Something very natural, very primitive was running through our blood. I was breathing loud and heavy, he was breathless. We gave in, we became one, amongst the thunder of the volcano we made love. It did not take us by surprise, it felt natural and right.

Afterwards we looked at the sky and breathed ourselves back to normal. In one mighty jump he landed upright and swung his long thick leg onto the tractor. I didn't move I just smiled up at him. He started the engine and I very slowly, very contently, joined him. We dressed each other and rode in silence to finish plowing the field.

At dusk he was done and pulled the tractor off of the field and parked. He split open a coconut from the back of his truck and we took turns drinking deeply of its nectar. We talked of animals. Jose told me that my idea for Juliana was what he wanted to do with several of his animals at the zoological station.

We talked about our dream of turning La Marina into an animal kingdom. I told him I wish I had more time on my hands, he said the same. I really needed to find someone with capital interested in our ideas.

I spent the night, most of it in the thermal pools. I felt like jello when I finally crawled out of the waters. I watched this mighty volcano begin her eruption. First the smoke from the cone shape top seeps out into the jungle tops. Then rivers of red blazing lava ran down her sides, carving everything in its path, glowing heat. I finally went to my hotel room and slept like a baby.

I woke at dawn and stood outside my door to listen to the volcano. It breathes, heavy and hard throughout the days. Like a heartbeat. I felt it come up through my legs, moving the heat inside of me. The energy it possesses bears respect. It was hard to leave.

I spent the rest of the week with Derek, who was a whiz on the computer, creating a computer disk of the dream we had for La Marina .

Lobo was always by my side. Fury was getting jealous of the attention I gave him, so I took some special time with her. She loved to chase bugs. She would stomp on the grasses to bring them out so she could see them better. I swear she was an entomologist.

That week, with my disk in hand, I went to meet Mario Sotela. He was a Costa Rican man with means, had done films in Hollywood and owned a television station. The appointment took place at his home in Escazu, a statuesque place. It used to be the home of the president when in office.

I knocked, no answer. I called out, still nothing. I pushed the already open door all the way and went in. Mario was walking down the magnificent spiral staircase, which looked like something out of Gone With the Wind. We were like twins, dressed in white button down shirts, blue jeans and black boots.

I said nothing, I watched him come down the stairs. He stared at me the whole flight down. If he was trying to make me feel uneasy, it wasn't working. I was used to this.

By the looks of him, so was he. He put out his hand and I mine. Then he spoke, "So you are lluvia salvaje?"

I took a deep breath and exhaled. "You are Mario Sotela."

He didn't know what to think of me. He was intimidated? taken aback? I knew I wasn't what he had expected. For a moment I thought, should I play this out, like something out of his films? then Jose came into my head and I thought, no, I will be Jose right now.

As if it was my house, I asked him to sit.

We sat. I first asked him the question I had foremost on my mind. There were rumors he was creating his own animal park. I asked him what he was up to.

He told me he was working on a personal project which would be a park of sorts, a private park. He had a piece of land close to Liberia, which is located north of Punteranes. It was a dry, arid area. He was planning on having African animals there. No carnivores, like lions and such. Just docile animals. Little did he know that fighting over territory or a mate will make any species roar. I asked him why, being a Costa Rican would he not put his efforts into saving the wildlife of his own country. I continued to state that putting African animals in a tropical climate was not to their advantage. Immune system changes were bound to lead to health problems. Skin problems and a new array of parasites would also be a concern. Not to mention the special type of grasses that may or may not be able to grow in Costa Rica. I was being blunt, but I didn't want to beat around the bush. I had precious little time to waste as it was. I showed him La Marina's project disk.

He was impressed by my presentation. I did a good job, if I say so myself. He wanted to take a little bit of the fight out of me.

He said, "Do you want to know why? Why I am doing my project? Because in a way I am just like you. I love wild life. I was in Texas a year ago. I came upon a herd of elephants so bunched together they could not move in any direction. They had blisters from the cold on their hides."

He asked the ranch owner what was he doing, the owner replied, "Oh, don't worry about the beasts, they will be dead by week's end."

They were part of an absurd, cruel hunting park, arranged for hunters to get their rocks off shooting them as trophies.

"And all this is legal." Mario continued. "I bought every last one of them. That is when I decided to make my park." As I heard this I went sick inside. What fashion of men could ever derive pleasure from such insanity. I sucked in my biting remarks on men. I realized not all are cut from the same cloth.

I smiled at him. He looked at my project again and said, "There might be a way to incorporate both."

He told me for the last year he had been growing the savannah grasses necessary for the species he wished to care for. They were doing well, because for most of the year Liberia had similar weather to Africa. He had also finished the perimeter fencing. He asked if I would like to see the place. He said we could fly with his helicopter.

I love helicopters. I said, "When do we go?" "Tomorrow," he said.

I left the disk and warmly shook his hand. If nothing else, there was somebody else out there doing crazy things like me.

The trip by helicopter was short. His creation was a wildlife paradise. It was done right, lots of money and professionals. A magnificent waterfall was located on the property, which he told me is why he bought this piece of land in the first place. It flowed thick all year long. Most waterfalls shrink to half their size during the dry season. Not this one. It created a sub-climate in the interior of the land. He had a mansion built right on top of it. It was first class all the way.

We walked around the whole property and talked. I learned that he did not know much about animals, but he loved and respected them, and he had the money to help them. His heart was in the right place. He took me on a tour with the helicopter . It was glorious. We flew home with a million different ideas racing through our heads.

At the end of the day he turned to me and said, "I want to help with what you're doing. Give me some time to sort things out."

He also asked if I would be part of managing the park. He liked all my various experiences with animals.

I told him, "We'll see. First things first."

Midmonth I received an invitation to attend a party bash in Los Angeles. It was a celebrity gala to support animal causes. I would have loved to go. It was a chance to present my project . But I was committed to another cause here.

I called Mitch in California and asked him if he would go in my place. Mitch didn't like crowds and having to talk to someone about fund raising, was not his cup of tea.

But he said yes, he would go.

I made it easy for him. I sent him disks of my project and a written summary. I told him to act like his Tarzan self and he would be a big hit. I told him jokingly, "Hey, maybe you'll find a girlfriend?"

He said, "I already have one." Oh, oops.

He went and had a great time. People were very receptive to him and asked all sorts of questions about Costa Rica. They even asked about surfing. Mitch must have loved that. He took lots of pictures for me with a throw-away camera. I smiled thinking of the picture he must have made. I asked him if he wore shoes. He never did.

He said, "Of course I did."

Then we both started laughing on the phone. He asked about Lobo.

I told him he was o.k. But I knew that we hadn't gotten all the cancer. I was just hanging on to him for as long as I could.

Mitch felt bad I was going this alone with Lobo. He had some surfer friends bring me a care package with little things he knew I loved, Island also added a few things.

He and Island spent time together which was good. They really loved each other.

I had to hang up, the phone bills were always enormous.

Time to see the puma. My visits to her were less frequent. I was planning that on purpose. Juliana was fine. She went wild seeing me. She was so very affectionate. I had to pry her off of me at times.

The male had been back around, Alex said. She had been rolling on his scent during the last walk with her.

The rains were heavy now. We had sun only until 10:30 in the morning. Then it rained into the night. Carlos and Alex told me to take some time off. They were home all the time now and Juliana, like everyone else, spent the time mostly inside. Not much to do for the next six weeks.

What I didn't know is that Mitch had called Carlos and asked him if it was okay for me to come to the States. He had gotten me a ticket and wanted it to be a surprise. Carlos told me, "It would do you and the puma good to be separated for a while."

I looked at him oddly. I knew something was up. I told him, "Thanks, I will think about it."

It would do me some good to take a break from everything.

When I got home a message on my machine from our local travel agent Guido, told me he had a ticket for me, to Los Angeles, waiting at his office.

I called Mitch. He said, "Just come Julie, and don't worry about anything else."

He had already secured someone to take care of the farm. He told me Island really missed me.

I missed her so much it hurt. I said yes. "Give me a couple of days to get everything ready."

I hung up and finally let go enough to get excited. Time to get out of the rain,

even though two weeks later I would be missing it again. It was always like that when I left this country. Costa Rica will always be in my heart.

I called my friends to let them know. Everyone thought it was just what I needed. Alycia and her daughter and Mariella, three wonderful power women, were on a journey themselves at this time.

They healed horses merely by touch. Alycia had used reiki on a horse getting ready to be put down. He had been lame for two years and nothing helped. Alycia not only had him walking but kicking as well after the healing.

I went riding with them. Every horse I saw was alive because of her. She truly is an inspiring woman. They all were. I learned so much from these women. Even Alycia's son Mauricio was a wizard. They are one of the most united families I have ever met.

I rode a beautiful red mare. She was thin, sleek, long-maned, and wildly spirited. It was good to run with the wind. We rode until dusk, then I kissed them all good bye and was on my way.

I planned to drive up to say good bye to the puma and bring some herbs in case anything should go wrong. I had schooled

Alex right from the beginning on all the herbs which I worked with.

But when I arrived home, everything changed.

Lobo was terrible. He was in such pain. No food was staying down. The cancer in the intestines caused them to stop functioning. They were rotting away. No matter how he ate, he was too thin. He didn't receive enough nutrition long enough to do any good. He looked at me with strong direct eyes. His eyes throughout the torment of his illness were pillars of strength.

I had to put him down. I knew he didn't want to go. It was the hardest decision I ever had to make in my life. I could not leave him like this and go to the States.

I called Kattia and Iala. Iala was in town for Loba was sick. She had something similar going on in her intestines. Iala was working with Dr. Bitters. When I went to the States, she wanted me to see Joel and give him Loba's hair sample for help with her problem.

Iala said it was best that Lobo not suffer any more. Kattia said the same. I just didn't know how to tell Lobo. When I tried later that night he cried, like I never heard an animal cry.

It tore me to pieces. I spent the whole night howling at the moon, cursing the gods for putting me in this situation. I stopped eating. I finally made the decision to do it. Iala and Kattia were with me. They communicated with him, for on that day I could not.

He didn't want to go, then finally he agreed. Upon that agreement he took my heart. We went up to Los Alpes and ceremonially helped him pass to the other world. We buried him with Spirit. We knew he would come back to us in some form again. He told me he was forever by my side. I was never alone he said. He is running with spirit. Wolf to wolf.

It was the worst thing I ever had to do. Lobo and I had a bond that time cannot steal. I cried not that day but I cried uncontrollably the next days. I took no calls.

Alycia came over. She said nothing, she just healed my pain. Alycia laid her hands over me. The warm energy flowed strongly out of them into me. It was filling the cold empty spot that I knew would stay inside of me for many years to come. I fell asleep. She left without a word. Fury stayed by me the whole time. I ignored her. She understood. Then I looked at her and knew she too had pain. Lobo was her family.

I pulled her to me and begged her forgiveness. She gently put her paw on my shoulder. I cried again till I fell asleep that night. Fury watched over me and never moved.

The next day I sent Alex the herbs he might need. I didn't want to go and see Juliana. I was too distraught.

Alex understood. He wished me good luck on my trip.

I told him I would call him when I landed in Los Angeles. I gave him Mitch's telephone number, told him to call if there was anything. He told me lightly that they would all be hibernating through the rainy season. He made me smile.

I hung up and felt guilty, then shrugged off the feeling and packed my bags. At the last minute, I decided to take Fury and surprise Mitch and She-Dog. Villalobos got the paperwork for me in hours. He felt sorry for me.

On October 16, I flew to Los Angeles. On the plane ride the movie was, I dream of Africa, with Kim Basinger, who I love. Great movie, but it depressed me. I feel the same about Costa Rica. I thought of Lobo, of burring him, of digging the grave myself. I cried again and then just dropped off to sleep. I woke as we were landing.

Customs was easy for once, and I had Fury out and about even before Mitch arrived. He had She-Dog with him. It was a joyous reunion between mother and daughter.

Mitch looked at me. Where's Lobo? I hadn't told him.

I couldn't answer him. I just let tears roll down my face. He held me close. We cried together over the lost of part of our family. We were lost there too for a while.

It was Fury and She-Dog that helped us. Fury went to him and She-Dog went to me. They healed us both during this time. They truly are angels.

One thing I learned was that not only can animals bring you to being...the now... they can take you away from it too...

Both the dogs did this without us having to know. They were working on both of us. The remarkable ability to pull one out of grief belongs to the animals. They make us see that life does go on... They can show you the other side... You look into their eyes, heir's carries you away.

You cry more then, they make you release first, they empty the void, the pain inside. Then, like a warm fire's glow, their deep soulful eyes, light your soul and carry your heart. Time doesn't heal wounds, love does... These dogs were the purest form of love. Animals' love is unconditional to those willing to accept it. No greater powers exist.

I stayed in Los Angeles till after my daughter's birthday which was November 5. I did mommy time with her. We had a wonderful visit. She was growing up so fast. She was turning into a very special girl. Where I had a drive to save animals, she had the same driven notions to help the homeless. She worked in a shelter in Santa Barbara and the homeless swore she was an angel who had descended upon them. I was very proud of my little pumpkin, as I called her...

I called and checked in with Alex almost everyday. Things were fine, nothing new to report. It was a time of quiet for the people of Amistad. I petitioned different people in the hopes of raising funds for my project. Things were coming together. It seemed our dream might become a reality. Everyone I had met on my last visit concerning funding was planning a schedule to include Costa Rica's wildlife.

We marched on in our causes for the wild ones. I had renewed hopes one more time.

Benefits took time and a lot of work. Most of the people I approached had heavy schedules. At this time next year, we were going to throw the benefit of the year. We would decide the where at a later date. It was possible we could do one in Los Angeles and then one in Costa Rica. The list of celebrities was growing. A lot of people cared and were willing to dedicate their time and efforts. Tippy and Martine were the ring leaders they were experts at raising consciousness and money.

I called Jose and told him what was happening. He was elated. He was doing a little renovating of his park. He asked me if I could bring him a few things from the States. I went shopping for him and the Solano family.

Then it was time to return. We decided Fury would stay with Mitch. It would be better for them, and I could manage on my own. I said my good byes and was on my way.

November 2000

It was the tenth of November. The rains were heavy. I felt weird. one part of me was glad to be home, one part of me wished I was back in California. I had hundreds of phone calls to return.

I called Alex and told him to expect me the next day. I sat on my bed and cuddled with Africa. She talked my ears off. She had missed me so. My neighbors had taken good care of her. She purred me to sleep that night.

It was still rainy when I woke the next morning. I packed the car with the gifts

and supplies for the Solano family, stopped by at the butcher's to pick up a half portion of a lamb. He was so happy to see me, he gifted it to me. I kissed him for it and was on my way. I couldn't wait to see Juliana.

The drive was slow as the weather was nasty and the rains were coming down hard. Few people were on the roads. As I climbed higher and higher up the mountains the air changed to a brisk blow. This was that time of the year the Chirripo mountain has huge long icicles hanging off it. One would think it would snow. But Costa Rica never gets snow. However one freaky year, long ago, it did snow in San Jose. That must have been a sight. I couldn't even imagine it.

I finally pulled off the main highway onto the dirt road to Amistad. They had done some patchwork of concrete on this road as the rains were playing havoc with its run off. Alex was waiting for me at the gates of Cuerici. He had a huge smile on his face. He missed me he said, and we hugged each other. Alex asked if I wanted to go down to the house first and wait out the rain storm. I told him thanks but no, I was anxious to see my other little girl.

I ran, slipped and slid in the mud to the puma. I called her. She returned my call with surprise. She was happy and relived to see me. She didn't know if I was ever coming back.

"Silly girl," I said, "I will always come back to you...."

I entered her cage and she went crazy. She was loving me, then attacking me. She was happy I had returned and mad that I had gone. Alex had to help me get back out of the cage.

I gave her a huge chunk of the lamb and went down with Alex to their house. It was a warm family welcome. They loved their gifts. We talked of what I had planned in Los Angeles. Everyone was excited about it.

The rains let off around midday. I had to leave and continued to the beach to check on the place. It was a muddy drive to the property. Things were o.k. Not much one could do about the mud and ever-present moisture. Mold was growing everywhere. I cleaned up as best as I could. Hoped for a little sunshine to dry things out and fell on the bed to sleep.

My friend Carol had come down to visit me. She lived in San Isidro. She too was from California and her kids, Casey and Terry, were school friends of Island's when she was growing up down here. Carol and I talked of California. We had dinner together and I slept at her house as it was closer for my morning drive to the city.

On my way into the city, I stopped in Cartago to see Memo. I had a small gift for him. It was nice seeing him again. We had lunch together and just enjoyed a smoke and some good conversation. He was leaving for Nicaragua the next day for a couple of weeks.

It looked like we were always missing each other. That was our relationship. A group of my friends got together with me that night and we took in a movie.

I called Mitch before I went to bed and spoke with Fury. She wouldn't stop barking at me. I felt homesick again. But I was home, I said to myself and dropped off to sleep.

The next day I got a surprise visit from Jose. He was in the city with his family for a get together. He had three days. He wanted to go up and see the puma.

So the following day we went back out. The winds up there that day were

monstrous. Everything was moving. Juliana was scared of all this. She didn't want to come out of her den. She had been chewing her tail again. Nervously.

Jose was astonished by the puma. He gave her a proud papa smile and talked to her in Spanish for a long time. Juliana listened from a distance and ran in circles. She snuck up on him and smelled him. He just remained still.

It really started to pour, so we said adios to her. The Solano family gave us a delicious meal of fresh trout and Jose took a bunch home with him for the family. Trout was a treat for them. On the other hand, Alex was so sick of eating trout he rarely wanted it.

I laughed at him. "You want some meat don't you?"

Jose invited the family out to La Marina. Carlos and Alex were dying to go. Since it was a slow time of work because of the rain, we planned the trip for the next week.

The drive home was brutal, the winds were gale force and we saw huge massive trees tumble down like twigs. As wild as the winds were, the following morning I woke to a perfect rainbow. Unpredictable, that's what mother nature is.

Juan Carlos had called. He wanted to do a Thanksgiving at the puma's with his family. He asked if I would help, I said I would love to. I would cook the turkey at my apartment and ride up with Juan Carlos. That Thanksgiving, as we ate the scrumptious dinner, another rainbow appeared. These Costa Ricans shared the American tradition of Thanksgiving for the first time. They loved it. They were amazed I could cook so well. I guess most thought I was not very domestic. They thought all I ate was chocolate candy bars and gallons of milk. Chocolate and milk were an addiction with me.

We ate till we couldn't move. The next morning I took the family members to see Juliana. She was a show-off. She did acrobatic leaps and random stalkings for everyone to see. Then she sat like a queen and let them admire her. She looked like a model poising for a cover of a magazine. She made cute bird like squeaks and enjoyed the attention thoroughly. The visitors told me they had never seen an animal in captivity so happy, so full of spirit. One could tell she loved the world she lived in.

Juan Carlos' daughter Stephanie idolized me. She loved animals and wanted to be just like me when she grew up. She was keenly interested in animal communication and wanted to get started right away. She told me she already had animals talking to her. I gave her a list of books to read and told her I would help her. We then piled into the cars and went back to the city.

I had to prepare my speech for the jaguar convention coming up. Jose wanted to start working with jaguars. We were to meet the people who were jaguar specialist from around the world. The convention was to take place at Simon Bolivar Zoo. Yolanda was pushing to save face to the animal world. By the end of the month I was ready.

December 2000

Our summer started. The rains were diminishing. Flowers bloomed again. Millions of butterflies were out. Juan Carlos had an exhibition of his art work. He specialized in photographing the great mountains of Costa Rica. He had the ability to capture nature as I have never seen in a photo. The pictures were alive. In one photo of the cloud forest I could actually feel the mists on my face.

Jose would be in the city that night. I asked him to come with me. I dressed to the nines for the event.

When Jose came to pick me up, he let out a long whistle. "Damn", he said, "You sure clean up good."

Even Juan Carlos took a step back. From tom boy to lady. I flirted madly with them.

Jose was very protective of the men folk surrounding me. "Don't want you getting in any trouble," he chuckled.

The exhibition was beautiful. If I had the money I would have purchased some of the photos. The evening ended late.

Jose took me home. He bent ¨down to kiss me. I accepted, then we felt weird and pulled away. Wasn't right to start a flame with him. I loved him in a way I will always love him. Two people with the same hopes and dreams. Two people taking a moment out from the chaos of our worlds. If only things could have been different I wouldn't have hesitated with this moment.

He would be back in the city at week's end for the convention. The week flew by and we were together again. We were back to our normal selves. Those who knew us could sense our desires. These we kept in check.

Another tapir had just been born at La Marina and Jose had pictures. I packed my notes and followed him to the zoo. Yolanda greeted us with a smile. We didn't smile back. We were cordial, that"s all.

About fifty guests attended the meeting. My presentation received a standing ovation. A reporter from the Tico Times was there. I wished it were Dan Fawcett. After the project jaguar and Inbio threats on his work, he had moved back to Canada. We kept in touch now and then by email. We knew one day we would tell our story to the world.

Jose came over and tapped me on the shoulder. "It's time to show our disk."

I hurried to set it up. As he watched for the first time what I had put together, a proud smile crossed his face. He gave me a nod.

Even Yolanda came over and told me she liked my project dream. I met lots of new faces. We were all " *cat people.*"

Then Jose introduced me to a couple from Oaxaca, Mexico. They owned the largest breeding center of jaguars. It was called *jaguar zoo.* They specialized in black jaguars.

His name was Juan Ramon and he and his wife planned to stay in Costa Rica for a week to see my work and the La Marina park. I spent the next week with them showing them around. We became fast friends. While we were at La Marina, Juan Ramon became enchanted by the tapirs. He and Jose talked about a trade. They wanted to exchange a pair of black jaguar cubs for a pair of tapirs. Jose was very interested. I was delighted.

The black jaguar is beautiful. They are larger than the gold jaguars. I had never seen one in real life.

Jose said, "Now you have something to look forward to after you're finished with Juliana. You can be mother jaguar now."

Juan Ramon invited us to see his place in Mexico. A new litter would be born the next month. We planned our visit for the beginning of March. My birthday. What a gift that would be. Two black beauties.

Costa Rica no longer had black jaguars. Rare sightings of black jaguars were of those which came from Nicaragua who followed the corridor passage of the mountain strongholds.

To reintroduce this species to Costa Rica would be monumental. But first we needed to do some research. We spent the night at La Marina, then we took off to the puma. Our Mexican friends fell in love with the place. Carlos was also with us.

Juliana was on her best behavior. She picked up that these two were animal people. She went up to them. Of course she was inside the pen and they were outside. She looked good. Her hair had finally grown back and it looked like she was content with herself.

Juan Ramon's wife sat by Juliana and made baby noises to her. She responded instantly. She talked back for a long time. She wanted to communicate with her. I took notes of what was going on between them. I looked at Jose, and in his eyes I saw the love he had for her.

I asked him if he wanted to go inside. He had never done this. I checked her mood, her body language, her tail and her ears. She responded to my questions, she was ready for him. I stepped in first, she was slow and easy with me, then Jose entered. Juliana remembered him in a way. I saw she was also a little taken aback by how big and strong he was. She smelled his legs, she smelled his hands, then she played with him.

He loved it. It was written all over his face. He knew how to handle her and she responded with love. At one point when she had enough, she came to me and put my hand between her teeth. She did this to me when she felt a little shy. She was ever so gentle and put just the right amount of pressure on my hand so that I could not pull away, yet without hurting me. The couple was enthralled with this bond between animal and human.

I spoke to them of my work with animal communication. They too knew this was possible and had communicated with their jaguars in different ways. It was a magical day for us all. It was time to leave her. I never wanted to over-do it when she was in contact with people. She opened their eyes.

Juan Ramon and his wife, Maria Luisa, left the next day.

The black jaguar cubs would be born the next week. They would stay with the mother for fifty days, till weaned. Then, if all went well with getting the permission from Minae for the trade of the dantes, La Marina would receive the cubs.

As we got ready to go, Juan Carlos came down the road. Introductions were made and J.C. told me he was here to measure off the new area which would be Juliana's research habitat. His friends had given him a modest price for all the material needed.

We were trying to use as little man-made material as possible. The area was a ravine with a ridge, a magnificent spot with views of the mountains. No one would be able to get to it from any way except through Carlos's property. This piece of land had natural barriers and edges which would make it easy to enclose with little material.

I spoke with Mitch. He told me that the only way to get the money would be to sell a piece of land. I wasn't to happy about this for I loved the piece and someday wanted to build a home there. If we petitioned to receive monies from the government, they in turn would also be in charge of the project. This was definitely out of the question. I decided to wait a bit. I needed time to think this through. Christmas was right around the corner.

My mother called and begged me to come home for the holidays. I had not seen my mom and family members in a couple of years. My schedule was clear, so I took advantage of the time and flew to Florida.

It was a pleasant visit. My mom was always worried about me. She thought what I did was terribly dangerous. I would laugh at her and hug her hard. My father had passed away a few years back and Mom needed the company more than anything else.

My father Julian instilled and understood my love of animals in me. Raised on a farm I spent endless hours with him. He too loved animals. We had the same birthday. I was his favorite and when mom would call me in to do some woman's work I would always rather be working by my father's side. I wish he could have been with me to see my work with the wild ones. I know he would have been proud.

It was a short trip. I flew back to Costa Rica right after the first of the year. My diary had come to its end......

The Workings 27

Right from the beginning, this New Year had a different feel
about it. My work load was still heavy but it was a year to see
promises fulfilled. I played the, hurry up and wait game.

Juliana walked the jungles daily. This was Alex's charge. She
settled into a regular routine, which suited her just fine.

I was now coming but one day a week to see her. I spent
this day going over my communication skills with her. It
became pure synchronicity. It was now being done in waves
of rhythm. Our minds read each others' even before the
thought fully reached my brain. Before it could be something
transformed into a sentence. She told me of her walks, I told
her of my work. When I was down or depressed she changed
the mode of communication. She listened intently to nothing sometimes, just seeing things going through my head.
She had that wise old look to her face as if she was a learned
old scholar. It was as if she nodded her head, taking it in. She
made me reach another level in my thought process. At times I
couldn't get there. She felt my frustrations and did not force it
upon me. She was giving me the time I needed to learn.

I knew I was spreading myself too thin. I was running in
to many directions. I needed to focus. This was hard. Not one
thing I was doing was lesser in value to me. How to choose?

At this time Juan Carlos was needed in the city. Even his
adventure hunting needed to be curbed for a while. He was
revamping the family business and welcoming a new baby
into his life.

Money was tighter now, so the wait for the new habitat at
Amistad began.

I worked on my herbal formulas. With the help of Tommy
and Pat at the Ark

Herb Farm, we formulated the jungles' medicines. We grew herbs from the jungles of Sri Lanka, too. Dostora sent us the recipes of the ancients. Tommy spoke of going to India the next year. We were learning the different processing necessary for our formulas. We were becoming masters. We tested everything on ourselves. Those were some funny moments, especially when we took some natural viagra. We were laboratory rats, yet we never got sick.

Our laboratory was growing. We worked with food grade and medicinal herbs. In my studies I came across a Texas-based laboratory in Costa Rica which extracted and manufactured a white powder from a red aloe vera plant. The plants grew in volcanic soil, rich in earth's nutrients. The type of aloe Mitch grew on the land at the beach was the same kind. The plant bleeds an extremely healing red juice.

The white powder went to the States. It was taken internally. It had run through a series of testing, being administered to cancer and aids patients. The results were tremendous. It was a detoxification of the bodies micro's and cell memory banks. It supported the DNA blueprints.

This could also be used on animals. A friend, who knew I was working on this, called to tell me that a doctor friend of his was coming to visit. His name was Vincent Giampapa and he worked with the aloe powder and in stemcell research.

I met with them in Jaco at weeks' end. A beach, an hour and a half's drive from the city, on the pacific coast side. They owned condos in a development called Los Suenos. This five star hotel/resort in Costa Rica was built by a Californian. It looked like a California development placed on the ocean jungles. All American standard. The marina, was the first in the country.

Vincent was waiting as I pulled into the gates. We took to each other right away. We talked for hours. He fascinated me and I him. We both thought alike. He gave me some samples of the aloe powder and some other herbs he was working with. We planned another meeting on his return in March. As I was spending the night I decided to kill two birds with one stone. I went into Los Suenos offices and asked to speak to the owner, Bill Royster. I had a copy of my disk and the fund raiser Tippy Hedren and I put together.

I had no prior appointment with him. His secretary was a friend of mine and she just pushed me through his doors.

We shook hands, sat down, and I gave him my idea. He looked the disk over. He liked it and would be glad to help. He offered Los Suenos to be the host of the celebrity fundraiser. Great, that was easy. I drove back to the city with Vincent and emailed Tippy the good news.

The next line of business was Mario Sotella. His manager had called and asked if I could come in. I went in the next day and was told that they were having difficulty with trans-porting the elephants. Types of transport were limited and customs, at both ends, threw them a red flag. My advice was to transport the elephants via banana boat. It is a steady, slow moving barge which should make the crossing in four to five days.

The paperwork was another thing. Mario would have to pull some strings for that one. He was also receiving African herbivores in herds from Columbia, from a breeding center. This didn't sound good to me. I didn't have the time to investi-gate. We could only wait some more...

Jose had the same problem with the international paper-work. Costa Rica had a law, one I admire. But there are exceptions to every rule. No wild animal of Costa Rica can ever leave the country legally. No trade, no selling, no nothing. It was funny, what left the country illegally was twice as much as what stayed in it. I told Jose he should just smuggle them out. He laughed. He was still going to Mexico. I told him I didn't know if I could come along. The timing was anything but perfect. I really wanted to go. I adore Mexico. The jaguar is a shaman animal to the natives and they too, have their powerful magic. It would be a great trip. But no matter how much I tried to juggle my schedule I couldn't get away. He left the end of February for two weeks.

My Birthday 28

March 4th is my birthday. I was invited down by my friends in Los Suenos, Karin and David, for a sail on a boat as part of a birthday celebration for me and Vincent. I didn't know Vincent and I had the same birthdays. No wonder we got along so good.

I loved sailing. I told them I would come down for the whole weekend. I called Memo. We had not seen each other in months. I had been thinking of ending the relationship. It was the type that would never lead to anything. It couldn't. His world was not one I could be part of. I cared a great deal for him though.

I invited him down for the weekend. He said yes. The morning of my birthday I awoke to his phone call wishing me happy birthday. He was so very sweet. He would pick me up at midday. When the time came, he called and said, family business needed him again. He would make it down if I didn't want to wait for the next day. I let out a huge sigh. I couldn't do this anymore. The relationship ended at that moment.

I left on my own for Los Suenos. I wasn't my cheery self. But I wanted to get out of this mood. I looked to the skies and asked them to bring me the love of my life for my birthday. Sometimes they hear us...

The beach was beautiful. The ocean beckoned me. I jumped in and swam for a long time. I missed the ocean. I always felt better when I came to her. I was a fish, I needed her. I lay on the hot sand and relaxed. I thought of all that was in front of me with this new year. I thought of Juliana. She was the driving force inside of me, that made me go on. Was I doing right by her? I sent her a kiss from my mind and gathered my things to walk to the condos.

Karin, one of my best friends, greeted me with a huge hug. I confided my whole personal life to her. She was disappointed for me that Memo and I broke up. But she had me laughing in minutes. Karin always was a lot of fun. She is a wonderful, unique artist. She designed frames which were out of this world. She was a beautiful woman inside and out. She introduced me to Susan, Vincent's wife, and another couple they had brought along. We made a good group and went out at sunset for parasailing. I remember feeling like I was flying when I was set off on the harness out of the boat. I didn't want to come down. My mood was lifting too.

We hit the town and local night clubs. We went home late and woke up early to sail the next morning. It was a gorgeous, tropical day. I wanted to see whales. The name of the sailing cat we went on was Pacifica. Meeting the captain was to change my life, again.

He was a tall, dark and handsome Italian with a pirates' swarthy gait. His eyes were satanic. Maybe alarms went off inside of me, though this danger is what I always liked to challenge in my own life with men. I find through my relationships that men are a lot less of a threat than we women give them credit for. In life I have yet to meet a man who rivals the women I have known in every walk of life.

We sailed to a beach called *Punta Leona*. It is the only strip of white sand beach for miles. Black and grey sand beaches surround it on both sides. Lunch was served and we spent the day swimming around. On the way in, I called to the whales again. The captain laughed at me. *"Calling whales"*? Close to the marina's inlet, an orca whale rolled onto the surface of the water. Everyone saw her. We were all excited. I flashed a "I told you so" smile at the captain. It had been a thrill. It was a good omen to me. I looked at the captain again and he to was smiling. I was happy. He made me laugh. He pulled me right out of my mood for good.

As it came time to leave everyone thanked him for a wonderful time. For some reason I felt like I had known this guy forever, even though it was our first meeting. He kissed the women goodbye and then he kissed me. I held on, for just that moment more. I fell in love with that very kiss....

The Hunter 29

After my birthday weekend I drove to see the puma. I was but twenty miles away from the turnoff when I heard a series of gunshots. I stopped the truck to listen. What direction was the firing coming from? It seemed to be a valley in the mountain pass. I heard another series of shots and then it stopped. Someone was hunting. There was no farm land in this area for it to be anything else. There was no way to get into the area except by walking. This could take hours and the hunter or hunters would have moved by then.

I saw no trucks parked on the road, which meant it was someone local coming from one of the small mountain towns sprinkled across the Cerro. I thought of calling Minae, but I knew this would be fruitless. All I could do is report it.

I drove to Carlos' house first before stopping to see Juliana. I told him what I had heard. He nodded. He too had heard the gun fire. Carlos told me that in the past certain local hunters had come in to shoot tapirs. They would shot anything else for that matter that came across their paths. He too had reported it to Minae but help never came from them. He said you had to catch them in the act, have two witnesses and then they might do something about it.

I was angry. I asked Carlos if he knew how to get into the area they hunted. He said he knew a shortcut which was only an hour's walk.

I knew the route well. I used to collect herbs with the indigenous there. The place abounded in ortega, the spiny plant which the tapir loved. It was what we would cut for Chepa the tapir at La Marina when we were filming. I told him I was going to go out there and take a look. I had a throw-away camera which I would take along in case I needed to catch something on film.

Carlos told me to be careful. Some of these men were ruthless. I told him I would act as if I was out for a walk gathering herbs if I ran into them. I didn't plan on getting that close to them anyway. I just wanted to see what they were up to. If they were hunting tapir their return journey would be slow as the meat alone of an adult tapir weighed in at somewhere around seven hundred pounds.

I checked the weather. It was going to be a dry, sunny day. I had a bow and arrows in my cabin. The arrows I had made when I was working with the indigenous people. The arrows had a unique head which was not a solid, closed piece. The arrow points had lined grooves in them which allowed for a great deal of bleeding to occur upon impact.. The regular type arrows did not let one bleed, it held the blood in as opposed to these. Very crafty of the indigenous people, I thought.

I packed a backpack up and was on my way. When I had walked about forty minutes, I looked for a ridge I could climb to get a better view of the area. I had not heard anymore gunfire. The jungle was thickening and one could be right on top of another person and not know it. I finally chose a strong, tall tree, easy to climb and with safe spreading limbs to sit upon. I had just settled into the nook when I heard voices in the distance. I turned and my camera dropped to the ground. I looked out and saw two men. One was pretty far off. I could barely make him out. With a rifle, the other one took aim at something I could not see.

In a flash, I readied my bow. I was aiming for his arm holding the rifle. Without a second thought, I let the arrow fly. True to its mark, it hit him just before he pulled the trigger. He let out a scream and the rifle fell from his hands. I wasted no time. I climbed down the tree, grabbed the camera and ran back through the jungle. I stopped after twenty minutes to catch my breath. I wished I had gotten a better look at the man's face. I wanted to know who he was, but everything had happened so fast. I was just happy I had hit him. I knew I was close enough to have done some serious damage to his arm. It wouldn't be shooting again for a long time.

When I finally made it to the cabin, Carlos was gone. He would be back in an hour, his daughter Anna told me. I told her to tell him to come to my cabin upon his return. I went to see Juliana. She could tell something was up with me. I tried to tell her what happened. I told her about hunters. I told her this was what she needed to guard against the most in her jungles. I told her not all people were good to animals. I know not whether she got it. I stayed but a short time with her, then went up to the cabin.

Alex was there, dropping off some wood for my stove. I told him the story. He looked at me incredulously. Then his father walked in. I told him. He asked if they had seen me, I said no. He asked if I could recognize them if I saw them again. I said no, but it would not be hard to find out who it was, for there would be talk about this for sure. How many people got shot by arrows anyway out here. Carlos agreed and suggested we go back out to the area the next day to see if there were any clues as to what they might have been hunting.

We all called it a day and I decided I wanted to sleep with Juliana. Alex helped me bring her to the cabin. She sensed my exhaustion and followed me like a dog right into the bed. I whipped up a fast dish of food and dropped off to sleep before my head hit the pillow. I slept in late. It was 9:00 AM, before

I was awakened by Alex's knock on the door. I rolled over to glance at Juliana. She was just awakening too. I couldn't believe how well we slept nor how long, when we were together. I let Alex in and he called us sleepy heads. He had brought me some fresh eggs and milk with homemade biscuits. I devoured every bite.

After breakfast, Carlos met me at his house. Alex was coming along. We put Juliana into her pen and started for the mountains. Since I had just come through the other day, the path was cleared of brush. Usually one had to walk with a machete, as all paths were covered over again within days. It quickened our walk. We reached the tree I had been on and spread out in three different directions to see what we could find. Alex and I found droppings from a herd of tapirs and Carlos found tracks and half eaten ortega all around the area. Alex told me we were not far from a good sized pool of water. The hunters were after tapirs. We set out to find shells left from the gunfires but came up with nothing. The jungle floor had to much camouflage and thickness to find anything easily. I searched for carcass remains. We looked to the sky for vultures. Nothing. All we could do was try to find out through discreetly asking questions of the locals in the area.

Just before dark we headed home and prepared to visit the truck stop restaurants on the main road. As we arrived at the cabin Magela, Carlos wife, was just coming in from the cows. Her sister, who lived on the other side of the mountain road, had news. The other day three men with shotguns had walked past her property at daybreak. She had seen them from the window of her house. She said they were too far away to know who they were. She recognized no one.

I spent the rest of the afternoon with the puma. I knew she heard the gunshots. I wondered what had gone through her head. I knew she had a horrible memory branded in her head. But this one could not be erased, only strengthened. This was one thing I always wanted her to be afraid of, or better yet, to be wise about.

Juliana had a way with things she feared. First she became afraid, and then she got furious. Since she was a wild animal, she had it in her to kill a man. I didn't fault her that. We all have that inside ourselves. In the history of Costa Rica, there had never been an attack on a man by a mountain lion. Yet every man feared them and would shoot one that crossed his farm in a heartbeat.

I was heading back to the city that night, so I kept Juliana in her enclosure. I readied my truck and went to the restaurant, followed by Alex and Carlos. We had coffee and bocas. We stayed an hour but found out nothing.

I had to get on my way. Carlos and Alex said they would hear something soon. Gossip was big around these parts and most hunters liked to brag about their sporting rather than hide it. It was the macho thing here. We parted. I drove along. Within an hour of driving, my truck got a flat tire. There was another truck stop restaurant up ahead. I pulled in and went in to get some help. Since there are no gas stations for long stretches of road and on the Cerro there is but one, people are always great about helping anyone with car trouble. A guy volunteered his help. When the job was done, I offered him a beer for his time. He accepted. We strolled into the bar. I paid for the beer, as I was turning to leave, a man walked in with his arm in a sling. I stopped and stared at him for the longest minute. I went into the bathroom to stall for more time. Sure enough by the time I walked back out he had downed a shot of whiskey and talk was starting. One of the other men in the bar had asked him what happened. The story he told was a riot.

He said he had been out shooting game bird, which was a lie, when he got lost on the path and was attacked by Indians. He said he had the arrow to prove it, for it was formed exactly like the ones he had seen in a camp just last year. In order for this man to have been anywhere near their camp, his hunting area had to be large. One did not need such a range for shooting game bird. Poacher was written all over his face.

I went to the bar, bought some peanuts, and ordered a coke. I pretended to be reading the newspaper and listened on. I wanted to burst out laughing for his story was so exaggerated. The arrow had hit on the elbow bone and broke it. It would be months before he could use his arm normally again. It would be twice that long before he could shoot a rifle. I left the truckstop with a smile on my face.

I rang Carlos the next day and told him. He roared into laughter. " The Indians. Well, that's good. It will keep him away from a lot of areas."

Alex said he had found out they were hunting tapirs for sure. He had talked to several of the farm lads which he plaid soccer with on weekends. We found out the hunter's name and made an anonymous report to Minae. They did nothing about it. I never saw the man again.

A year later Minae sent reinforcements to check out the poaching problem. It was Alex who helped them uncovers a ring of hunters which would hunt no more.........

Sailing and Summer 30

The next months were months of waiting. Everything I was working on was for one reason or another pushed into another time. Jose's visit to Mexico had gone well. He told me it was just as well that I had stayed behind for if I would have seen the baby black jaguar cubs, I wouldn't have come back. I giggled into the phone. He said he had pictures and to get my ass down to the park. Tempting. As for the permits, it would take at least six months for Minae to give the approval for the exchange. Sotella also had been denied paperwork for his animal transport. It seemed the planets were just in the wrong position.

We also postponed the decision whether or not to create the new place for the puma. I was falling into a depression about the puma. I wanted her to be free by now. That kept coming back to me again and again. Even though she was content with where she was, I wasn't. I felt I wasn't doing enough. I was judging myself again.

The sailor I had met at my birthday was now a steady in my life. We spent all our time possible together. He knew my troubles and told me to take some time for myself and just enjoy being in love for once. I deserved it, he said. So I did. We sailed the oceans blue. We did a trip to Panama which took two weeks. It was beautiful. The coastline is something to see. There were several islands along our journey which would be perfect to release Juliana. I started fantasizing about buying one of the islands and living on it with the puma. The Panama Canal was being worked on. They were enlarging it. International leaders. It was hotter then hades in Panama.

On the sail back, we came upon a humpback whale which stayed and swam along our current for a long time. The nights under the stars on the boat were gorgeous. We ran with schools of dolphins. At night the dolphins throw off phosphorus light as they dance through the waters. It was like a wizard's wand touching the sea to perform a moving kaladescope show. When we finally made it back, I was sorry it was over.

I needed to make a trip to California. It was time to do the final plans on the benefits. I also missed my daughter. Mitch would be coming back with me. His work was done.

I stayed with the puma for the remainder of the time before I went. She too, had missed me and as I told her of my adventures at sea, she merely looked at me like I was loco. I took her for long walks. I noticed she was maturing in many ways. Her appearance, her disposition and her communications with me. She knew I was stuck in my head with her future for the moment. She would gently swat at me as though to say, "Let it go. Let it go. I will tell you when I am ready."

I put it out of my head and thanked her for being in my life. She graciously accepted the praise and just nodded at me.

I left for California. It was summer. A lot was going on. My daughter came and picked me up. She was growing into a woman. We laughed till our sides hurt . We did everything together. Shopping, out to her college campus and took in the latest movies. Island was planning a trip to Costa Rica for Christmas. It had been a long time since she had visited Costa Rica. She never forgot her Spanish, and a lot of her friends in California were Mexicans. She loved to speak the language.

The next week I sat down with the committee for the fundraiser. The guest list was growing daily and a warm wave of encouragement coursed through my body. It was going to be quite a party. The date was set for sometime in October. The first fundraiser was to take place in Costa Rica.

My daughter and I went to see Mitch in the mountains. It was a nice reunion. We were just as we always were with each other. All too soon the visit came to a close. Mitch was excited to be coming back to Costa Rica. I helped him ready the dogs for their flight. It was good to see them again. They had both gotten so fat. City life.

We flew out on a red eye flight and woke in the airplane to a painted sunrise. The first thing Mitch did when we landed was take in a deep breath of air.

"God, this feels good," he said.

The dogs ran around and knew they were home. Fury hated flying. She rolled in the grass for ten minutes. She wanted the smell of life on her again. They were glad to be home.

We stayed in the city that night and then went to see the puma. It was a wild reunion. She knocked Mitch down. The dogs even gave her a playful nip hello. The city they left behind was gone in one yelp and a resounding howl. You could see Juliana was bringing back the wilds to them. She showed them how to play again, jungle style. She chased them, then stalked them and danced in bountiful leaps above their heads.

One thing my puma had was style. No animal I had met ever had that type of natural grace. Her eyes told you that. They shone with perfect balance.

I saw every muscle in Mitch's back unfold. The load on his shoulders was lightened. What is this that makes that happen to us? It is a fill into the sensory preceptors throughout one's body. These sensors trigger a release of endorphins which balance every nerve. Everything we see, smell and feel is pleasing to the soul. Our spirit wakes from a deep slumber...

Mitch talked late into the night with Carlos and his family. We slept in the cabin and then he went to the beach with the dogs and I went to the marina to see my love. I had to do some work at

Nine Eleven   31

On September eleventh the whole world changed....

We were brought back to thinking of the world as a whole. It touched all of us.

October' s fundraiser was cancelled. Travel stopped.

The whole world came to a halt. The calm before the storm...

The following months were quiet and full of wondering and waiting...

A New Year Cometh 32

I had given up my apartment and moved in with my lover. I spent my time between him and my puma.

My daughter was on her way down. She too had to postpone her vacation with me for some months. It was the talk of the town. Everyone that knew her, missed her, mucho!! I picked her up from the airport with her favorite flowers, *mille de flores de San Jose*. Then we launched into talk and caught up with stuff, driving through a whirlwind tour of all her friends and favorite places. She was greeted with hugs and kisses and smiles and tears. Island took time to talk with all of them. It was nice to see old friends.

We went to bed late and woke up early the next morning. This was the first time she would see the puma. Up to now it had only been pictures. I could hardly wait to see my two daughters meet each other for the first time. I called Alex as we were leaving. I told him to put Juliana in the cabin.

The drive up was breathtaking. Island was enjoying herself like I had never seen before. We stopped and had gallo pinto, her favorite for breakfast. The sun was shining, it was hot at Amistad. We pulled up to the gates. Island went out of the truck to open the gate. She swung like a monkey on it. Island had shorts on. She has incredible long light legs. I went into the cabin first.

Juliana was on her leash inside my bedroom jumping and pouncing on everything and hiding under the comforter blanket and tangled her leash all around it like a giant ball of yarn. Outside Alex and Island had just met. They hit it off great together. They both made a cute couple. I put Juliana on her leash and sat on the couch with her in the other small room of the cabin. I called to my daughter to come in. As she

entered, her long blonde hair cascaded down and Juliana's
eyes popped out of her head. I'm not kidding, they did. What
a reaction. I laughed so hard that I dropped the leash and
Juliana took one leap and was wrapped around Island's legs.
Playfully, curiously. My daughter made a move to get her off, I
stopped laughing and pulled missy whoha back.

My daughter was a bit scared. That was normal. She was
also so enthralled by Juliana. I took her out behind the cabin
and talked to her for a bit. She had to realize that Islandia was
mine. Juliana thought her to be very different. She was also a
bit intimated by her. I knew she sensed she was a part of me,
my young, not just another human. There was a similarity
between the two which was evident by watching both of them
at the same time. I saw them as my two daughters, .

We stayed for a while, then drove to San Isidro. Island
wanted to see her first boyfriend and some schoolmates. You
would have thought the president had come to town. She had
such a welcoming party by literally the whole town. All her
schoolmates had gotten together in the local pulperia. Her first
boyfriend, Fabian, took one look at her and asked her to marry
him. For the next two hours it was a non-stop stream of conversation.

We made plans to come back in the next days. We would be
spending the rest of the week at the beach. We picked a quiet
hidden hotel close to our farm. The beach was a private paradise. There were barely any tourists this year so we had the
whole place to ourselves. Mitch called Island a mayonnaise jar
because she was so pale and suggested she get some sun. They
laughed and they joked like this all the time. It was what we
all needed to lift our spirits.

We took the dogs and went out to the waterfalls . Everyone was so happy to see her. She had been sorely missed. The toucans sang her to sleep at night and the monkeys woke her to the rising sun. All too soon it was time for her to go. I really didn't want her to go. It was hard saying good bye. I wanted to spend more time in her life.

I had to come to a completion with the puma. They both looked to me for guidance. With a responsibility like that, one grows immensely with wisdom. I drove Island to the airport. We hugged and kissed and promised not to cry. I waited till she had flown into the sky and cried anyway.

Jaguars 33

Jose called and told me it was jaguar time. With three different ones. The first jaguar story he had for me was that he had been out in the jungles of Cabo Blanco national park. He had spotted a female black jaguar again which he had only seen once, a year before. He had assumed she had come through from Nicaragua and didn't know that she had come back. She was big. The black jaguars are bigger than the gold ones. He was planning to go tracking her and asked if I wanted to come along.

"I'll be ready whenever you are," I replied.

The second story he had for me dealt with a humorous incident which occurred in his town. It happened that the local jail had a wild jaguar in one of its cells. They said it had gotten trapped, closed into a barn of one of the farms which bordered the park. The police had been asked to come and deal with it. They didn't know what do with it, so they put it into a cage it in the cell. Then they called Jose. The jailer was so frightened of the jaguar and the cell mates had the same shivers, that he had emptied out the cells. Jose went on down with a net and a rope. Jose is a large man. He barely fit into the door of the jailhouse. The bars of the cells were rusty and old. It would take no time for the jaguar to break through the bars with his powerful jaws. All a jaguar's power is in this area. They have a pit bull's jaw structure, only ten times greater. The men gathered around the windows to watch. Jose stood before the jaguar and calmed it. He remembered what I had told him about communicating. I could feel it in his voice. I heard that he had heard. I smiled inside and hugged the phone.

He had a natural way of communicating with the animals. It came from his whole life of living around them. He had his own way of communicating. He threw the net around the cat. In one sweep he had him out the cell and into the carrying cage in the back of his pick-up. The men were in awe.

Jose said, "I got some more of that reputation stuff you always told me about." I laughed and made fun of him. "Wow, even I am impressed," I jested.

I'm sure he was blushing on the other end.

He drove the jaguar as far as he could into the jungles where he was found and let him go.

He needed my help on the final jaguar saga. Minae was giving us a medal. They liked the work they saw us do. They were giving a five month old jaguar to Jose to work on releasing back to the wilds. He was most excited about this. I was so happy for him. I knew I had instilled this will in him to begin releasing animals back to the wilds. Minae would be delivering the jaguar in two weeks. It was a male. Jose already had a name picked out for it, Libertad, which means freedom. I told him I would help him all the way.

The coming weekend I went tracking with Jose for the black jaguar. We picked up her trail by days' end. Darkness was moving in fast, so we called it a day and went back to the house. The next morning we followed the tracks again. It seemed she was walking heavy, more weight on the hind legs and clenching deeper with her fore paws. She might be pregnant. We spent the whole day out but didn't catch a sight of her. We did pick up some scat by the rivers edge. As evening fell we walked back to La Marina. We had just topped a crest in the mountains when we saw them. The sinfully beautiful black female with the golden male. They were on the move. We saw them only for a glance, yet what a powerful image remained in our minds. She must have a den in the area. I guessed her to need three more weeks gestation before her due date.

We left them alone. We would go back after a few months and check on her. We didn't want to cause any disturbance to her and her cubs. I never did get to go out to see her again, but Jose did. He had the luck of seeing her but not the cubs. The jungles had a new queen......

We choose a good area for the arrival of Libertad. The enclosure was to be much like the puma's, away from the other animals and people. Only one person would be working around him. His contact with humans would be limited. One thing in this jaguar's favor was that it had been with its mother the entire time in the jungle. The mother had been hit by a car and this cub was the only one found. He already had survival skills under his belt and the blueprinted knowledge was fresh from instinct experience.

Jose had to come up with a couple thousand dollars for materials. I told him I might be able to help him. I went home the next day.

Sold 34

It was time to make a decision about money. The fundraisers were now postponed till when??? The terror of 9/11 made it difficult for people to travel. Everyone's schedule was being rearranged. Jose needed money and I needed money for Juliana. I decided to sell my property. It was a beautiful piece, and selling it was one of the few regrets I have in my life.

It had spectacular ocean views with sunsets. A river with seven waterfalls ran through it. Wild and exotic bamboo and groups of tree ferns, my favorite tree plant in Costa Rica, grew all over it. I signed on the dotted line and sold it to a friend of mine in Dominical for peanuts. I felt an empty spot in my stomach.

I called Jose and told him I had the money he needed. He thanked me, and the next day he came into San Jose to buy what he needed for our new project. I then decided to wait until September to attempt another release of the puma. If she came back, I had the money to go ahead with Juan Carlos' plan and change Juliana's destiny. I invested my money with a group of investors called the Villalobos brothers.

They had been in business for twenty-five years. Most foreigners invested with them. It was my first time investing with anyone. I never before had money to invest.

Mitch took over most of the work with the puma now. I wanted to go away. Really go away. I wanted to get out of Costa Rica for a spell. My head needed to get right. I needed a break from my animal work. I was running out of steam. To much waiting. To much wanting.

My lover suggested we go to Italy. A change of scenery would do me good. I loved to travel and had not been able to go really anywhere in ten years. I spent the next five months in Italy…

The Return   35

During those months, I knew what I wanted to do. What-ever it took, I wanted to return Juliana to the wilds. I thought about it enough to know that I would be satisfied with nothing less.

Mitch had been in touch with me the whole time I was in Europe. Everything was fine with the puma. I knew this stretch of absence from her was more for my benefit than hers. I had to get used to her not being around. She was so much a part of my life, my very being. I knew she had been training me to bring the conversations of the wilds to others.

As soon as I landed, my friend Oscar picked me up and drove me to the puma.

Oscar, one of my dearest friends, was a taxi driver by trade. He knew me better than anyone, and he was there for me, every time. He was my right hand. He took care of things I entrusted to no one else. We talked the whole way up.

I flung open the gates of Cuerici and ran as fast as I could to Juliana. I screamed to her, I'm home. How's my little girl?

She couldn't believe her ears. She stalked me and then charged against the mesh to grab me in her arms. She would actually spread her two long front legs out and try to squeeze them through the holes. I walked into the pen and never wanted to let her go. The tears spilled into her face, she turned and licked the salt away. She purred so long and loudly, I heard nothing else. It flashed through my head that I should just build a house into the jungles and live with her. She meant that much to me...

I stayed with her a while. She had so much to talk to me to. I remember every thought she sent to me. She didn't want to understand why I wanted her to go. Go for good. Why? Had I done something wrong... Didn't I want her anymore?

I told her we had different lives as humans and animals. I told her I loved her from the bottom of my heart. I told her she awakened my soul. I told her I didn't want her to go. I told her I didn't go away from her, I needed to go away from myself. I told her when we were ready it would happen. I told her my heart was breaking already now just thinking about it. I looked in her eyes and showed her a mother puma's strength. I showed her children. I showed her life...

In that instant our communication stopped and she jumped out of my arms. She showed off for me. I watched for a long time, my vision blurry, my heart weak, but my soul strong.

I saw how man can teach the wildest beast through love. I saw a wild beast teach a man love. I saw the oneness which we all really are. I felt a special sensation come over me, knowing that in this life I was chosen to feel this love. That I had shared an experience few can. We can love completely with animals even though we do not understand them. I sat and went over in my mind my life's paths, I laughed at myself. I looked at Juliana and she told me to tell the world. It was then that I decided to write my book.

A yell came out of the woods. It was Carlos and Alex. I went to grab Oscar and we reunited over lunch. After lunch Carlos took a walk with me. He wanted to talk to me alone. He sat me by the trout pond. We watched the ducks for a long time. We didn't speak.

I broke the silence. "Carlos, you know how I feel, don't you?"

He replied with a nod and held my eyes with his. "Never be afraid," he said. "Always look into my eyes for your strength. Any decision you make will be the right one. Trust in yourself. You need nothing more."

I turned and put my arms around him. I held on to him for a long time. My home- coming was bittersweet. Oscar came out and told me we needed to get going. We were returning back to the city. I stopped by Juliana's and fed her for the night. I told her she would see me soon, and left.

I slept the whole ride. I was getting rid of jetlag and emotions.

A Change Of Pace 36

Changes began occurring in every way. I had vivid dreams. They were as colorful as they were intense. A week after entering the country, I received bad news. The country received bad news. The investment firm of the Villalobos brothers was under investigation and they had to shut their doors to all their investors. Not only did I lose all my money but thousands of others did, too. Millions of dollars were gone. The heartbeat of the economical world of Costa Rica stopped. People were desperate and were selling everything they had just to stay alive. These were maddening times.

Basically I closed my eyes to any dreams I had. It was like starting from the beginning all over again. My lover had sold his boat and we took a house in the city together. My work force changed. Minae was closing projects left and right. They had no more money for anything either. I no longer was running all around the country helping with projects.

I worked with my herbal remedies again to make money. I had only a few clients now and life was back to the basics with me. I went out to the puma twice a week. Mitch and I saw each other only on rare occasions. He too was in a slow time of work. We both agreed to wait for now with another attempt to release Juliana. We had so much to sort out. It would all take time. Many of my friends' lives had changed, and we helped each other out as much as we could.

Jose was doing okay. He called to let me know he had seen the mother female jaguar again. She had two cubs, one which was like her, black and the other one golden. He said they looked well. He was lucky to have been able to see them. But Jose knew his jungle better than most people know their home.

I went out to see him. Libertad was soon to be released. The project was going well.

Jose was very proud of himself. I was proud of him too. He had a newcomer on the line .

"Tell me tell me," I begged.

"Curiosity killed the cat," he said to me.

I retorted back, "Cats have nine lives. I'm not finished yet."

He laughed at me and gave me the biggest bear hug. We walked to Suzie's, the jaguar. She remembered me and rolled over and over for me to play with her. I stuck my hands through the bars of the gate and teased her. She was getting fat.

Jose finally let the news out. "A zoo in England contacted me. They have a lioness they want to give me."

"Wow a lioness! How did this come about?" I asked.

He said he had been working on helping them establish a proper tapir center. His success with tapirs had many zoos and parks throughout the world interested in his methods. They were giving him an African lioness in return. They were also funding the transport of the lioness and sent the money needed for a proper compound at La Marina.

Jose had a way with felines. I thought it odd to ship an African lion to Costa Rica, but things were what they were in this planet of changes.

He showed me his plans. The compound would be beautiful. It was to be natural, spacious and replicate the African plains. A natural pool would act as a barrier border for the compound. I saw the excitement in Jose's eyes. The money would also supply a quarantine area and an animal hospital.

Jose turned and said to me, "You could work here."

I kicked him and ran, shouting, "You'll have to catch me first."

He knew I was kidding, but he ran after me anyway. He caught up with me at the house and just then Marta, his wife shouted out to grab the phone. Jose picked up the call.

I couldn't believe what I was hearing. Someone else was on the line wanting to get rid of two lioness ASAP. As he hung up the phone, a big grin spread over his face.

"Well, looks like I am going to have a pride." "And you will be the lion king," I giggled.

We both went to work on the felines coming our way.........

Libertad was released without pomp and circumstance but with much anticipation. He was tracked and was doing fine. Hunters were still about at times and Jose told me that Libertad always killed the hunting dogs which were sent out for him. Libertad was getting a reputation now and the spirits of the wilds were keeping him safe and strong.

By the end of the next month the compounds were ready. They were perfect. A divider had been placed in for the felines to first get to know each other. They also would have an inside, enclosed area for the nighttime.

Jose took no chances of something happening to his new charges. His new ladies, I should say. Even the quarantine area was spacious and set amongst a group of beautiful trees.

"I love my new laboratory," I told him as we went past the animal clinic which was getting the finishing touches.

The first to arrive of the group would be the lioness from England. Then two weeks later, the two from Columbia would arrive. So instead of black jaguars, we were getting African lions. Expect the unexpected... Again

Roar 37

I spent the next week with my own lioness. One morning, I took her out into the forest. We were on our way to turn back when her collar came off. Warning flash. Here she goes again. But she didn't. She dashed around a bit. Then she played hide n' seek for a while and then just like a dog came over to me when I called her.

I put the collar back on her and walked home. I wondered at her behavior. Had it been too long for me to be able to let her go?

She answered me immediately. The wilds had never left her, she could come and go as she pleased. It was a solemn statement from her.

I joked at her, "If it pleases my queen."

The next morning Alex came by on a motorcross bike I had given him last year. He had just ridden up from Rivas, the town down below and had seen puma tracks. A mother and cub, and wondered if this had anything to do with Juliana not wanting to be out in the jungles. I told Alex to keep his ears open at night in case Juliana should start screaming again. But I also thought that with young, a mother puma would not come close to any human habitation.

I told Alex I was going up to La Marina to greet the first lioness. I asked him if he wanted to come.

He burst out, "Sure, I do."

We planned on meeting in San Jose at the beginning of the following week.

I then went back to the city and read up on as much information as I could on

African lions.

On the international news that night was the story of the famous magicians, Siegfried and Roy. Their horrible experience with their white tigers was headline news. One thing people that worked with wild animals had to realize was that you could take the animals out of the wilds, but one never could take the wilds out of the animal. Felines do not like to be commanded. They will take direction only through the desire to do so

for you. A love for you, a respect which must be shared. The answers are always in the tail. They will always push limits and boundaries. That is their strength. Look to them as if they are your god, for gods they are... No matter the gilded cages which man makes for them to live in, it does not come close to one day walking the mighty forest and returning to the kingdom which is theirs to behold. Even those born in captivity always have this dream playing in their minds, a calling which some will chose to answer above all costs.

I went to bed that night and again had dreams.

Alex was early the next day. He had jumped the first bus. He was grinning ear to ear. I could tell he was excited. He had always wanted to go out to La Marina but the time never was gotten.

I was happy for him. I told him he worked well with animals and had that thing that made them want to work with him. This trip would show Alex some possibilities. When we reached La Marina, Jose was already with the lioness. Marta said he does nothing but hang out with her. I told her I knew the feeling, every woman does for that matter....

I first took Alex around the park. I wish you could have seen his face. He was in heaven. When we reached Suzie, the jaguar, she immediately starting talking to me. She was so happy to see me. She took to Alex right away. I didn't tell Alex she was dangerous to everyone but me. I waited and watched. He went right up to the bars and started to talk to her. She responded so fully to him. She played with her ball for him. She patted softly at him. She moaned at him. I smiled, softly inside. Yes, Alex had a thing...

We went off to find Jose. He was in his glory with the lioness. She was a magnificent animal, the largest lioness I had ever seen, with a golden coat. She was in good condition, both physically and mentally. I stared in awe for the longest time.

Jose and Alex were talking. I went closer to the cage. She rose,came over, and let out that low moan which makes one know they could only be in Africa. Such a deep baritone sound. She was friendly. She wanted to be scratched. I knew Jose was just about to caution me about touching her, but he didn't. I could feel his hesitation, I could feel his eyes on my back.

I took the chance before he changed his mind and reached in to touch her. She rubbed and rubbed alongside the fence to me. She rubbed hard. Her hairs were falling, little pellets of golden fur. She was a love. You could tell that about her. It was good. She had come from a place where she had been treated well. We stayed for a while with her.

Her temporary pen, the quarantine area, was bordered on one side by rolling hills which held the dairy cows on Jose's farm. Upon spotting the herd, the lioness moved. Such power in her motions. She was regal. Her movements were like deep drumbeat rhythms, pacing back and forth in a looping gait. She was doing hunting moves. Everything about her was stately. We stayed until dusk with her. As we were about to leave, the lioness began to roar. We stopped in our tracks. Her roar shook the jungle. I remembered seeing a tiger roar and in that roar came the power to paralyze their prey and their enemies. I know not why or how I knew this. I just felt it so. `The vibrational energy from a roar is mighty indeed. The other animals followed, the jaguars moaned, the coyotes howled. The cackle of the birds added to the din which created a powerful music. We left amidst the symphony.

MY BURIAL 38

Throughout my years in Costa Rica I have come across, come to know and learn from the many different tribes of Indigenous People. They too are an endangered species. One who carries our ancient spirit and with that a knowledge and power beyond the grasp of most white men. Their many rituals and ceremonies, unique and coveted, allowed me to enter into a time and space which is never ending and we know not yet its beginning. I have seen the Indigenous banish plagues, heal man and the animals with an understanding of the inner mechanisms, the rhythm, the sounds we cannot hear. Knowing flesh and bone without having looked through a microscope.

I am about to share an experience I had with one tribe in the mountains.

On a cold, foggy morning in the cloud forests I was brought by a small boy a beautiful fox. He lay still in the boy's arms. His coat was the color of dark autumn's splendor. His tail long and thick a masterpiece of fur hanging softly by his side. The boy told me it had been hit on the road. I felt for a pulse, it was very weak. I told the boy I would take it to the settlement beyond the trees. I knew it to be of the Indigenous. The boy handed over the fox. I smiled down at him, squat and kissed him on the cheek. He slowly turned and walked up to the highway mountain and disappeared into the foliage. I began my descent, carefully, down the slope, latter turning into a sharp ravine where the going became very slow. I stopped several times to check on the fox. He seemed in a deep sleep. I sent him picture message not to worry. He was safe. I coddled him and felt warm rushes of blood spark inside of me. My every heartbeat on the trail walking, sent a signal to his heartbeat to keep going… 2 hours later we reached the settlement. This tribe did not speak to white man. They would not let me pass an entry point through a rock cavern. I was tired. I sat down with the fox and signaled for water. A woman in the background, very small, very brown, and a face drawn with many lines of life, looked over to me and met me eye to eye. I knew not at the time what was being said of me. The dark woman was the medicine keeper. She allowed me through the entrance after telling the guardsmen that I wore Puma medicine. She was referring to my scar of Juliana's on my mouth. How she could see and tell what it was and where and how I got it took me back. I drew a deep breath, bowed my head and entered into the settlement. It was a page out of a book. The carvings of the mystic animals, the simple dwellings formed into a semi circle. The acceptance of living in the jungles and the artistic harmony within it. Colorful embroidered rugs and cloth. Two other girls came and looked at the fox and laid it on a huge red boulder. The medicine woman had them cut long, big green leaves while she mixed herbs and clay which she had brought from her dwelling. The mixture turned to paste and this was rubbed on the fox. He still lay very quiet. Dusk was falling. The sky was clearing. The stars would be out soon. I was taken by one of the girls to a cleared spot of ground on the other side of the boulder and was instructed to dig a hole. I knew not what for but as if in a trance I did their bidding. After 15 minutes they stopped me. I sat down on a log. They came back with a blanket and a leaf full of fruits, fish, banana, nuts and seeds with a heavy dark bread soaked in a bitter honey. I eat everything. I was starving. The girls then undressed me and covered my nakedness with an indigo blue blanket. The medicine woman came. This nite was to be my initiation that was needed in this time of my life. A rebirth. I was to die the old me, that which needs to be forgotten. I remember little else from that moment on as I was placed into the grave. The blanket was put over the opening. It was pitch black, one you could touch. The earth was warm. I spent a nite of screaming, clawing crying and singing. I sweated and I shivered. My fingertips were raw and bleeding, no nail to be seen. I went black. My dreams were projecting me out of my body. Everything I was frightened of came to life. I begged. Would waken then drift off again no matter how hard I tried to stay awake. I tried to climb out, finally I was dead. I awakened to sunrise, the blanket removed as my eyes found the sun. I never felt more alive in my life.

They dressed me and escorted me back out of the jungle. The fox? He had gone to, well and on his way.

Animal Communication 39

How does one talk to the animals? For each of us it is different. Some of us have an instant connection with the animal world. Children have this. Those who have lived in the wilds have this. But sometimes they do not know how to start or sometimes they simply doubt that what they are hearing is interspecies communication. Those who have not experienced any other type of life but city know not that it exist inside of them, therefore harder for them to access. But there is no golden rule for who can and who cannot. There are exceptions to every rule and I have found that there are no rules in animal communicating. It stems from our instinct, our trust in ourselves, in our first premonitions. An instinct opens outward and lets all life in. It seems impossible that we could hear this sound. A vibrational frequency comes alive in our minds. All we have to do is burst free from the old husk and cast our energy upward, to fly.....many times as I communicate or am open to being communicated with, I am not conscious of emotions yet it comes physically, in waves of tears or body-shudders or bursts of laughter, breathlessness, sometimes it seems I just hold my breath. Breathing as the Buddha or Hindus do helps to open that floodgate to a different reality.

Some communication is obvious. Take for example our domestic cats and dogs. We know when they are hungry, we know when they want to go out, we know these little things from their actions. What we don't realize is that at the same time they are communicating also. Though we are blind to it, the truth is sitting right in front of us, daunting us everyday to try...

They look at us as mutes. Unable to talk to them so they take it upon themselves to talk to us in sign language, in their case, body language. A dog brings you his leash to let you know he wants to go out for a walk. He brings you his ball so you will throw it. He is teaching you.

From the moment you first start to communicate with your pet they go alittle berserk. It excites and dumbfounds them that you have the ability to talk to them. Wild animals are different. They expect it from us for they know things about every species that we have yet to know.

It is important to practice knowing your thoughts. Thinking for your self, listening to the answers to every question you ever had from your own little voice as it is sometimes called. In the world today we go to everyone else, or the "Experts" for advice when all we really have to do is listen to ourselves. Whatever we think we will pass on to our animals. Think clear good thoughts. Get to know your own thoughts first. Get to know yourself. Do this in nature. Throughout the millennium of time man has always found his greatest solace in Nature. Return to this now.

To start communication with your animal, I first suggest you practice an exercise with a group of friends. Of course they all must be willing to want to do this. The first step is a simple fifteen minutes of quiet meditation. If you have never meditated nor know how, don't worry, just quiet the mind. Become content with yourself. Clear your mind of everything. Focus on nothing. This is hard, so just focus on breathing. Then arrange partners and have each pair face each other and be a bit apart from the rest of the pairs. Each pair choices a receiver and a sender. Meaning one person will receive the picture the other is sending. Choose a color for the whole group to concentrate on and the sender will then send the receiver an object or thing which has the chosen color.

For example, if the color blue is chosen, the sender from one group sends his receiver a blue jay. From another group a blue sky. A blue ball and so on. The sender does not need to have eye contact, sometimes it is better not to. Both parties can keep their eyes closed. It depends on what makes the individual feel more comfortable. At this time the sender does not have to strain to send his partner the message. Relax. Repeat the image again and again in your mind. Breathe. See what happens. At times a receiver from another group may pick up what is being send from another sender. Minds are connecting. Anything can happen. Minds are read not just by one at a time.

This method is a simple exercise. It begins to expand the minds' horizons on its infinite abilities. Transfer this practice to your animal. Instruct it via your thought to do something which normally you tell it to do by a voice command. Reiterate it calmly and patiently until your animal moves. Keep direct eye contact which will help the focus of your message. It will come. It always does.

One of my favorite first steps is to show your pets how much you love them. It conditions them to open to you. Love is a powerful symbol we all get, whether we know the language of the receiver or not. The other method, the one I most frequently find myself using, is that of instinctive call. Letting go of our egos. Believing in other powers you possess which are still considered the unknown. It is a feeling, ever so slight that one may miss it, that tugs at your center core. It steers you into the direction of the animal at hand. You let go of yourself, you allow them to control your thought patterns. Only when enlightenment occurs do we know it exists.

An easy exercise to try with this method is to become the animal you are trying to communicate with. Allow yourself a couple of days for this. Remain in your animal form. Try nothing else but to be exactly like your animal. In a few days you will find with your animal's help, for they will pick up instantly on what you are trying to do, that there is something. You can't put your finger on it right away but this something is an open door between you and them. Look at your animal as if it was a child, feeling every emotion you do. Wonder what they must feel, how they would react. Be quiet. Try not to speak during this time period. Spend one whole day not talking at all. You will release that which blocks the other senses. On another day be blindfolded and again release. You will awaken something deeper. With practice this will become second nature.

Finally there is the power of animals. Some animals have such a power that without knowing anything about it or having ever experienced it before, they will communicate to you by sheer will of the force within them, which is able to bridge century old gaps of the human mind versus the animal mind. They know how to get inside you. They know when to use feelings to make you understand and/or when to use communication. It may seem as if you are dreaming while being awake. In a way, that is just what is happening. It is a higher level of talk. Words are heavy in tone, in weight, on the mind. This communication is a light form. It travels as a light beam does into space. Your space, empty in a mind of which we use but a small portion our entire life time.

The mystical perception, which is only mystical if reality is limited to what can be measured by the intellect and senses, is remarkably consistent in all ages and all places, East and West, a point that has not been ignored by modern science. Psychics use this space. They have this knowing of how to access it. It is natural. We are all born with this ability. If you put a child in front of an animal, they are talking. With their minds. No false words, no misinterpretation. An honesty of innocence we are born with. We all are born free. Society and its rules and rigidity starts the cycle of putting the chains around our brains. They are afraid to be honest.

Very emotional people scare those who are not. Emotions are so brutally honest. The others living in a cloud or fog are offended by its huge force.The force comes like a heat, warmth to our bodies, most people do not know what to do with this. So they become afraid and by this fear we have always been ruled by those who have tried to shut down our own thoughts and feelings and destined us to become robots.

Love is honest, honesty is Love

As quoted from The Snow Leopard by Peter Matthiessen:

In Tantric practice, the student may displace the ego by filling his whole being with the real or imagined object of his concentration; in Zen, one seeks to empty out the mind, to return it to the clear, pure stillness of a seashell or a flower petal. When body and mind are one, then the whole being, scoured clean of intellect, emotions, and the senses, may be laid open to the experience that individual existence, ego, the 'reality" of matter and phenomena are no more than fleeting and illusory arrangement of molecules. The weary self of masks and screens, defenses, preconceptions, and opinions that, propped up by ideas and words, imagines itself to be some sort of entity (in a society of like entities) may suddenly fall away, dissolve into formless flux where concepts such as "Death" and "Life", "Time" and "Space", "Past" and "Future" have no meaning. There is only a pearly radiance of Emptiness, the Uncreated, without begining, therefore without end.

Natural Medicines, Part I 40

The curing of animals comes second nature to me. It is a gift. I have a great deal of respect for all those in the medicine field, be it natural or not. What I do not agree with is that they are separate. These two forces must join together to better suit every problem we have our world today. Animals taught me how to heal them. Animals communicate with all plants and trees. They tell each other what they need to know. Whenever possible I let the animal sniff, see, taste and feel a variety of different herbs and grasses. The ones they linger with are always the ones they need. I then gather those together and make them into a remedy which has never failed me in curing the sick ones.

Herbs cure the cause of a dis-ease, pharmaceuticals simply relieve the effects and prolong the body's dis-ease. They weaken our immune system, while plantlife invigorates it. Plant life carries "Chi" energy, life force. Drugs are dead matter. Everything in life is either organic or inorganic. Bodies are organic, herbs are organic. Drugs, chemicals are inorganic. Antibiotics are just that anti-bodies, against the body.

There are always negative side effects to our drugs, whether they are felt instantly or over a long period of time. Primarily the lymphatic system, the kidneys and the liver, house the most burden of toxicity when overloaded with chemical medicine. Herbs, if not needed, are expelled from the body instantly.

There are three levels of healing. Physical, emotional and spiritual. Physical is what is tangible. Spiritual is the higher self. Emotional deals with emotions, which create physical poisoning. Most caged animals suffer emotional strife, in turn breaking down the physical state of the body. As often as pos-

Thy Kingdom Come

sible when working with sick caged animals, I remove them from their prisons first. Many live in the emotion of fear. "Why are we caged? What have we done wrong?"

I study their mind first, watch their behavior, instill in them a reason to want to survive. I give them importance. They need and understand this.

It takes great dedication and patience to break through the walls built up inside them. No animal is unworkable. No animal is hopeless. If they do not work with us, it is because they are not supposed to. It is up to the individual in charge of an animals' life to make the crucial judgement call of what an animal lives for in their and our lives. One is never to try to break the animals' spirit. Cruelty is a double edged sword. Once one does this, they will forever have to watch their backs.

Emotional scars take love, not time to heal. Bach flowers helps to assist those with deep-rooted problems. This is a homeopathic tincture easy to administer. Animals, just like we do, also carry memories of ill treatment, grief, seperation from their own kind and lonliness. They harbor despair. They weep, yet we do not see their tears.

Trust and respect must be established first. This takes time. Most animals who do not respond quickly enough to satisfy the owner, are then discarded.

Remember they, too, have a soul and a heart. Herbal remedies are not as easily available for animals as they are for people. I am working on solving this problem. In the distant future via a website and DNA diagnosis we will be able to reach every animal far and near. Today, we cover a broad spectrum of maladies and one is able to receive formulas worldwide by overnight mail.

Parasites create a multitude of health problems, even cancer. The proper formula to de-parasite is one of the foremost products I urge people to use. Veterinarian wormers carry detrimental toxics.

Vaccines are another poisoning of the bodies.

Herbs are not a quick fix. They need the time and process to allow the body to strengthen itself. This is crucial to maintaining healthy happy animals. In the long run, you are saving yourself a lot of time and money and eliminate the animals' suffering.

Create the atmosphere needed to allow the animal to want to be healed. Their state of mind may quicken or prolong the dis-ease depending on what is done for them.

Never bring your fears with you. It is an unnecessary thought pattern placed.there by you.

There are two types of herbs, food grade and medicinal. Food grade is available by order or at healthfood stores and holistic pharmacies. They are easy to use. Safe, yet effective. Medicinal herbs are a stronger force, which need the supervision of a herbologist.

The gene pool of our captive wildlife is less than half of those who still remain in the wilds. Once taken from the wilds, even the new species succumb to the same old problems. If a breeding center or zoo is to be successful, it must mimick what the animal had in the wilds. Few, very few are able to do this.

New species are constantly forming. They too are adjusting to a new planet, an ever-changing one. Cloning is an unacceptable answer to an age-old problem. Only in preserving whole areas of the wilds in our world, without interference from man, can Mother Nature reverse the damages which most feel are irreversible. But I have a great belief in Mother Nature. It brings to mind a saying I once heard.

"Man in his greatest humility has neither the power to save nor destroy the earth, only himself."

Natural Medicines Part II 41

My work with herbal remedies was growing. My experiences with natural medicine is a book in itself. The growing toxicity ever present in all life forms comes most directly from the huge array of chemicals, whether in our food or our medicine. They even are in products we use to clean. The green life forms which make up our planet are laden with cures for every ailment. I was curing diseases which never stood a chance with modern medicine.

Tommy and I worked around the clock with the jungle botanicals. I created a line which I call Vida Verde, meaning green life. I wanted to create a network on the web to correspond with wildlife centers around the world. This would enable me to diagnose, via hair samples or feathers or scales, thus formulating natural medicines to cure the diseases. The line contained the formulas of some of the notable masters in herbology. Dr. Udo, Joel Hyman, Ed Burnheart and my shaman Dostora Warnisuyeria were finally giving me the secrets of their formulas. Dostora Warnisuyeria had asked me if I wanted to take over his practice in Los Angeles. He would be returning within the next year to Sri Lanka, for good.

His medicine is truly that of the gods. I witnessed a perfect harmony which the body needs to live disease free. It is a great shame that mankind does not realize, that which he turns his back on, is that which he needs the most. The great ones' medicines needed to be preserved. Mankind is not whole without them.

Some of the remedies are so simple. With the red seed of the achote plant we cured stomach ulcers and perforations of proportions which normally needed to be operated.

We cured the Parvo virus with clay. The mud, taken internally, collected the poisons. A homeopathic tincture was added. The juice of cabbage was given to drink. It flushed the harboring virus from the cells.

I remembered a walk in the jungles in my first year in Costa Rica. I was sitting up on the banks of a large stream and witnessed my first jaguar. It was a female, and she looked like she had just given birth. She was slow and wobbly as she walked down to the stream. I thought she might need to drink, but instead she buried herself into the mud clays along the banks. She lay for a spell. She spotted me, shook herself off and with one powerful leap was gone. She was whole again. The muds are part of their natural instinct.

There are many varieties of muds and clay. Some can be taken internally. Others for use externally.

I have used them repeatedly. I have detoxed internal parts of the body by applying it externally where the organ is located. It cleanses the lymphatic system.

We cured feline leukemia.

We cured cancers with blends of herbs addressing each personal blueprint of every patient, be it two legged or four. We cured mange in every variety of animal with pau d'arco and curcuma.

We cured gum disease with a blood red root, called Leche de Tarrogon.

We created positive green life forms to sustain the cells. We raised immune systems.

We grew echinacea, Augustafolio. This is one of the worlds most effective immune system builders and antibiotic. Goldenseal is another. Cloves, Blue Flag, and St. Johnswort are others. Together they form powerhouses of safe effective remedies.

We worked with reproduction problems. Donq Quai is an excellent female hormone balancer. Wild yam is another. One is the estrogen side, the other progesterone.

Mating in captivity is difficult at best. One of the reasons is the lack of a natural habitat. The animals' mindset needs to be nurtured. This was proven through our success with the tapirs. Their environment was natural. Think about zoos. How can animals stay in the mood when surrounded by a million faces of another species they know little about, man?

How would you feel? Being among natural things stimulates reactors in all of us. That element of comfort. Endorphins are released through plants and flowers, from earth, trees and green grasses. Not from concrete. The sounds affect them also. What do you like to listen to when you make love? Now think of them.

I worked with everything imaginable. The animals respond so much quicker and more positively to the use of natural medicines. There are no lethal side effects. The nutritional value concentrated in every herb is also a food source for the sick. We treat the cause of a disease, not just the effects.

After a disease is treated, we do a cleansing of the whole system. Food grade herbs are given over a period of two weeks. Then we fortify it. We make the body stronger than it was before. Blends of green life are given daily into food. We restore the body back. It becomes rejuvenated. The indigenous people taught me a great deal about the forces of nature and their healing powers.

The phases of the moon are a strong force, and I religiously worked by them.

When one is dealing with taking something out of the body, ridding it of a foreign matter, virus or bacteria, it is done when the moon is waning, when she is going down in size. When it is necessary to add something to the body, fortify it, this is done when the moon is waxing or growing in size. As powerful as the moon is in ruling the great oceans of the planet, so to it rules the waters in our bodies.

Darkness and light are keepers of another energy. Each one has a different power for a different purpose. Cells rejuvenate under sunlight, unless they carry negative traits which darkness holds in check until the illness passes.

Touch therapy is important. We hold energy in our hands. Women receive through their right and give out through their left. For men it is the opposite. They receive through the left and give through the right. This field of energy gently stimulates healing when one learns the technique. The Tellington touch is a good representative of the many facets of healing we possess in our hands.

Most of my animals far outlived the so called normal lifespan. I logged every patient into my notes. I had so many pieces of paper with so many important things written on them. It was hard to stay organized. I moved around so much.

That year my mother bought me a computer for Christmas. I finally got to be better organized.

The Dream 42

The new year hit me hard. Everything was fine with my work, but now my body was caving in. Of late, I had taken great care of everything but myself. I became very sick. I wasn't even able to go out to see the other two lioness' arrival at La Marina, nor was I present for the release of Libertad. But they all were doing well. Libertad was free, doing the wild thing. Juliana was doing fine also. When I last visited with her I felt she had grown up.

She was an adult puma now. It was time. I sensed her waiting was over. In my mind her release was planned for March. I wanted to release her on my birthday. Before I got so sick, I held her paw and told her so. It would be the greatest gift to me. In that moment, Juliana saw a longing inside me, a love that gave her the courage to let me go. Her eyes softened to me. They held me in a trance. I finally saw the confusion of the past year leave both of us. She never pulled her paw away, and she listened to me. I hadn't even realized that my mind was talking to her like that. From the deep recess inside my buried thoughts I too, was finally letting go of all the doubts about us and what we meant to each other. I saw her as a spirit.

Her eyes changed to a bright, warm glow. She moved her head so close to mine, that I gasped. She sent me pictures inside my head of life in the great outdoors. She showed me her children. I saw myself there coming to see her, and when I saw her little ones, the overwhelming desire to touch them. But I didn't. They were born free. Juliana pulled her paw away. The pictures stopped.

I took a deep breath and put my head down. Acceptance. She felt this and meowed. I pulled away and stood up. I left without another word between us.

I was home but a day or two and then I got horribly ill. I was hospitalized for a week. For one month I could do nothing.

By the begining of March I started to feel right again. But I was so weak, I couldn't walk, let alone run. My lover needed to make a short trip back to Italy and wanted me to come. He wanted to fatten me up again. I lost so much weight this past month. I weighed one hundred and seven pounds. I could use some good Italian food. I was crazy about this guy, and he drove me crazy too. So I went. I told Juliana I would be back, and when I did we would finish our walk.

I was in Italy for two weeks. In those two weeks my life turned in a direction not of my making. I had a horrendous nightmare just three nights before flying back to Costa Rica. In my dream a street cat I had befriended on my first visit in Italy was being torn to pieces. I was holding it in my arms and dogs were ripping it from me,

Then the dream changed. I saw my puma. I heard her cry for me. Bewilderment in her voice broke my heart, halfway around the world her presence was still with me. Another scene, gruesome came through, "as the ax-like machete swung down into her flesh, the bone crushing agonizing blows sounded in my head. I woke up in a sweat.

I was shaking. I told my lover the dream. He held me close. I sobbed into his chest. Morning came. I went to check my email. There was a letter from Mitch. He only wrote when there was trouble. I dreaded opening it.

The message read,

Sorry, but I have bad news,

Juliana got out of her pen on your birthday. She

came back three days later. She walked through

```
Fernando's property again. He attacked her with a
machete. She was cut badly. I was out of reach,
Carlos called Jose. Jose came out with his new vet-
erinarian and stiched her back up. They took her
back to La Marina She was doing okay. Again I am
sorry. Hurry home.
Mitch
```

My heart was in my throat. I called and left a message on Jose's phone. Then I emailed him. I went out into the snow and meditated to Juliana. I told her I was coming. I told her I was sorry I wasn't there. I checked my email throughout the day. Finally Jose responded.

Don't worry, she is in good hands. I will fill you in when you arrive I am taking good care of her. She is right by my house. I haven't left her side since I got her. Call me when you land.

Jose

I flew out the next day.

La Marina-Full Circle 43

My flight landed late in the day. I wouldn't be able to go
out to Jose's right away, like I wanted. I called him from the
airport. His voice was serious and calm. The story unfolded.
Carlos told me what had happened and that Juliana was
bleeding badly.

He had her in a stable by his house. He said she was to weak
to get up. Fernando had said she had tried to attack him. Fernando also had put a call to the local police and Minae.

Carlos was furious with him. He knew the story was not
true. But he had no time to lose with the man just then. He had
to help Juliana. He said she came with him and Alex just like a
puppy.

After I heard everything he told me, I got my new vet Christian, and jumped in the truck . We drove straight through.
We reached Carlos' house. It was already dark. We rigged up
lights and prepared to treat her. It took sixty-one stitches to
close her up.

Alex and Carlos were there the whole time. They took some
pictures to show me the before and after. When Christian was
done, they put Juliana into the truck and drove all the way
back to La Marina. I took her there for two reasons. She needed to be watched by Christian over the next 48 hours to see
if there was any complications. I also needed her out of there
before we got the story straight.

I didn't want Minae going up and causing any more problems for the moment. Christian told me she had eaten a lot
today and there was no infection. The stitches were holding.
She was in a small area so she couldn't move around and open
a stitch. The cut on her back was the worst. It had been opened
by the machete all the way to the bone. The muscle had been

hanging out when they first saw her. I breathed not a sound
for a long pause. I wanted to go and machete Fernando the
same way he had done Juliana. I was sick to my stomach.

I took a deep breath and told Jose thank you. He said, it
wasn't necessary. He told me Alex had called every day. They
were worried sick about Juliana. Alex missed her. Jose suggested I bring him out with me when I came.

I told Jose I would be out the next morning.

He told me to wait until the following day for he was going
to be gone the next day with business in town. Christian was
there round the clock with her. She was fine with him. Jose
said she let him touch her and check the stitches. I marveled
at that sense this animal had. She had just been brutalized by
man again and yet when faced with a new stranger treating
her she knew the difference of what men were right and which
were not.

The first day Juliana had arrived at La Marina, an incident
occurred. One of the workers carried a rake to clean up her
pen. When she saw the man with the rake in his hand, she
hissed and snarled. Jose told the worker he need not come
close to the cage. Jose said he would take care of her. Since she
was a cub, she never liked anything raised at her. Her memory
at what happened to her mother never waned. I hung the
phone up and told Jose to tell Juliana I loved her and I would
be there soon. Yes mama, he replied...

I then called Alex. He told me the day after next was better for him to come. Minae was coming out tomorrow and he
wanted to be there. We decided it was better for me to stay
away. With the way I felt I knew I wouldn't be able to control
my anger. The next visit I planned to Amistad I would be tak-

ing care of someone once and for all. I needed to release a lot
of pent-up fury. I took my lover that night, again and again.

The passion between our lovemaking was fire and water. We
were fire and water. Two forces of nature which were always
hungry for more.

I was getting my strength back. I slept into the next afternoon, and then spoke with Mitch. I was angry with him. He
hadn't been there for Juliana. Fate steers us in different ways.
In this way it had been for the best. I just didn't know it at
the time. I ended up hanging up on him. Then I called Alex.
Minae had come and gone. The meeting had gone in our favor.
Carlos Manuel Rodriguez was in office again at Minae. He
was on our side, both mine and Jose's. When he heard of the
denouncement of Fernando's against my puma, he told the
men who were to come out to leave no stone unturned in their
investigation. He knew my puma was not a man eater.

It was dry season. The tracks from the incident with the
puma were still there. The Minae men had found that the
tracks and direction of Juliana's trail clearly showed she had
not been the one attacking. It had been the other way around.
There was also not one mark on the man. If a full grown puma
wanted to attack a man, she would have ripped him open.

His complaint was thrown out. Now it was up to us to press
charges against this man for what he did to her. I'd rather take
things into my own hands.

In my black mood, my tiny voice came through. I was Juliana. I was soft and gentle. I saw a subconscious intelligence
in this animal which left me in awe. She had the empathy of
a powerful wild foe and the strength to master the wisdom to
necessitate change in mankind.

She could have killed him, yet she chose not to. Man and beast. Who then is the beast?

I told Alex to thank his father for me and to let him know I would be up to see him the next week. Alex was anxious to come with me to see Juliana. I told him to bring her ball. We left early the next morning. Alex was in a different mood. Everything had changed so suddenly, and he was still in a state of shock. I knew how much Juliana was a part of his life. He had spent every day with her and felt empty without her. We talked about everything and nothing. We both were afraid to think about what might come next.

Juliana would not be able to return to Amistad.

Fernando might wage war and even have someone shoot her in her pen. We didn't put anything past him. I thought of the lecture I would receive from Jose. Could I make him understand? I pulled into the gates of La Marina with mixed feelings. It was hot. The temperature here was very different from that Amistad. Juliana wouldn't like it. She liked the cold. La Marina was wetter, more humid, and at a lower elevation.

I parked the truck. Jose waited by the front door. I sent Alex to him, waved at him and ran to the pen where I knew Juliana was. I wanted to see her alone first. She had been sleeping. I slowed my pace as I got close. I didn't want to scare her. I softly called to her. Her head went straight up. She cried softly to me. I went to open the door. It was locked, I didn't even wait to ask for a key. I broke the handle and went inside. The pen was very small. It was tucked under a tree. We couldn't move around much, but that was o.k. I just wanted to pet her and to feel her.

She was shedding like crazy. She was a bit thin. Her wounds looked very good. She was healing fast. We said so many things in that moment. We felt so very much. I went quiet and treasured this moment with her as if it was my last. We were under each other's spell. She made me feel everything she was feeling. She told me something. She wanted to go home. I told her yes, she needed to really go home. Her home, her world...

The arrival of the veterinarian Christian broke the spell. He asked if I would help him with her. I did. I liked the way he worked. He had a gentle bedside manner and a love for animals that showed. He listened to everything I said. He gave me respect. He wanted to learn my medicines. I told him he would. He stayed only a brief time for he knew I needed my time with her.

As he left, Alex and Jose walked up. As soon as Juliana heard Alex's voice, she jumped from her box onto the ground in front of him. I witnessed a rare, touching moment between these two spirits. They were like brother and sister. Juliana thought for sure we were taking her home.

A lump rose in my throat. I didn't have the heart to tell her, not yet. Alex gave her the ball. She swished her tail in happiness. She played with it, then turned again to me, asking, "Let's go home."

I left Alex with her and walked with Jose. Jose started a speech he must have rehearsed in his mind over and over again to me. "Julie," he said. "I know this is hard on all of you, including Juliana. I see no way for now that we can do anything but build her an area and have her stay at La Marina. We have a male puma that we could eventually introduce to her and put them together."

I looked up at him. "I will not put her in a zoo, ever, even one as wonderful as yours. She was born free and to freedom she will return. I gave her my word. I gave you my word. No matter what it takes I will set her free."

Jose knew not to push me right then. We changed the subject for now.

I spoke with the vet on what she was taking, and added some herbs of my own to her food. Then Marta put lunch on the table for all of us. We ate mostly in silence. Jose's children lifted the cloud on us all by running in and out of the house and talking up a storm of questions about Juliana. They were spoiling her rotten with all their attention. Jose finally told them to go do their schoolwork. Time to let the puma be.

I walked outside to smoke a cigarette. I couldn't believe what I saw. Since I had broken the door on Juliana's cage, it was simply closed by a piece of rope. Jose said he would fix it later. Juliana had opened it easily and was sitting in the back of my truck.

I finally cried for the first time since I had come back to Costa Rica. Every emotion tore me down. The tears burned my face. I couldn't look at her.

I called Alex to slowly come out.

Jose heard the tone of my voice. "What is it?" he asked.

I told him never mind. Just stay where he was and keep the kids inside. Alex stopped when he saw her in my truck. The first tears I ever seen him shed spilled down his face. We said not a word to each other. We did what we had to do. We put her back into the cage and said our goodbyes.

Jose fixed her door. We would return at weeks end to help Christian remove the stitches. Jose hugged me hard. I started my truck and Juliana screamed at me. Please don't leave me. Alex and I drove in silence back to the city. Alex slept at my home that night. We knew we had to come up with something soon.

We were up at the crack of dawn, both of us pacing. I drove him to the bus stop and kissed him good bye. In two days I went up to see Carlos. I needed his wisdom. He told me to see the signs which were around me and to follow my heart. The rest would come. As hard as this experience was on Juliana, she had learned without a shadow of a doubt that man was not to be trusted. Carlos said our greatest fear of her coming in contact with hunters was one we could put to rest. She had learned a very hard lesson. And she had learned it the hard way. We both felt she would never trust man again.

Carlos then did a healing on me. It was beautiful. He was becoming a shaman. He always had it in him. He said we all would be starting new lives. We needed to let go. I was more than ready. I walked to the cabin before I left. I didn't want to do anything with it but leave it as it was. It had been the best home I'd known.

I drove back to the city and called Mario Araya. We met the next day. He knew my history with the puma. He had been through it all with me. His life had changed too. He and Tatiana had divorced. We would get together and go target practicing. I had a beautiful silver engraved 9 mm which Memo had given me as a Christmas gift when we were together. I told Mario I was going to sell it.

He joked and said, maybe I should use it just one time before I did. I laughed in return. I knew he meant Fernando. I told Mario I would dress like a puma and scare the living daylights out of the man, then I would castrate him. Evil thoughts. We laughed at how we both were. All my men friends that

340

heard of what happened, were willing to help, no matter what I decided. I wished I was god ...for a day...

Thy Will Be Done 44

Alex called and asked me if I wanted him to bring his tent. We were leaving the next day for La Marina. He said it would do me good to sleep with her again. He was being so sweet. I cared so much for Alex. He always thought with his heart. It is probably why the animals loved him so.

"Thank you for thinking that Alex, I would love to sleep with her, bring it along," I said.

The following morning he took the bus to San Jose, then I picked him up and we drove to La Marina. We were in no particular rush. We still had not come up with a plan for Juliana. We arrived shortly after noon. Jose was in the local town buying supplies. The kids were in school and Marta was taking a siesta.

I had brought some choice pieces of lamb for Juliana. I heard her calling for me. She knew the sound of my truck. She was screaming her baby call to me. I ran to her. Alex followed. Juliana rubbed herself against the fencing, dying to get at us. We couldn't open the gate. It was locked. So we put our hands through the gate petting and rubbing her, hard.

She purred like a tiger. She looked good. Her wounds were closed. Her fur was growing back. She was still shedding. I sent Alex off to find Christian and bring me the keys to her cage. I feed her morsel by morsel. She was so excited and happy to see us that she barely ate, and I knew she always had room in her belly for lamb.

I whispered sweet nothings to her. I asked her, "What am I going to do with you?"

She smiled at me, then she grabbed my hand with her mouth and just held it, lovingly for a long time. I stopped thinking and just felt her. I went inside of her and never wanted to return.

Every animal comes to teach us something. It is never suffering.

Facing our fears Needing to know love Companionship Giving us strength

Giving back our powers Showing us death Showing us life

Opening a door....but never suffering

This we put on ourselves They know our purpose As they know theirs

It is not by chance that they come into our lives

It is because on a higher conscience level, we have asked them...

I heard at that moment the call of the wild, I felt the wind, though no wind blew. I felt the earth, strong and constant, warm and still beneath my feet. I grounded myself to her.

Juliana felt everything I was feeling in that moment. She looked out at the jungles and mountains surrounding her. I saw a look come into her eyes, one I had never seen. She was listening to a voice I could not. I closed my eyes and prayed...

Alex came up the path. He had the keys. Christian would join us shortly. I let Alex in the cage with her. I left him alone with her. I don't know why, but I felt he needed this time with her. Alex never asked for anything for himself. I told him I was going to see the lions.

I would return in a little bit. I ran into Christian, and he took me to see the new lionesses which had arrived from Columbia. They were smaller than the one from England. The habitat for the lions was finished. It was indeed a bit of paradise for the ladies. Christian showed me the area Jose had designated for Juliana and the male puma. I barely noticed nor listened to what he said. It wasn't his fault. He was trying to do the best he could for all the animals. I told him he was doing well. He told me that Julianais his favorite charge. He said there was something about her, he couldn't put his finger on it, but that she was different from any other wild animal he had ever met. I told him, I know...

We returned to Alex and Juliana and helped Christian remove the stitches. Juliana was a bit weary of Christian this time. She wanted him to stop fussing over her. She also just wanted it to be me and Alex. When she started to jump away, I told Christian to tell me what to do and I finished the work for him. There was just one stitch on her face which she did not want touched. So we left this one.

Jose drove in just then. Christian went to see him. Alex and I tidied up Juliana's cage. I hosed down the ground so it would be cooler for her. Alex added some greenery. We fixed two bowls of water for, as usual, she was defecating in the water. We both told her that we would be spending the night with her.

She went to her box to lay down. Alex and I went to see Jose. We spent the rest of the day with the animals and visited all of them. Suzie the jaguar made us laugh. She reminded us of Juliana in so many ways.

As day turned into night, the symphony of animals started. Alex and I sat with Juliana. She listened to the roar of the lions. She listened to the eerie howls of the coyotes. She was not afraid, she merely listened. It was feeding time for all the carnivores; we fed ours too.

We pitched the tent close against Juliana's cage, then Alex and I shared a dinner with Jose and his family. The talk was light. None of us spoke of Juliana's future. After dinner Alex was shown to his room and Jose and I took a walk around the park. We walked in silence. As we came round back to Juliana's cage, Jose spoke.

"You know Juliana came from these jungles, and now she is back here again." I nodded. Fate had brought her back here. I only said, "But for what purpose?" Jose bid me goodnight. I climbed into my tent and laid there, listening to the night sounds. Juliana made her own sounds to me. I answered her back. Alex came outside to make sure we were all right. He couldn't sleep just yet. He went in to play with Juliana.

The lock was off for our visit so we could come and go as we pleased. Jose had a family of deer loose in the park. They had made their way over to us. The male buck was in full sight. The moon lit up the night. Juliana looked at the buck, then turned back to us. Finally we called it a night.

Alex returned to the house and I to my tent. I was just about to fall asleep when I felt a warm scratchy tongue lick my arm. I opened my eyes and stared right into the amber glow of Juliana's eyes. She had gotten out of her cage and had come into my tent. I lay on my side and just looked at her. Then I thought of the family of deer. I had to put her in again. Just as I lifted myself up and started to call her to stay, she bolted out of the tent like lightning and was gone. Great, I thought, I really need this right now.

I went to fetch Alex. Jose heard us and got up too. All three of us went out to go get her. We had her leash with us. I had been hoping to take her for a walk the next morning, early, to stretch her legs.

She was not far from my tent. She was not bothering the deer. That was good. She ran from Jose. I told him to just stay in one spot. Alex went to her with the leash. She lay there and let him put it on her. As he tugged on it to turn her home, though, she stood her ground. She wanted to go for a walk, not back into her cage. I went over to help coax her. She did not listen. I instructed Jose to fetch the carrier kennel so we could put her in the box and carry her back. When Jose came with the carrier, she snarled and growled. She knew what we were up to. We half pulled, half dragged her into the kennel. At the last minute, I told Alex and Jose to stop.

"Take her for a walk," I said. I hated seeing her so angry.

Alex walked her for an hour. Jose and I sat and waited. When they were close again Alex called and told us that she was fussing again. She did not want to go back into the cage. I didn't blame her. We ended up having to force her. She hated every minute of it. We put her back into her cage and Jose gave me the lock.

"Just keep it," he said. I locked the gate and we went back to bed. That night I had dreams, so many of them, vivid and in color. Too much information came at me. I couldn't put it together. I woke at 4am and went to Juliana. She too, was awake. I communicated a strong message to her.

Juliana, you are back to the place where you were born. Alex and I will be returning home today. You must make the choice to go free now or not. You must not come close to man. I will come some day and see you again. You are ready to go free. I am ready to let you go. I will love you forever. I will talk with you again. Thank you for being one of the most wonderful things in my life. You need your life now. You make up your mind, and let me know.

I lay by her gate and slept again. She watched me the whole time…

At 5:30 AM, Jose and Alex came by. I wanted to leave. I told Jose I would return in three days. I left Alex with Juliana and walked into the house with Jose to clean up. I told Jose I would have an answer for him soon. I needed some time by myself right now. He understood.

Alex and I got into the truck and blew Juliana a kiss. I looked into her eyes for one brief moment and knew she knew... Then we were gone. I still remember hearing her cry as the truck rolled away. I never forgot.

Alex and I no sooner were entering the city limits when my cell phone rang. It was Jose. Juliana had broken through the roof on her cage and was loose in the park. He said she was trying to follow us. He said if it was possible for us to turn back and help him with her.

I looked at Alex who heard the whole conversation. We both had that same look in our eyes. We were about to make the decision, once and for all. I took a deep breath, then got back on the phone and told Jose I would call him right back. I clicked the phone shut and pulled off the road.

Alex spoke first. "You know that without our help Juliana won't go back in that cage. She will not come look for us, she knows better. She knows we went. Now maybe it is time for her to go, too."

I looked at Alex and I knew he was right, I thought the same. "Alex, on one side I know what you are saying, on the other side I am going to worry about her. She doesn't know that jungle."

Alex then looked into my eyes with all his innocence and replied, "You will always worry about her, one jungle is much like the rest. She knows what to do, but it is your choice."

"No Alex, it is her choice, and she will make it in the next day or two." We both smiled at each other and grabbed each others hand.

"Thy will be done," I whispered and then called Jose. He picked up immediately.

"Jose, I think its best to just try to keep an eye on her today. Alex and I will come out as soon as we can, but not today. Do you know where she is now?"

Jose took a deep breath. "Okay," he said, "The park is closed today so that will help with no visitors being about. She is still around here, she hasn't gone up to the road. More likely she will go into the jungle. Then I don't know if we will be able to get her."

I held my breath in that moment and looked to Alex. He smiled. I told Jose, "Never worry that I will not be able to find her. She will always come to me. These years have formed a bond between her and me, a bond that will last forever. The choice is now hers Jose. Whether you agree with me or not, she came home to take over the throne, where her mother was queen. Now it is her turn to fill those shoes. Let her be. Help her if she needs it. I will check in with you and you do the same with me. If there is trouble, I will be there, whatever the time."

I stopped talking, my hands were begining to shake. Alex squeezed them harder. Jose finally understood. His deep voice sighed. "We will take this one day at a time. I guess all I can do right now is trust you."

"Jose, all I want you to do is believe in her, to believe in everything I have taught you, to believe in everything the animals tell you. Listen to your little voice inside… And thank you."

There was a long silent pause and then Jose said he would call us later in the afternoon.

We both hung up. "So Alex, we wait. I will call you as soon as I have news about her."

I started the truck up again and drove Alex to the bus station.

"Tell your father to call me after you have told him our story," I shouted out to him as he ran to catch the bus pulling out of the station.

I slowly turned the truck towards home. I drove slower than I had ever driven in my life. One part of me wanted to drive like mad to go see if she was all right. Then I saw her face as clearly as if she was in front of me. There was slight confusion in those eyes and yet simultaneously there was acceptance.

I didn't want to see anyone just then. I drove to a spot high above the city and just parked and sat. I sat for the longest time, staring into space. I rolled a joint and left the world for awhile.

The phone rang. It was Mitch. I told him I couldn't talk just then and hung up. My lover called, worried, wondering where I was.

I told him I was okay. I would be home soon. I didn't know why, but I didn't want to share my story with anyone. It was a thing between those who were with her in that moment. It was an unspoken chapter. It was a secret of my heart.

I couldn't explain to someone even if I tried, what had just transpired between Juliana and me. But as I gazed up to the skies I know that there, they knew.

I drove home and lay down to sleep. I dreamed as if in a movie, everything about her which I have just written. I woke with the sinking feeling of what it would be like to live now without her. Suddenly the world seemed so empty. I knew I would fall into a depression. But I knew it would take the time

it took to heal and then it would go away. It would turn into
joy. It would turn into honor. I reached to call Jose and as I
held the phone in my hand it rang. It was 4:45 PM.

Jose's voice boomed loud and clear, "Well, Juliana is in the
jungle now. My worker saw her leave. What now?"

A great smile creeped onto my face. "Jose, just leave some
food for her in a place where she will know. Lets see how the
night goes."

Jose agreed and told me he was going to keep the park
closed the next day , just in case. I also told him to keep his
dog on a leash so it wouldn't scare her away in case she
wanted to come back. He told me he had already put the dog
away. "Have a good evening Jose, get some rest." "You too,
good bye."

Carlos then called. Before I could say one word, he said,
"She has made her choice. Be happy and proud of yourself.
She is free. We will cry rivers, you will cry oceans, but let them
be of joy, for you returned a great one back to her world."

Jose called the next day. Juliana came in the night and took
the food Jose had put out. She stayed around the park for
one more day. Then she went into the jungle and didn't come
back anymore. I knew she was waiting to see if I would return
for her. It was the hardest thing not to want to see her one
last time. But I knew it had to be this way. I had moved from
where I used to be in my life with this experience and knew I
could never go back.

This mystifying command was related to an earlier intuition.
Every day I spoke to her with my mind. After one month's
time, Jose went into the jungles to see about her. He picked up
her trail and then he saw her. She had been watching his walk
the whole time, this he knew. She looked well. She looked

wild. She snarled at him. She didn't come close. They stared at each other for a long time. Then she was gone.

Jose called me to let me know she was doing fine. It was then that I too, decided to leave. It was time for me to leave Costa Rica for a while. It was time to write my book. I packed up my things and stored them with Kattia. I saw all my friends. Kinder words were never spoken, as those my friends spoke to me that week. I am bathed with feelings. They said good bye to a wild heart that captured theirs.

The hardest good bye was to Carlos. This was between him and me. He bade me godspeed on my return. He would be waiting for me, for however long it took.

As I sit here and write these last lines I think of Juliana. I think of when I will finally return and go to her. I know she will be there.

As I complete my Story, news reaches me. Carlos Rodriquez is elected minister of

Minae for another term. Yolanda from the Simon Bolivar Zoo has been thrown out.

Minae is taking over the zoo. Such news for one like myself gives me the nod from above that my work was not in vain.

Carlos may very well become the greatest force in Costa Rica's animal life and environment. He grew by leaps and bounds. May you rule as a lion over this majestic kingdom called Costa Rica.

As I write this, it has been seven months since I last saw Juliana. Jose has constantly been in touch with me as to her well-being. From time to time a guard, which Jose instilled in the jungles surrounding La Marina spots her. She is well. She never comes close to man or his kind. She understood everything I told her. She is an original of the species. Juliana is living free.

When eye to eye

That chance meeting, with a wild one

A wild animal comes and goes, as it pleases...to you

They fall not for tears, sweet talk, nor bribes

They know no lies

What one faces at that moment

Is pure, direct readings of your mind, your being Whatever is in your brain at that moment, they know..... In the blink of an eye

You are right in front of them

You move not a muscle

For they have you in a trance

When eye to eye

La Fin.

From the Author

My name is Julia Bindas. I have gone by many others...

My passion for animals and my cat-like behavior towards life itself lead me down a road less traveled in the world. From the physical to the spiritual, the mystics and the scientists, the world was my territory. I traveled it most of my life. I went from the concrete jungles of Los Angeles to the jungles of the rainforests. I was unguarded. I was called formidable and fierce. I was as soft and sweet as a kitten too.

This has been an intense year, but I think positive. Always... My rapid-fire, full- tilt instincts spring from this mind-set. Any great change or trauma is an opportunity for me to grow. That's why I can take it so well and go on. I like to grow. I get to reinvent myself. I believe in strength, wisdom, and courage. I believe in freeing, your mind, being alive...

This part, my book, was about opening myself to be read. I have kept so much locked inside my mind. Rather than putting on layers of a character in order to be read, I had to come out. Remember through me come the animals. This was always hard for me to project to those who were human.

Overwhelmed, exhausted, all thought and emotion beaten out of me, I lost my sense of self, the heartbeat I heard was the heart of the animals

When asked did I ever think about committing professional suicide, I replied, not while I'm doing it. The animals call it listening to that little voice.

My experiences are breathtaking to me. I wouldn't change them for any other path in this world. What made me so strong was that I had learned my fears and battled them.

I love to learn, it's a turn on. Einstein, one of my heroes, said, "Imagination is more important than intelligence."

My imagination has turned on all that have met me. The wild ones who share our earthspace, are worthwhile to get to know. They give us balance. They give us powers back we lost. It is easy to talk to them. They are everything you imagined and more. Whether one is young or old, weak or strong, race or creed matters not to them. They are without judgment.

The minds of animals are a kaleidoscope of moving colors. Their emotions are like ours. They feel all we feel. They have a rainbow inside which is that array of senses we dare not touch. The sixth sense, the seventh. Their physical ability is far keener than ours. They have parts far more developed than ours. The minds of animals are beautiful in their thought. They love in a way I have not seen in other life forms. They know how to live. It is far from true that it is merely survival.

We know so little about our own minds, we use such a small part of it. The wild ones use it all. That is the difference which separates man from beast. Who then is the beast?

This book was written in the Italian Alps.

Upon my first visit to this country, my thoughts went out to the wolves. Once aplenty, they are no more.

My second visit I called to those spirits, I howled into the mountains. And it was returned...

Sightings of wolves in the northern region were a first in so to many years. I closed my eyes in order to see. Was there a connection with me and their return, was there a message to be sent out again for the wild ones?

For those of you interested in natural animal remedies or animal communication, please feel free to contact me via my website.

The continuing saga of my life with animals will also be available to see and enjoy. I encourage all of you to get to know the animals we share our world with.

They are waiting for you!

About the Author

About her:

She –Will woo your heart, while her voice seduces your soul

It is all about delicate power

She grips you in one moment, hard, and then melts you in sensual smoothness the next

She never gives up

To often she gives in

And puts not herself first

Her emotions rule her, she cries... She is liquid, like the sea

She was made to move

Her passions in everything she does inspired a small country to do better

Every animal who met her felt at home She was born on the day of the animals And to them she will return

An Anonymous Onlooker

Epilogue

Everybody thinks I found this broken little cat and fixed her

But they are wrong

She fixed us, everyone of us

She touched the whole part of us

So many fans she had at her finish line

I found a truth in Costa Rica and I brought it to the people

We live in a time where there are real power animals in our lives

We are connected to animals as we are connected to our families

Each and everyone of us is each and every animal

I work on showing the people their animal side

There need not be a lifetime with one to know the reason they

Are in our life's path

Devote yourself to an idea, strength will follow

As I devoted myself to the idea of wild animals so I Too

followed the strength of them throughout my life

The mountain lion, the tiger, the jaguar

Symbols of a power which is mine

The three together formed the animal inside of me

May this book open the minds of man to search out the truth.

May he return back the kingdom from whence he came

These writings are my prayer to all the wild ones

May cages be open and chains unbound

That respect replace fear

For the wild at heart...

Julia Bindas

Made in the USA
Columbia, SC
05 October 2021